Sushi

鮨の魅力とは？

① 素材を選別し、旨さを引き出す必要最低限の仕事を施し、お客さんの眼前で素早く美しく握る。やり過ぎない単純明快な職人仕事による旨さこそが、江戸前ずしの凄さであり、旨さの秘密のすべてとなる。

② 「すし種」と「シャリ」と「山葵」に、「醬油」と「海苔」を加えての単純明快な組み合わせの中で、それぞれの旨さを超えた、まったく新たな「握りずし」という世界を瞬時につくり出す。

③ すし種を替えていくだけで、千変万化の素晴らしい握りずしの旨さを、少量ずつ気ままに、数多く、楽しみながら食べることができる。

④ 個々の食べ手の姿勢と能力次第でも、旨さの世界が簡単に変貌してしまう、特異な食の世界を持つ。

⑤ 職人の個性と人間性、お客さんと職人との相性をも合わせて食べるという、食の世界では他に類のない、極めて人間関係の濃密な、異端の世界をつくり出している。

⑥ 江戸の食文化と、粋で、いなせで、単純で、見栄っ張りで短気、意地と誇りの心意気を持つ、江戸っ子気質を今も色濃く残している。

⑦ 食べ手と、つくり手の職人たちとの切磋琢磨による伝統的な旨さの維持と、新たな旨さの創造と発展は、今も着実に継続されている。

「仕入れ」と「選別」

——最高に旨い魚を仕入れるための選別
すしの旨さの大半は、素材の選別の優劣によって決まる。仕入れは、店の経営方針と力量によって、様々な違いを見せることになる。選別される魚によっては、2倍から10倍程の大きな仕入れ原価の開きとなり、それが高級店と大衆店との決定的な違いとなる。

——素材の選別
① 魚種の識別が正確か？
② 天然か養殖か？
③ 旬が最適か？
④ 産地・漁場の選定が最良か？
⑤ 漁法、輸送の違いによる鮮度の維持管理と熟成の旨さは最良か？
⑥ 旨さのための量目、大きさは最適か？
⑦ 脂の乗り、旨みが最良か？
⑧ 魚介の種類と格付けによる旨さの評価は最適か？
⑨ 雌雄の違いによる旨さの差異はあるか？
⑩ 特殊な条件（希少性の高い）の中でも、あえて追いかけるか？
⑪ 相場の暴騰のときも、あえて挑戦するか？

以上を厳格にチェックし、選別することによって、最高に旨い魚を仕入れることができる。

食事作法

江戸前ずしのカウンター席での食事作法
① あらかじめ、店の平均客単価等を承知し、店の方針に、ある程度合わせられる度量があること。
② 信頼とくつろぎと謙虚さの中で、素晴らしいひとときを共有し、隣の方に迷惑をかけないこと。
③ 店とすし職人との間に、適度で心地よい距離を置き、すしの旨さを楽しむ余裕と心意気があること。
④ エセ通よりも、程よく、たくさん食べる客が一番歓迎されること。
⑤ 同業他店の評判、評価の話は嫌味になることがあり、程度をわきまえること。
⑥「おまかせ」、「おこのみ」、「おきまり」と、食し方は分かれるが、自信がなくわからないときには、職人への信頼である「おまかせ」にすると良い。
⑦ すしの順序は好きなものから食べればよいが、淡白なものから食べるのが結果的には無難となる。
⑧ 種とシャリの温度も、旨さの大切な要素であり、握られたすしは、なるべく早く食すこと。
⑨ 醬油は種に適量をつけ、シャリにはつけない。
⑩ 食すときは、箸でも手でもどちらでもよく、口に入れるときに種が上か下かも好みの問題となる。
⑪ 山葵の量は各人の好みで、注文次第で加減できる。
⑫ 生姜とお茶は口直しで、お代わり自由。

旬

——旬とは何か？
すべての魚介類は、四季の移り変わりとともに旨さの持ち味を、微妙に変化させていく。その中で、身肉が最も充実し、脂が乗り、最高の旨さを発揮する時期をその魚介類の「旨さの盛りの旬」と言う。しかし、旬のとらえ方はもう少し多様で、魚種によってはかなりの長期にわたる旬を言われることがある。旬のとらえ方の錯綜と誤解があるからで、整理すると次の3種類の旬に分類することができる。①「季節的先(はし)りの旬」②「旨さの盛りの旬」と③「漁獲量的盛りの旬」。さらに②「旨さの盛りの旬」と③「漁獲量的盛りの旬」とがほとんど重なり合うものがある。また資源保護のために、漁獲量と漁期が定められている魚介類は、漁期の後半と「旨さの盛りの旬」とがほぼ重なることが多い。しかし、魚介類の旬の真髄は、「旨さの盛りの旬」の中にある。

① 季節的先(はし)りの旬
やがて来る「旨さの盛りの旬」の季節を先取りし、旨さはまったく未成熟ながら、文化的な伝統・行事・慣習・地域的なこだわり等を背景に、季節への期待と憧れを持って愛でる、日本独自の旬のとらえ方である。漁獲量の僅少さと、こだわりと熱狂の需要により、魚種によっては異常

な価格に暴騰することが多い。

② 旨さの盛りの旬

ほとんどの魚介類は、産卵の時期を中心にして、旨さの旬を特定することができる。やがて来る産卵のために、食欲を増進させ、身肉が太り、肝は大きく成長し、卵・精巣も大きくなりはじめの頃、身肉は充実し、脂が乗り、旨さの最盛期となる。

③ 漁獲量的盛りの旬

産卵の準備のために、海面近くや浅瀬に移動し、餌の食いが激しくなり、漁獲量が増大する時期で、釣り人たちを楽しませる時期でもある。卵・精巣がさらに肥大し、産卵直前の時期となっていることが多い。身肉の旨さは、卵・精巣の肥大化のために吸収され、旨さの盛りの時期を通過してしまっていることが多い。

④ 「漁獲量的盛りの旬」と「旨さの盛りの旬」の同時到来

鯖、秋刀魚、鰯、鯵、鮭等の大群で回遊する魚は、旨さの盛りの時期に大量に漁獲されることになり、その時期が最高に旨い時期となることが多い。

⑤ 禁漁期と漁期の設定による旨さの旬の特定

海胆・鮑・赤貝・平貝・ズワイ蟹等は、産卵時期を保護するため、禁漁期が設定されているのだが、漁期の終わり頃が旨さの盛りの旬となることが多い。漁業資源の保護のために、漁獲量と漁期が定められている。

What makes sushi so special?

1 Ingredients are carefully selected and with a minimum of steps, their flavors swiftly drawn out to create a tasty, attractive treat right before the customer's eyes. The signature flavor produced by the masterly but uncomplicated, unassuming craftsmanship of the sushi chef is what makes Edo-mae sushi so special, and the whole secret of its irresistible, delectable appeal.

2 A totally new realm of flavor transcending the taste of each individual component – that of 'nigiri-zushi' – is created on the spot through the simple combination of vinegared rice, wasabi and neta (fish or other topping or filling), plus soy sauce and nori.

3 Simply by swapping one neta for another it is possible to sample a multitude of delicious nigiri-zushi flavors at whim.

4 Sushi is unusual in the world of food in that its flavor can be transformed by the attitude and ability of the individual diner.

5 In the intimacy of its connections between people, ie the combination of the chef's individuality and human qualities, and the match between customer and chef, the world of sushi strikes an unorthodox note that sets it apart from other cuisines.

6 Edo-mae sushi retains a strong flavor of Edo food culture and the stylish, smart, simple, slightly show-off, short-tempered, stubborn and staunch spirit of the born-and-bred Tokyoite.

7 New flavors continue to be created and developed while maintaining traditional tastes, thanks to the dedication and cooperation of sushi eaters and makers.

Sourcing and selection

Sourcing only the tastiest fish

The taste of sushi is largely determined by how well the ingredients are chosen. The sourcing of ingredients varies according to how a shop runs its business, and its capabilities. The price of fish sourced by one sushi shop can be anything from double to ten times that purchased by another, this cost marking the definitive difference between high-end sushi restaurants and more everyday establishments.

Choosing ingredients

1 Is the fish correctly identified by species?
2 Wild or farmed?
3 Is it the best season?
4 Is it from the best location/fishing ground?
5 Are freshness/aging according to differences in fishing method and transport the best they can be?
6 Is it the perfect weight and size for optimum flavor?
7 Is the spread/quantity and flavor of any fat the best it can be?
8 Does it rate appropriately in terms of flavor for the species and its status?
9 Are there any differences in flavor between male and female?
10 Is it worth deliberately seeking out even under special conditions?
11 Is it worth persisting with even if the price is high?

By scrupulously ticking off these points when selecting fish, sushi shops can ensure they source only the tastiest specimens.

Etiquette

Edo-mae sushi eaten at the counter:
1 The customer needs to be cognizant of factors such as average customer spend, and have the capacity to match the shop's approach to some extent.
2 The aim is to share an enjoyable moment amid an atmosphere of trust, ease and modesty, and not to disturb adjacent diners.
3 There should be an appropriate, comfortable distance between customer and chef, and the latitude and desire to enjoy the delectability of sushi.
4 Customers that eat a decent amount are more welcome than self-styled connoisseurs.
5 Talk of the reputation and rating of competitors is disagreeable, and should be kept to a minimum.

6 Customers can be divided into those who leave their choices entirely to the chef, those with certain preferences, and those who choose the fixed menu, but if lacking in confidence about what to order, it is best to trust in the chef's choice.

7 It's fine when eating sushi to start with your favorites, but ultimately the safest route is to begin with milder flavors.

8 The temperature of fillings and rice is another important element of flavor, and sushi should be eaten as quickly as possible after making.

9 Put a suitable amount of soy sauce on the neta, not the rice.

10 Eat by hand or with chopsticks; either is acceptable. Whether you place the sushi in your mouth with neta upside or down is also purely a matter of preference.

11 The quantity of wasabi can be altered to taste on ordering.

12 Ginger and tea cleanse the palate; consume as much of these as you like.

Seasonality

What is meant by 'season' when it comes to sushi?

All seafoods alter subtly in flavor with the changing of the seasons. The period during which a species is at its fleshiest, has fat, and exhibits its finest flavor is referred to as its peak season for taste. But interpretations of season are in reality more diverse, and depending on the species, the period referred to as the season can be quite long. This is due to the intricacies and misunderstandings surrounding what is meant by the term 'season'. Season can refer to any of the following three things: 1. 'Coming into season', ie when a species first comes on the market; 2. When a species is at its tastiest; and 3. Peak volume for catches. 2. and 3. in many cases virtually overlap. Furthermore for species deemed off-limits for certain periods to preserve stocks, the latter half of the fishing season and 'tastiest' season often overlap. However, the true essence of season when it comes to seafood is when the species peaks for eating.

1 Early seasonality

A peculiarly Japanese approach to seasonality, in which foods are treasured with a sense of seasonal anticipation against a background of cultural tradition, custom, ritual, and regional preferences even though the 'tastiest' season is yet to come, and the item in question is still far from mature in flavor. Demand due to paucity of catches and obsessive pursuit of the species in question can lead to astronomical prices.

2 Season for peak taste
A specific period of peak taste around spawning can be identified for most seafood. Appetite increases and fish become fleshier and fattier ahead of spawning. Livers grow engorged, and when eggs and testicles also start to grow, flesh becomes full, fat is acquired, and the pinnacle of flavor achieved.

3 Season for highest volume catches
To prepare for spawning, sea creatures move closer to the surface or into the shallows, and feed more intensely. This is when catches grow, and also when fishing is at its most enjoyable. In many cases the taste of the flesh is absorbed in order to fatten eggs/testicles, by which time the species is past its most desirable in flavor terms.

4 When highest catch volume and peak taste coincide
Fish such as mackerel (saba), saury, sardines, Japanese jack (aji), salmon etc. that migrate in large schools are caught in large volumes when at their most flavorsome, this high-volume period often coinciding with when they are prime eating.

5 Peak flavor season specified by setting of fishing and non-fishing periods
To protect species such as sea urchin, abalone, blood cockle, pen shell and snow crab during spawning, fishing of these species is prohibited at certain times, and they tend to peak in flavor toward the end of the fishing season. Quotas and fishing periods are set down in an effort to conserve fishing resources.

20	spring		64	summer
22	春の魚　spring fish		68	夏の魚　summer fish
24	春の素材　spring variety		70	夏の素材　summer variety
28	春の握り　spring nigiri		74	夏の握り　summer nigiri
32	鰊　herring		78	新子　gizzard shad fry
34	白魚　icefish		80	縞鯵　striped jack
36	星鰈　spotted halibut		82	平政　yellowtail amberjack
38	白鱚　Japanese whiting		84	飛魚　flying fish
40	墨烏賊　golden cuttlefish		86	真鰯　sardine
42	槍烏賊　spear squid		88	真子鰈　marbled sole
44	鰹　bonito		90	鮑　abalone
46	真鯛　red sea bream		92	蛸　octopus
48	蝦蛄　mantis shrimp		94	真鯒　flathead
50	海胆　sea urchin		96	煽り烏賊　bigfin reef squid
52	蛤　common Orient clam		98	真鯵　Japanese jack mackerel
54	青柳　Chinese mactra clam		100	鱸　sea bass
56	小柱　clam muscle		102	鮎魚女　fat greenling
58	帆立貝　scallop		104	穴子　conger
60	鳥貝　Japanese cockle		106	伊佐木　chicken grunt
62	春子　sea bream fry			

108	autumn		136	winter
112	秋の魚　autumn fish		140	冬の魚　winter fish
114	秋の素材　autumn variety		142	冬の素材　winter variety
118	秋の握り　autumn nigiri		144	冬の握り　winter nigiri
120	鯖　mackerel		148	鰤　Japanese amberjack
122	新烏賊　young cuttlefish		152	真鱈　Pacific cod
124	皮剥　thread-sail filefish		154	鯥　saw-edged perch
126	秋刀魚　Pacific saury		156	真梶木　striped marlin
128	間八　greater amberjack		158	細魚　Japanese halfbeak
130	イクラ　salmon roe		160	黒鯥　gnomefish
132	海松貝　geoduck		162	魴鮄　red gurnard
134	甘海老　pink shrimp		164	鮪　Pacific bluefin tuna
			166	鮃　olive flounder
			168	小鰭　gizzard shad
			170	蝦夷鮑　Ezo abalone
			172	平鱸　blackfin sea bass
			174	車海老　Japanese tiger prawn
182	巻物　rolls		176	平貝　pen shell
184	干瓢巻　kanpyo roll		178	赤貝　blood cockle
186	カッパ巻　cucumber roll			
188	紐キュウ巻　himokyu roll			
190	鉄火巻　tuna roll			
192	穴キュウ巻　conger & cucumber roll			
194	沢庵巻　takuan roll			
196	梅巻　pickled plum roll			
198	山葵巻　wasabi roll			
200	ネギトロ巻　scallion & tuna roll			

spring

春の魚

3月に入ると、水温を下げきった海は、清澄な透明度を増している。その中で、春を旬とする魚たちは、やがて訪れる生命の最盛期と、その後に来る初夏の産卵に備え、少しずつ身肉を太らせ、充実させはじめている。4月に入ると真鯛、白鱚が最盛期となる。墨烏賊、天然の帆立貝は身が太り、食感と甘みが強くなり、産卵前の命の輝きを見せている。白魚は卵で腹をふっくらと膨らませ、舌に触れる微かな卵の食感を楽しむことができる。一年生の鰊が程よい脂をたたえて旨くなってくる。江戸時代から伝説的な魚としての輝きを持ち続ける鰹が、南の海から爽やかな感動とともに北上してくる。この時期の蝦蛄はみなメスに転化してしまい、弾けるような卵をパンパンに膨らませ、人気の高いものとなっている。最高級の格付けをされる星鰈は、真子鰈よりも一足早く旬に入りはじめ、淡白な旨味の中に、しっかりとした身の締まりを味わうことができる。漁獲量が極少となっている蛤は、鳥貝とともに春を告げる代表的な貝となっている。最近の鳥貝は柔らかで心地よい食感と甘み・旨みをより一層楽しめるようになった。産卵前後の脂の薄い本鮪の群れが、脂が乗り、香り高い冬場の鮪たちに代わって、久方振りの登場となる。旨さでははるかに及ばないものの、爽やかな季節の到来を感じさせる。

spring fish

By March, chilly winter seas take on a bracing clarity. In these cool waters, fish that reach their prime in spring gradually grow sleek and fat ahead of the imminent pinnacle of their life cycle, and the early summer spawning that follows. By April, red sea bream and Japanese whiting are at their best. Golden cuttlefish and wild scallops glistening in pre-spawning prime condition grow fatter and acquire a more intense mouth feel and sweetness. Icefish acquire a bellyful of roe, the subtle sensation of eggs on the tongue adding to their appeal. Yearling herring acquire just the right amount of fat and added flavor. Bonito, species of legend since Edo times, arrive in the north from southern waters to great excitement. Mantis shrimp (shako) during this period all turn into females, and bursting with plump roe, are a favorite sushi option. Among flatfish, the highly prized spotted halibut starts to come into season a step ahead of marbled sole, and though mild in taste, has a fine-grained, robust texture. The scarce hamaguri (common Orient clam) is, alongside the Japanese cockle, one of the main mollusks heralding the start of spring. In recent years cockles have grown more tender, their texture, flavor and sweetness increasingly agreeable. Schools of bluefin tuna, lean around spawning, acquire fat and reappear to replace their delectable winter forerunners following a lengthy absence. Although far from equal in flavor terms, they offer a taste of seasonal pleasures to come.

鰊
(nishin)

３月に入ると、春の到来を待ちかねたように、まだ若い一年生の鰊が入荷してくる。うっすらと乗った脂は同種の真鰯(まいわし)のものよりははるかに淡白で品がよく、爽やかな香りさえ持っている。真鰯と同じように持つ、細くて長い無数の胸骨を完全に取り除きながら開いていく。うっすらと乗った脂によって乳白色に染められた表面の身肉は、包丁で十文字に切られた下からのぞく赤身との対比が美しい。すしに握ると、身肉はとろけるように崩れながら旨みをあらわしていく。そして春爛漫(はるらんまん)の到来とともに、さらに旬の最盛期に入っていく。

Young herring, just a year old, appear at markets in March as if eagerly awaiting the arrival of spring. Their thin layer of fat is much paler and has a more refined quality than that of their cousin, the Japanese sardine, and even has a refreshing fragrance. The herring are split and splayed, in the process removing a mass of long, thin sternal bones akin to those of the sardine. The surface flesh is rendered milky white by a thin layer of fat, an alluring contrast to the red flesh revealed through the cross slashed by the chef's knife. Made into nigiri, the fish virtually dissolves, spreading its fragrant flavor. And as spring progresses in earnest, the herring reaches its peak.

herring

白魚
(shira-uo)

1月の終わり頃、半透明の華奢で小さな魚体での初入荷となる。生のままの白魚の握りは、活きのよい白魚の群れの一部のように見える。頭部にある微かな苦みと、小魚のわりにはしっかりとした骨とによって、大人の味覚と食感を楽しむことができる。旬も終わりに近づき、卵を満々と抱えはじめる頃には卵の旨さも楽しめる。無数の小さな卵の粒々が、舌に歯に微妙に触れつつ、つぶれていく食感を味わうのだ。塩を打ち、蒸してから急冷すると、魚体は美しい乳白色に変貌し、旨みの増した食感を味わうことができる。

These translucent, sylph-like fish arrive on the market around the end of January. A nigiri of raw Japanese icefish resembles part of a darting, flashing school of these tiny creatures. With their hint of bitterness in the head, and unusually robust bone structure for their size, icefish offer a treat for the seasoned palate in both taste and texture. Another delightful sensation awaits as the season nears its end and the fish begin to fill with roe, the mass of tiny eggs tickling the teeth and tongue as they burst. Salted, steamed then quickly chilled, the fish turn a brilliant milky white, this different texture only highlighting their exquisite flavor.

icefish

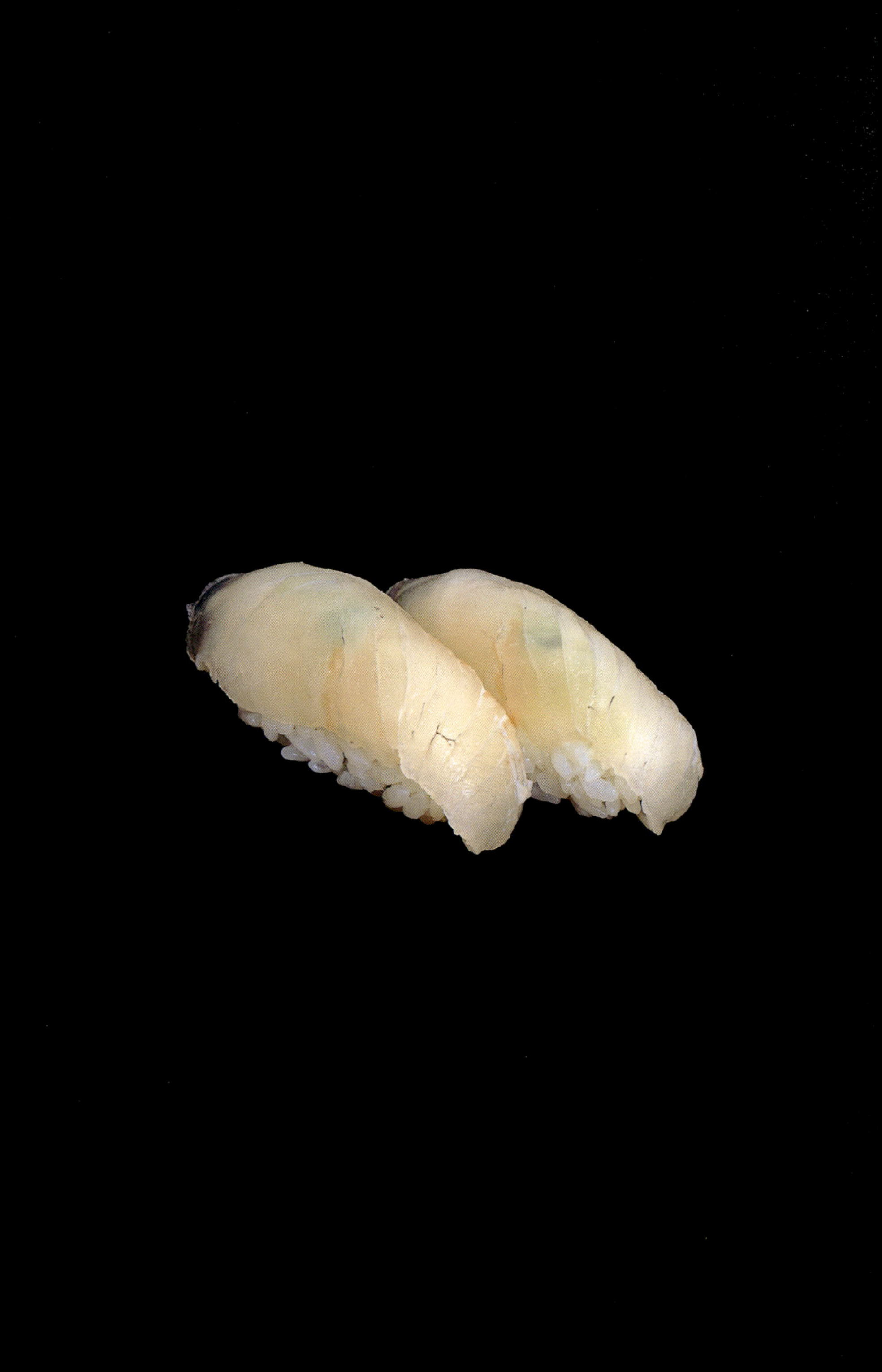

星鰈
(hoshigarei)

生態系が弱く漁獲量があまりにも少ないために、常に最高値をつける最高級の格を持つ白身の魚だ。身肉はしっかりと締まり、味わいはあまりにも淡白であるがゆえに、河豚以上に繊細で微妙だ。この旨さを堪能するためには翌日まで熟成させ、微かで繊細な旨さを最大限に引き出してやる必要がある。熟成された身肉を、少し厚めに切りつけて握ったすしは、繊細で品のよい緊張感のみなぎったものとなる。目をつぶり、意識を集中しないと星鰈の旨さを充分に満喫することはできない。エンガワの部位はさらに徹底的に咀嚼する。にじみ出る筋肉が持つ脂の旨みを充分に味わいつくすためだ。

Scarce and ecologically fragile, this high-status species invariably commands some of the highest prices. Firm-fleshed, its mild flavor makes for an even subtler, more delicate taste experience than fugu (puffer fish). The fish must be left to rest until the following day to maximize this subtle flavor. The aged flesh is sliced slightly thick and formed into nigiri of exquisite tension. To enjoy hoshigarei to the full one must close one's eyes and concentrate. The flesh from around the base of the fins should be chewed especially thoroughly, to fully appreciate the savoriness of the oil that oozes out of the muscles.

spotted halibut

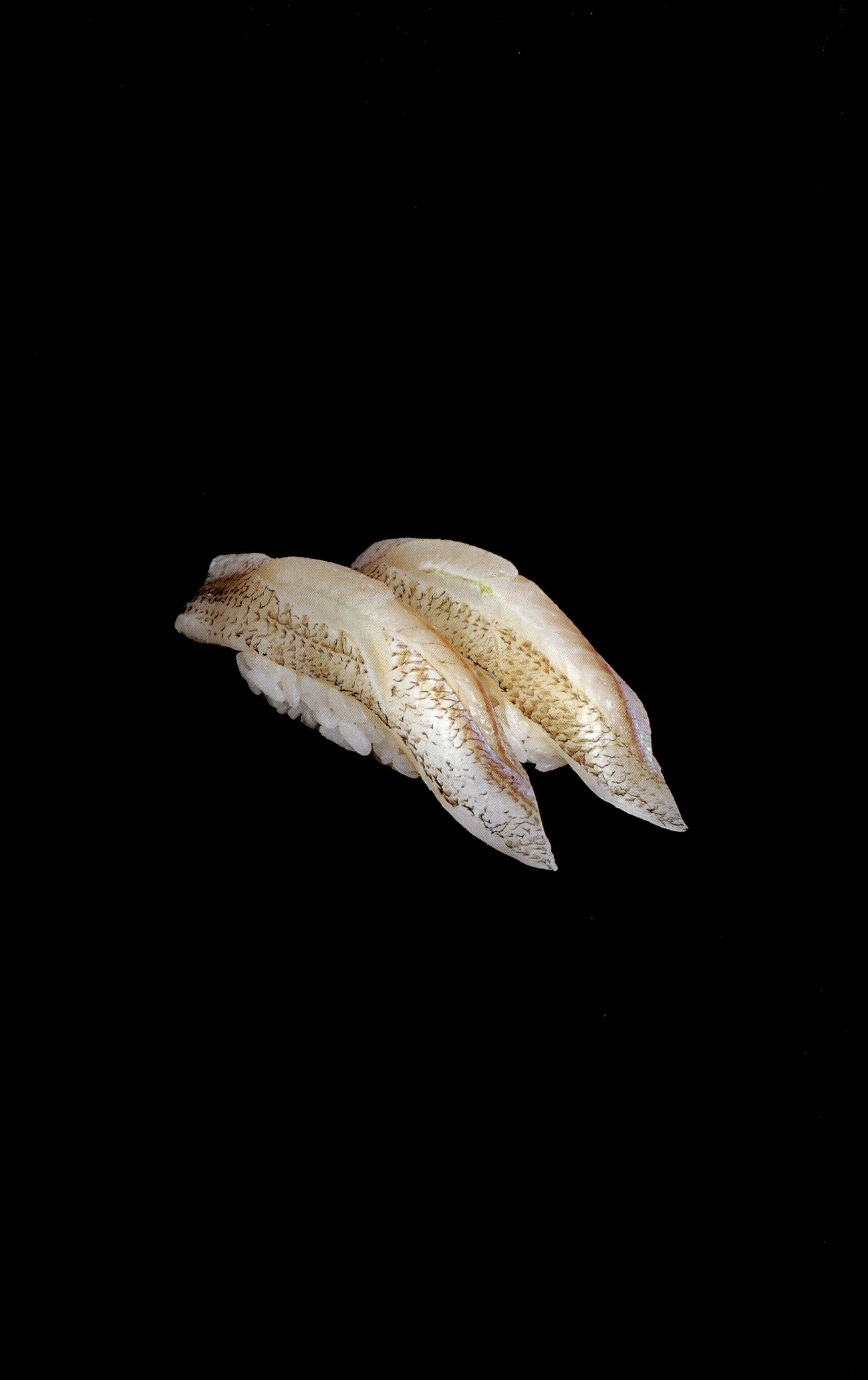

白鱚
(shirokisu)

春先の水温が上がりはじめる頃から卵持ちの頃までが旨さの旬となる。さらに晩秋から冬場にかけても餌をたっぷりと食い込み、旨さの時期となっていく。これは水温の変化の少ない深場に移行していく"落ち鱚"の時期の旨さとなる。白鱚は品のよい美しい姿をした小魚だが、生で食べることはしない。塩と酢とで軽く締めることによって、皮を柔らかくさせ、淡白だが厚みのある身肉に新たな甘みと旨みをつけ加えることになる。これをさらに昆布に挟み、昆布締めにする。身質の密度はもう少し締まり、微かに昆布の旨みをきかせた、新たな味わいの誕生となる。

Shirokisu peak from early spring when water temperatures begin to rise, to around incubation. They also feed ravenously from late autumn through winter, making this another prime season for flavor, the time for *ochi-kisu* (falling whiting) who move to deeper waters where the temperature is more constant. Japanese whiting has a sleek, refined appearance but is never eaten raw. Its thick flesh is not particularly rich in flavor but imparts a smooth, sweet taste. The skin is softened by marinating lightly in a mixture of salt and vinegar. The flesh is then lightly firmed between sheets of kombu, the flavor-enhancing properties of the kelp act subtly to create a new kind of richness.

Japanese whiting

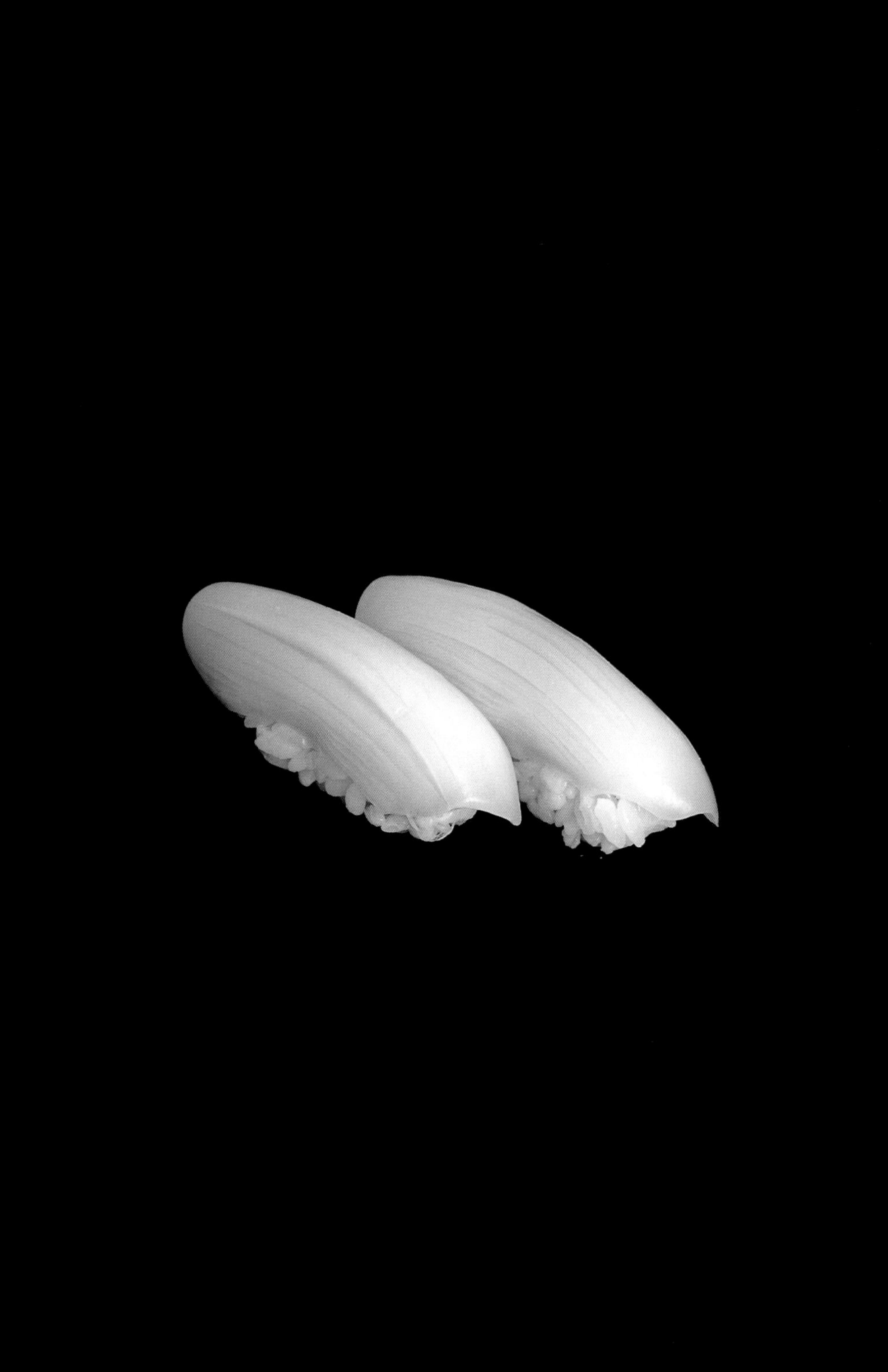

墨烏賊
(sumi-ika)

8月上旬、煽り烏賊と入れ替わるようにして墨烏賊の子供の新烏賊が登場する。江戸前ずしの世界では、小鰭の子供の新子とこの新烏賊は、初物ゆえの驚異的な高値をつけることになる。東京のすし屋の間では、意地と誇りと見栄をかけての戦いが始まるからだ。柔らかだが心地よい食感を持つ新烏賊は、2ヶ月もすると大きく成長していく。やがて春の到来の頃には、片手のサイズを超えるほどの大きさに成長し、強めの食感と微かな甘みをあわせ持つようになる。そして春の終わりの頃には産卵し、一年生の命を終えていく。

Young sumi-ika appear in early August, as if just in time to take over from aori-ika (bigfin reef squid) in Japan's sushi establishments. In the world of Edo-mae sushi, as the first of their species for the season these young squid, along with shinko – the fry of gizzard shad – fetch astounding prices, their arrival setting the stage for a battle of wills, pride and vanity among Tokyo sushi restaurants. Within a couple of months, still tender yet satisfying to the palate, they have grown large, and by spring are bigger than a hand, firm in texture, and with a hint of sweetness. Spawning around the end of spring completes the sumi-ika life cycle.

golden cuttlefish

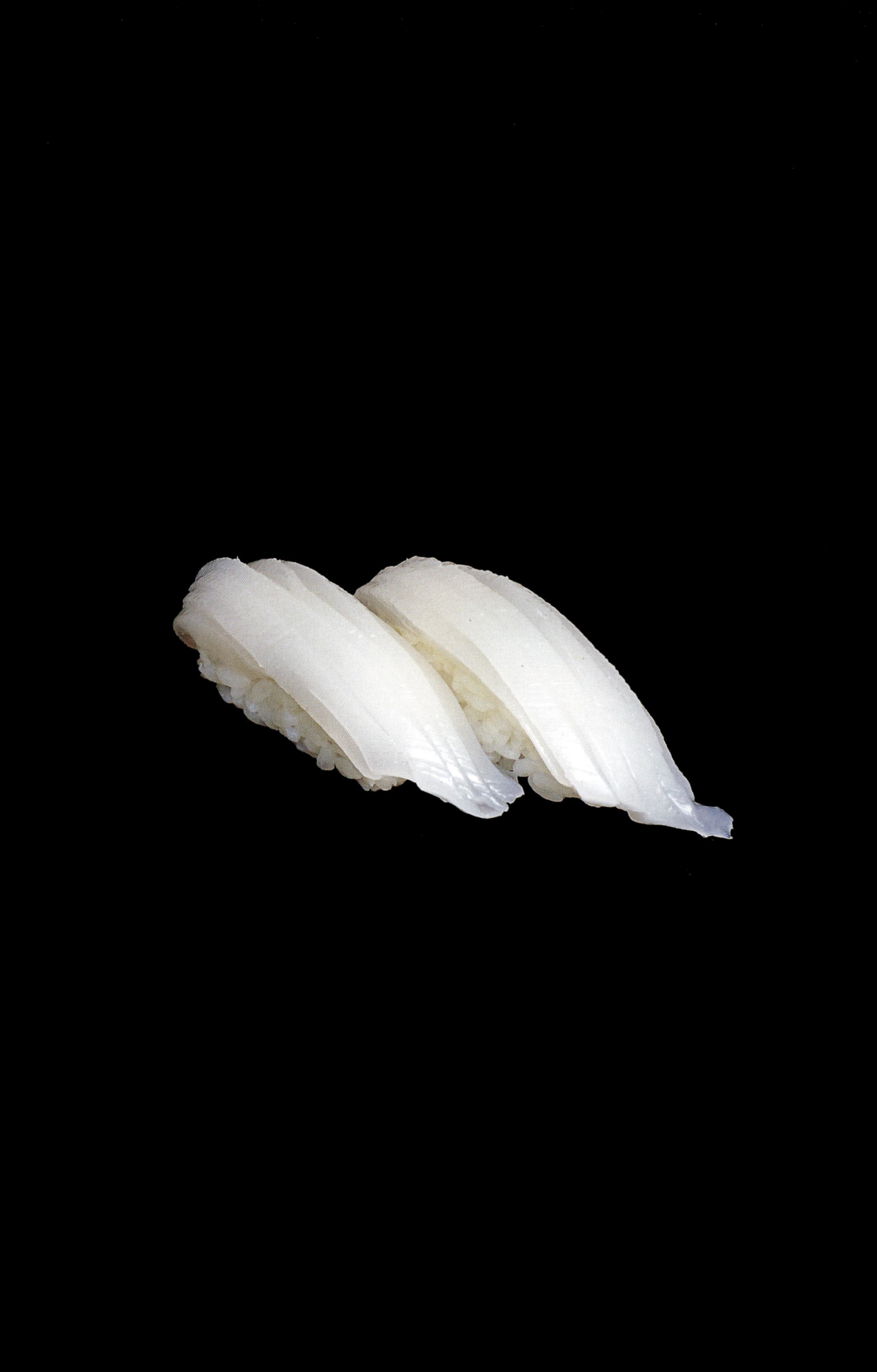

槍烏賊
(yari-ika)

晩秋に出はじめる槍烏賊は、2月頃には俄然大きく成長し、薄く柔らかだった身肉も厚みが増し、甘みもさらに強くなってくる。活きた身を糸造りにしたうっすらと透明な槍烏賊のすしの姿には、清々しい美しさが感じられる。それでも槍烏賊の最高の旨さを楽しむためには、もう少し熟成の時間の経過を考慮に入れる必要がある。丸々1日位の経過と、透明感がまったく消えてしまった頃に、さらに槍烏賊本来の甘さと旨さが増してくる。この槍烏賊の握りは、ほとんど真っ白にまで変色した身肉の中に、槍烏賊の熟成の旨さのすべてを楽しむことができる。

Making their first appearance in late autumn, around-ika have a sudden growth spurt, their tender, growing thicker and sweeter. Diaphanous yari-ika straight from the tank and cut into strips for serving as sushi is an irresistibly refreshing sight. But sampling yari-ika at its most delectable requires a little more aging: left a day before going under the chef's knife the squid acquires its true sweetness and flavor just as it loses all its translucency. Nigiri made from this yari-ika contains the mature flavor of the species, in by this stage almost pure white flesh.

spear squid

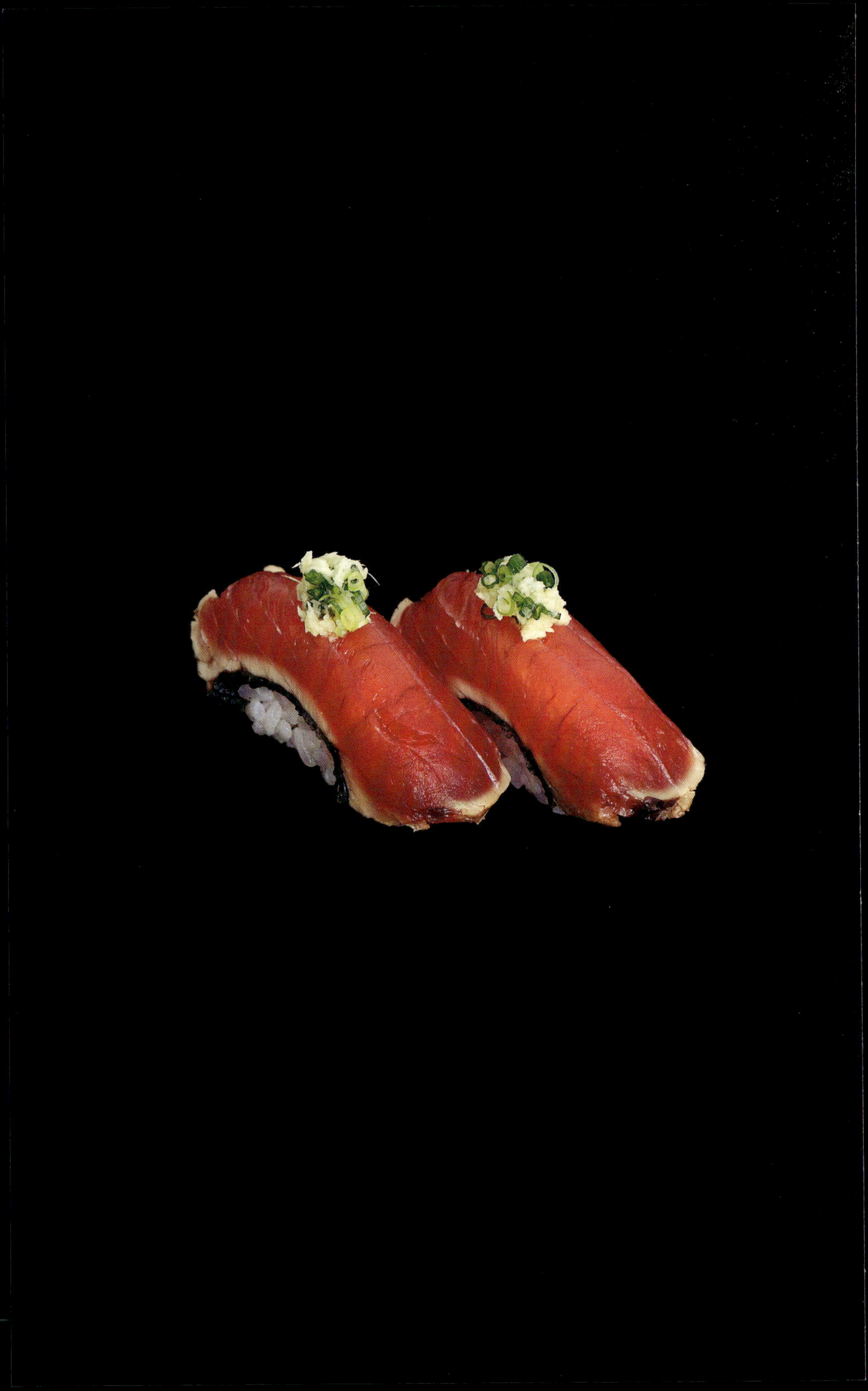

鰹
(katsuo)

日本列島の最南端から北上して来た鰹の群れは、４月から５月に入ると、皮目にうっすらと脂が乗ってくる。この時期の鰹を「初鰹」と呼ぶ。身肉は鮮やかに赤く、軽い脂の旨みと微かな酸味、血の香りまでもまとっている。鰹は旨さの選別が最も難しい魚だ。見事な鮮度で、丸々と太った姿をしていても、脂も旨みもまったくなく、渋みさえも持っているものが多々混じるのだ。最高の鰹は皮を焼いてすしに握っても旨い。薬味となる黄色の新生姜と浅葱の鮮やかな緑色が、視覚的にも美しく楽しめる。

During April and May, schools of bonito (katsuo) migrating north from the southern reaches of the Japanese archipelago acquire a thin layer of subcutaneous fat. These fish are known as *hatsugatsuo* (first bonito) and have vivid red flesh, a mildly fatty quality, a subtle tartness, and even a whiff of blood. Of all fish, good taste is hardest to pick in bonito: among the specimens at market there will always be many that are plump and fresh, but totally devoid of fat or flavor, astringent even. The very finest bonito tastes wonderful seared and made into nigiri, the addition of yellow new ginger and vivid green chives as condiments making it a visual treat too.

bonito

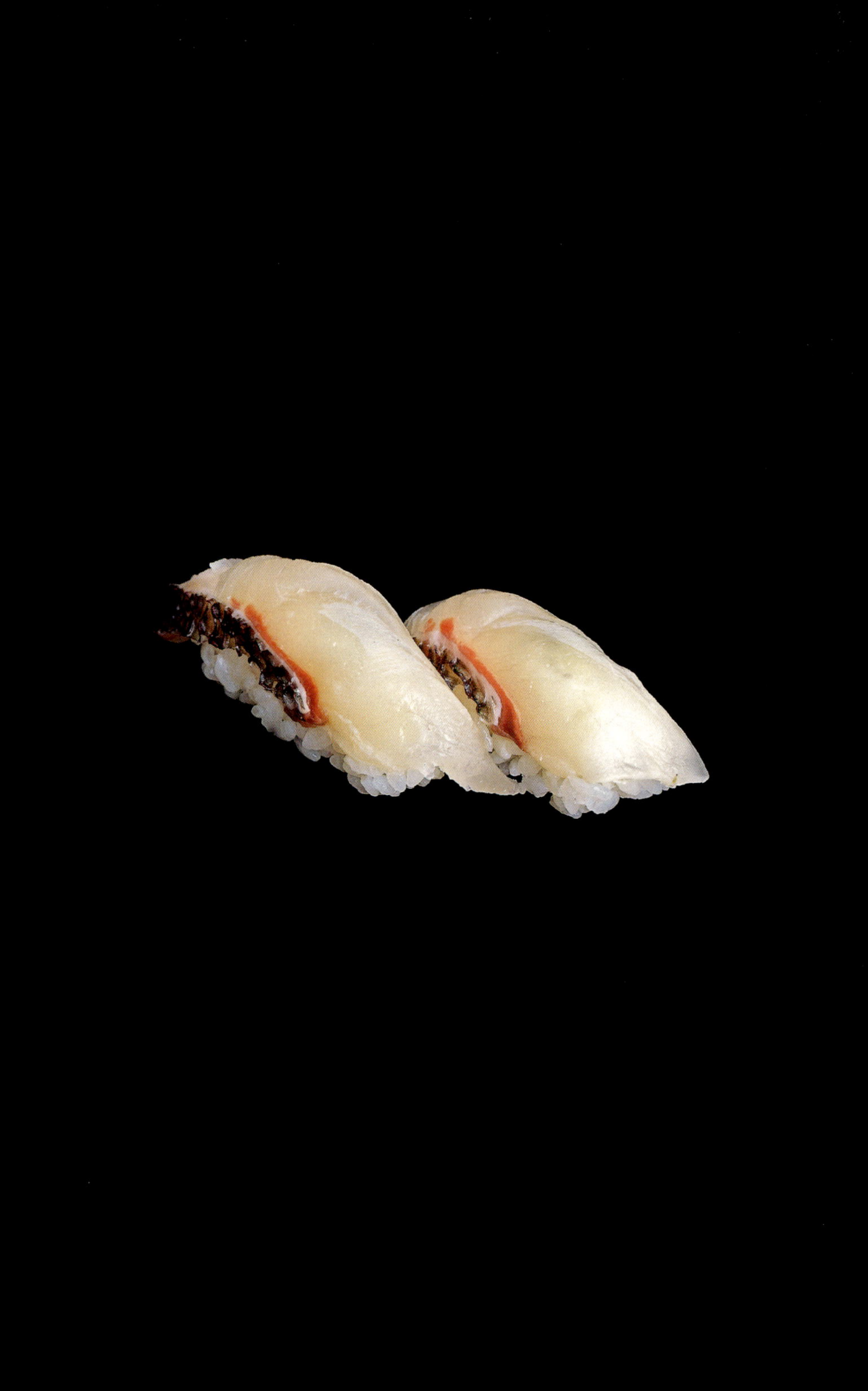

真鯛
(madai)

魚の王者と称される真鯛の旨さの旬は、冬場から4月の終わり頃までとなる。真鯛は5月から6月の産卵の時期に合わせ、餌をたっぷりと食い込んでいくからだ。旬の最盛期の身肉は琥珀色に色づき、雌の皮目は婚姻色と言われる美しい朱色に輝いている。真鯛のおいしさの特徴は、皮目の美しさと身肉の甘みの濃い旨さにある。1.5キロ前後の雌は、皮目に熱湯で霜降りをすることによって、美しい朱色の皮付きのまま刺身にすることができる。この真鯛を握ると、艶やかで姿の美しい握りずしとなる。皮目の朱色と甘みのある脂の旨さ、程よい皮の食感もあわせて楽しむことができる。

This 'king of fish' is in its prime from winter to late April, due to prodigious feeding ahead of May-June spawning. At season's height madai flesh turns amber, the subcutaneous flesh of the female also acquiring its beautiful red nuptial coloration. Madai is prized for this visual appeal, and its intense sweet flavor. Female madai, weighing around 1.5kgs, can be blanched leaving the color intact for vibrantly hued sushi, the fish's shimmering scarlet and sweet, succulent fat combining with just the right degree of texture in the skin.

red sea bream

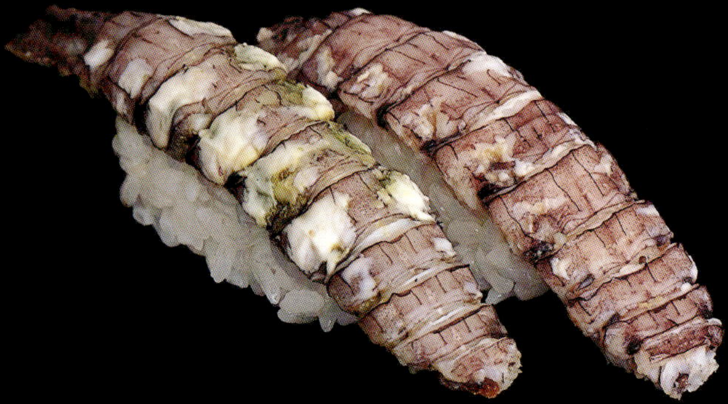

蝦蛄
(shako)

４月から６月にかけての蝦蛄は、はちきれんばかりの卵を抱いている。身肉の甘みは薄くなるのだが、卵の旨みと食感を楽しむことができる。蝦蛄にはもうひとつ、異なった旨みを見せる時期がある。晩秋の脱皮の直前には、身肉がたっぷりと太り、濃厚な甘みと高い香りの旨みを楽しむことができる。握る前に少し炙ると身肉がふっくらと膨らみ、甲殻類の一種である蝦蛄特有の香りと甘みが、さらに強く立ちのぼることになる。両手の「爪」の身肉はことさらに甘みが強く、希少な部位として珍重される。

Between April and June, shako are bursting with roe. While their flesh is less sweet, the flavor and texture of these eggs make the crustaceans a gourmet delight. Shako offer a different taste experience again in late autumn, when they grow fat and acquire an intense sweetness and fragrant succulence just prior to molting. Searing slightly before pressing into nigiri plumps up the flesh, highlighting the unique aroma and sweetness. The flesh of the claws is particularly delectable and a much-desired delicacy.

mantis shrimp

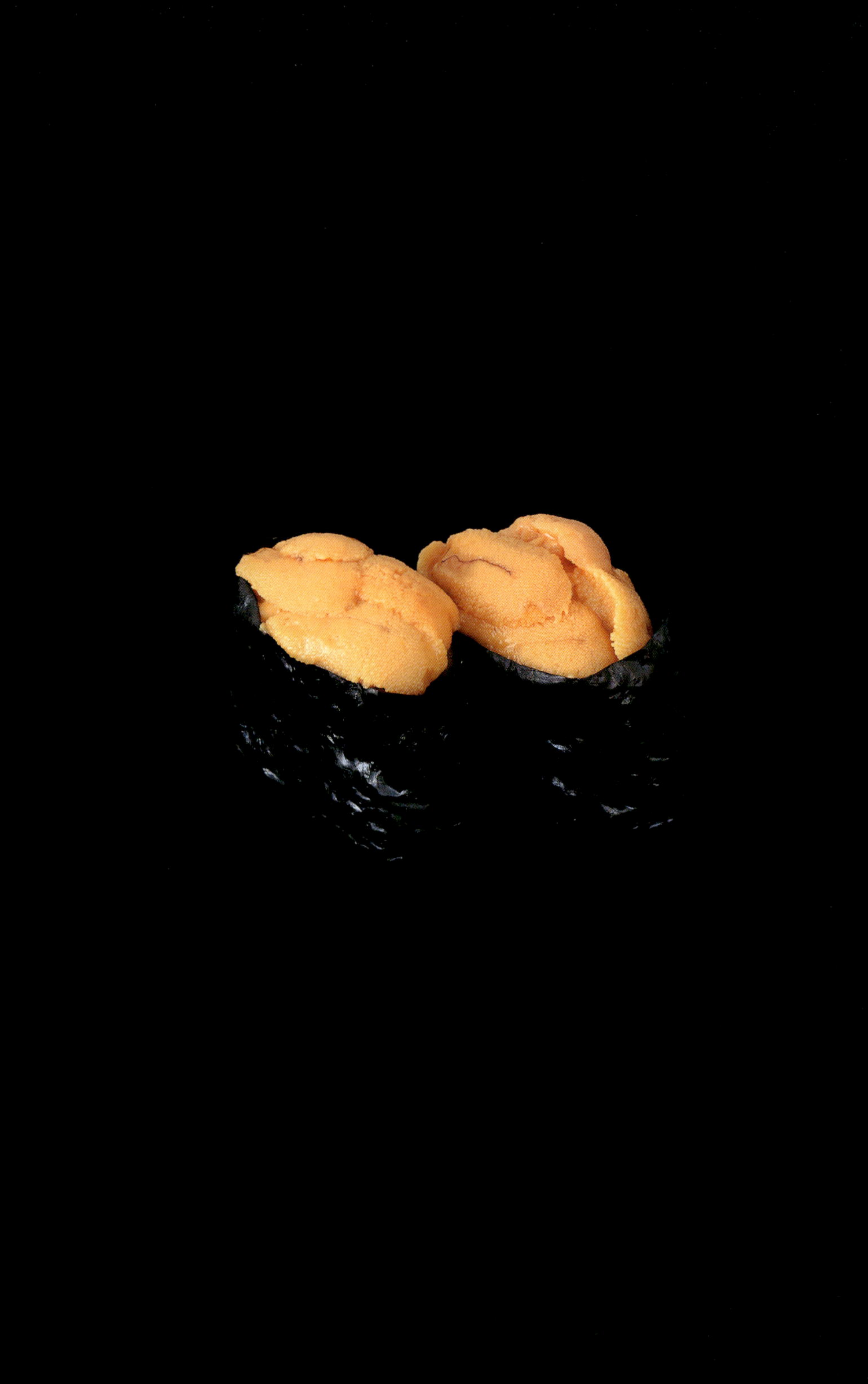

海胆
(uni)

日本海の海胆は夏場が、道東の海胆は晩秋から春の終わり頃までが旨さの旬となる。海胆の旨さの識別は特に難しい。鮮度・色・姿・形ではなく、食すことによってでしか識別することができないからだ。蝦夷馬糞海胆は黄朱色で粒が小さめで身崩れしやすいが、旨み甘みが濃厚で軽い磯の香りも楽しめる。北紫海胆は黄褐色で粒は大きく成長する。蝦夷馬糞海胆よりも身質がしっかりとし、見てくれはよいが甘みは少し軽い。海胆と海苔と醤油との相性は抜群で、すしの上にたっぷりの山葵を乗せて食すと旨い。

Uni from the Sea of Japan are best in summer, while those harvested off the east coast of Hokkaido peak from late autumn to the end of spring. Identifying the tastiest specimens is especially tricky with sea urchin. Freshness, form, color and appearance offer no clue; flavor is all. The short-spined sea urchin is yellowish-brown, fine-grained, and comes apart easily, but is rich and sweet with a slight salty tang. The northern sea urchin meanwhile is yellowish-brown and coarser, firmer fleshed than the red sea urchin, and more attractive, but not as sweet. Uni, seaweed and soy sauce make an outstanding combo, further improved by a generous garnish of wasabi.

sea urchin

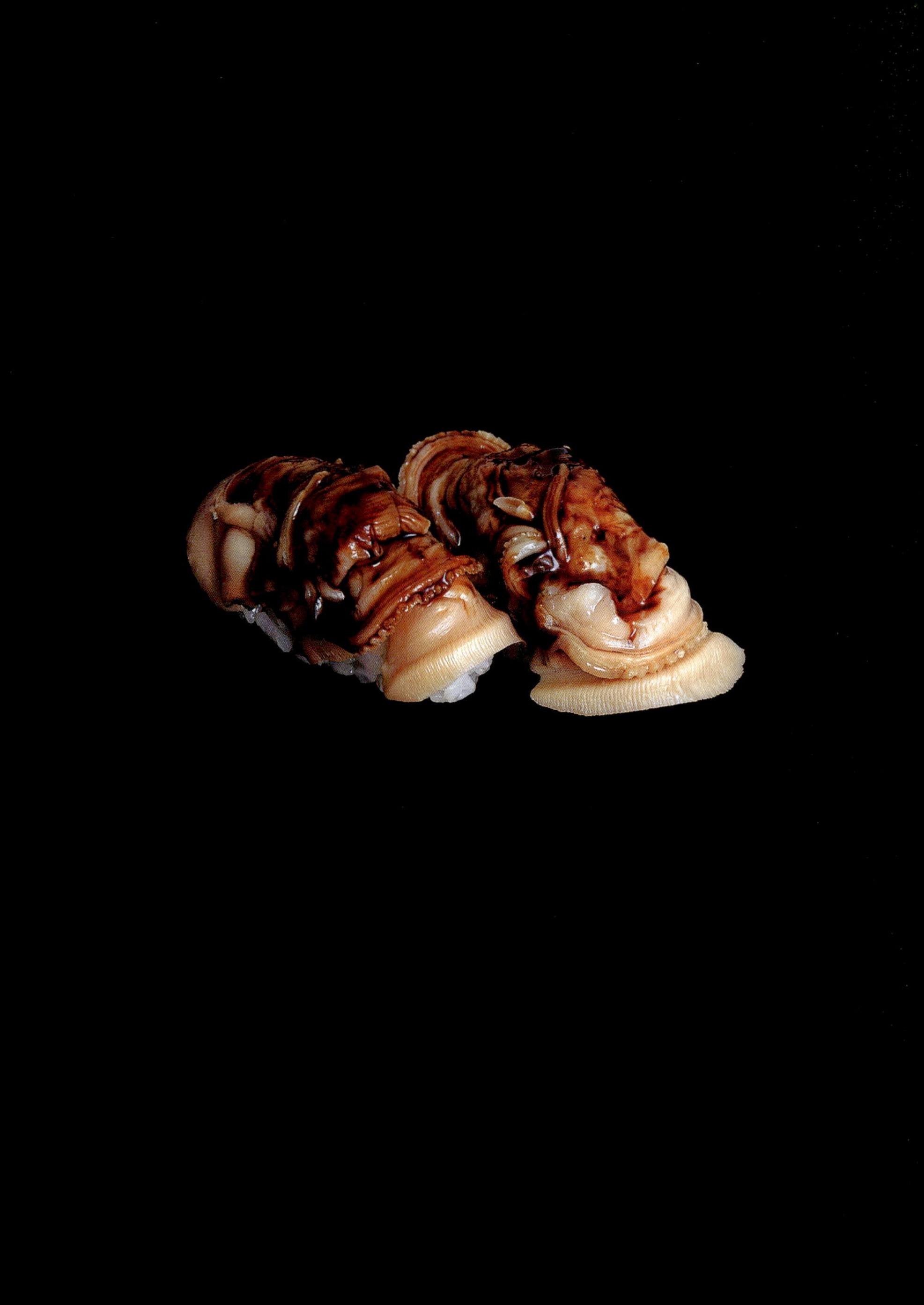

蛤
(hamaguri)

蛤の旨さの旬は春先から夏場にかけてとなる。蛤には内湾に生息するものと外海産とがあるが、身肉が太って柔らかい内湾産が特に旨い。しかし近年、貴重な内湾ものは絶滅に近いほどに減少している。"煮"蛤の仕事は江戸前ずし独自の希少な技のひとつとして伝承されてきた。日本には蛤を生で食べる食習慣がなく、必ず煮含めてから使用する。まず貝を剥き、身を熱湯に通してから開き、蛤の煮汁でつくった汁に漬け込み、味を十分に染み込ませてからすしに握り、さらに上に甘いツメを塗る。

Hamaguri are most delectable from early spring into summer. Found in both inshore and offshore beds, inshore hamaguri with their tender, plump flesh are particularly tempting, although in recent years have declined almost to extinction. Cooking hamaguri is a traditional technique specific to Edo-mae sushi. The Japanese have no custom of eating the clams raw, preferring to simmer them in broth before use. Shelled, blanched, then splayed open, they are marinated in a stock of simmered hamaguri juices to intensify flavor, then made into nigiri and coated with sweet tsume glaze to finish.

common Orient clam

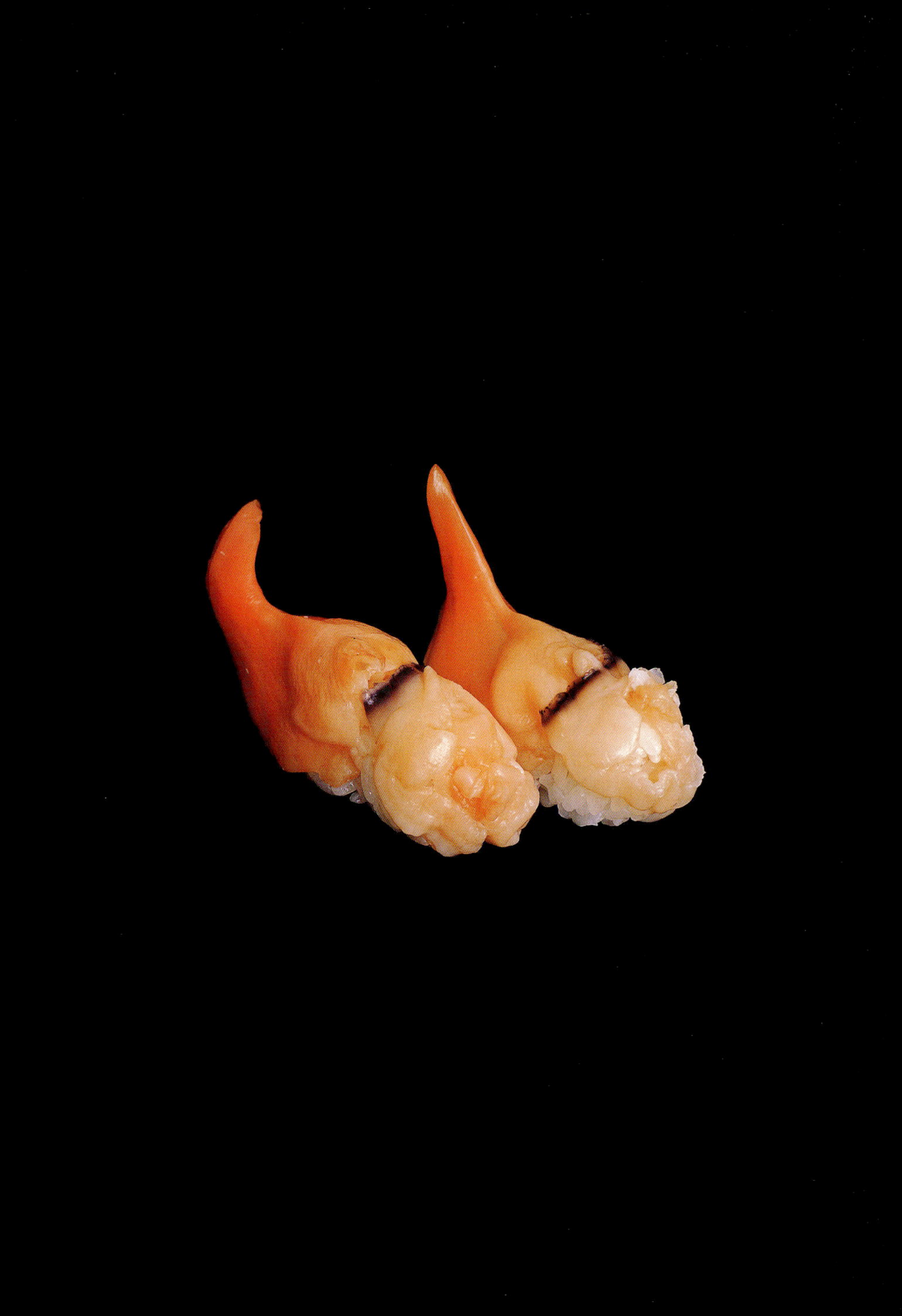

青柳
(aoyagi)

旨さの旬は冬から春にかけてとなる。卵持ちとともに身肉は痩せ、6月には産卵が始まる。近年は入荷する産地が南北に拡大し、旨さの旬が長くなった。塩揉みし、ヌルを取り除き、湯に通して身肉を固め、舌の先端をツンと突き上げるようにさせて開く。柔らかく、優しい歯ごたえには心地よいものがあり、独自の癖のある香りと甘みが旨さとなる。大小一対の貝柱は「小柱」と呼ばれて珍重される。最近は色が美しい黄朱色の大サイズのものが極少で、良品は高値となっている。正式和名は「馬珂貝」だが、名称の持つ響きの悪さのために、最近では青柳と言われることが多くなった。

Aoyagi are at their peak from winter to early spring. Losing flesh during incubation, they commence spawning in June. Recent years have seen a north-south expansion in the clam's grounds, lengthening the season. Salt is rubbed in to deslime the clams, which are then rinsed in hot water to firm, and the tip of the tongue flipped up to split open the flesh. Of a tender, pleasant consistency, they are distinguished by a marvelous fragrance and sweetness. Aoyagi adductor muscles, one large, one small, are known as kobashira and greatly prized. Catches of the attractive larger reddish-yellow aoyagi have plummeted of late, with good-quality specimens at a premium.

Chinese mactra clam

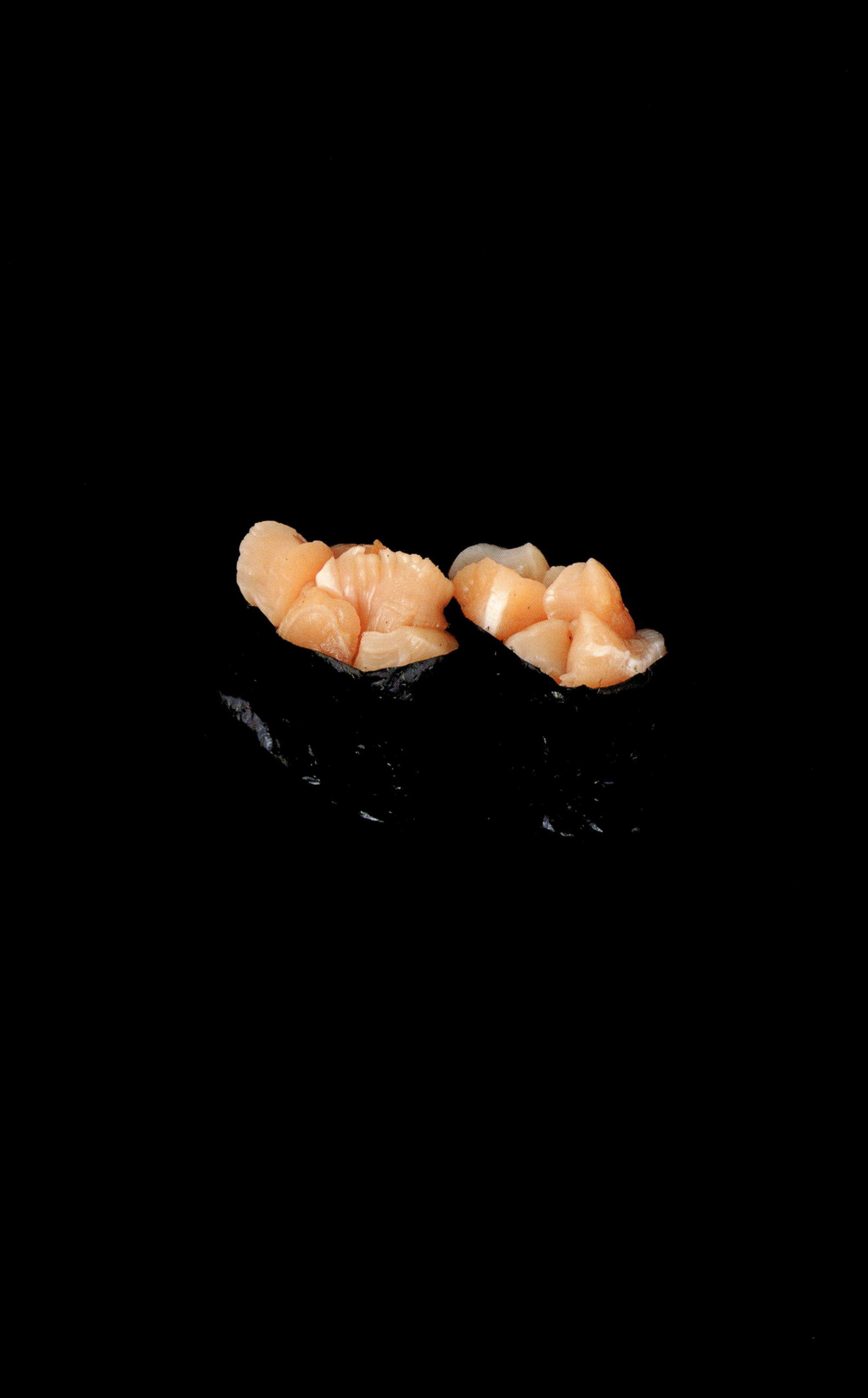

小柱
(kobashira)

青柳（馬珂貝(ばかがい)）についている大小２個の貝柱は、小柱と呼ばれ珍重される。大きいほうを大星(おおぼし)、小さいほうは小星(こぼし)と言う。江戸前ずしではこの小柱を生の状態で握る。大ぶりの艶々と黄朱色に輝く貝柱は、色鮮やかで見事に美しい。本来の主役となるべき身肉の舌よりもはるかに甘みが強く、水っぽさもない。鮮度が良く、活きているときの生態反応による軽く爽やかな噛み心地には、痛快感さえある。高級料理の中での応用範囲が広く、舌の部位よりも５倍以上に値付けされるほどに、商品価値は高く評価される。

The twin adductor muscles of the Chinese mactra clam (aoyagi or bakagai) are a delicacy known as kobashira. In Edo-mae sushi kobashira are used raw. Impressively large, their bright yellowish-red hue gives them a vivid beauty. Far sweeter than the clam's tongue, they also lack its watery flavor. The light, refreshing sensation of biting into fresh kobashira caused by the shellfish's biological response, can be intensely pleasurable. A firm favorite of upmarket dining establishments, kobashira sell for over five times the price of clam tongues, proof of their high market value.

clam muscle

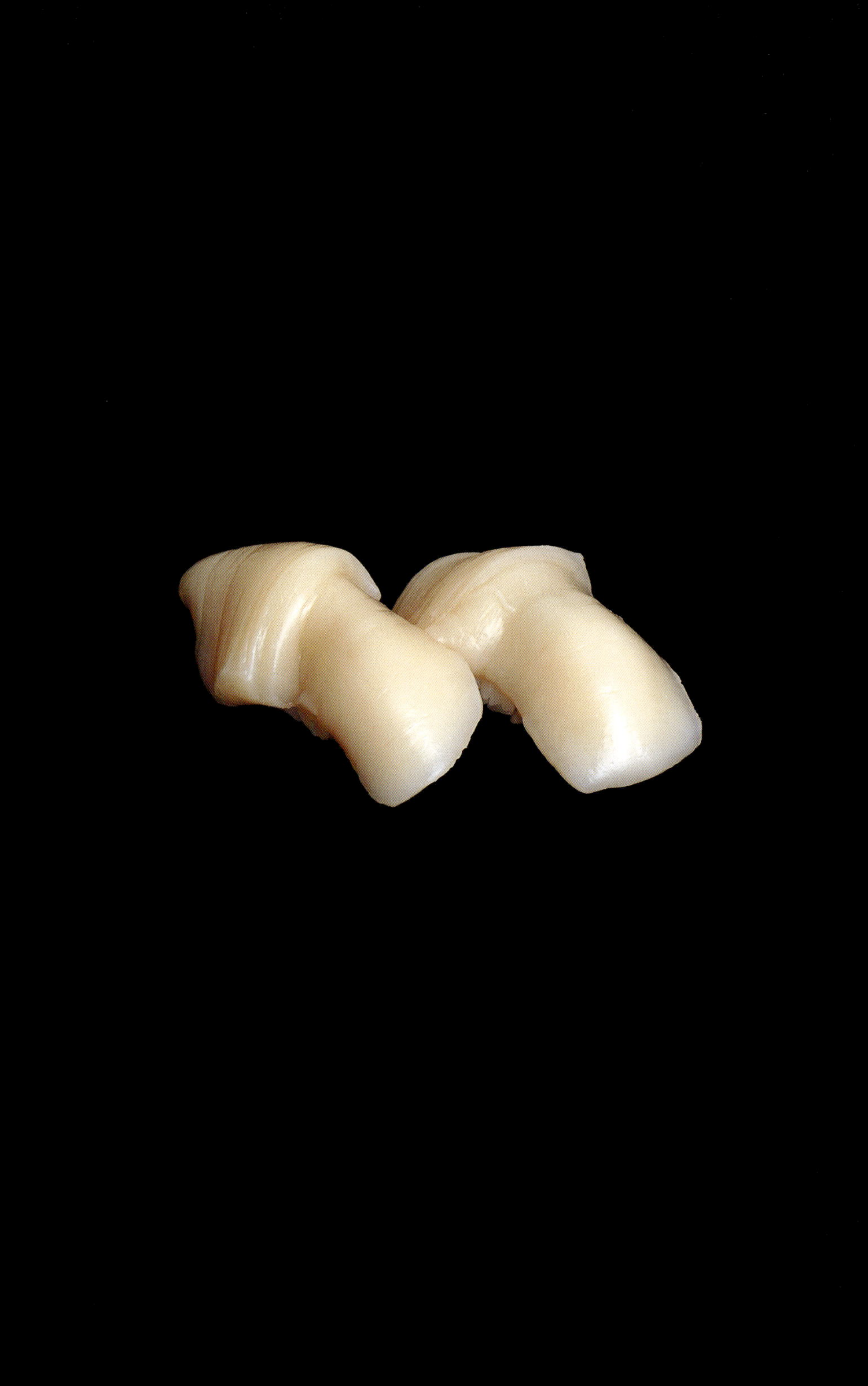

帆立貝
(hotategai)

オホーツク海南端の低水温の急流で鍛えられた天然の帆立貝は、養殖ものにはあり得ないような心地よい食感と強い甘みを持っている。産地から殻付きで活きたまま送られて来る帆立貝は、4年生のサイズが最も旨く使い勝手もよいため主役となる。12月上旬から解禁となる漁は、翌年の4月には旬真っ盛りの最盛期となっている。帆立貝は成長していく卵巣・精巣の肥大とともに貝柱の旨さもさらに増大させる。豊富なプランクトンを餌に、6月頃の産卵期直前まで旨さの旬は続いていく。この時期の卵巣・精巣は、まるで海胆のように甘く旨く、産地でも特に珍重される部位となっている。

Wild scallops, tempered by the swift cold current on the southern edge of the Sea of Okhotsk, have a pleasant texture and intense sweetness absent from their farmed cousins. Shipped live in the shell from their catching grounds, they are tastiest and most versatile aged four, making it scallops of this size that dominate the market. The season opens in early December, and peaks in April. The adductor muscle becomes more succulent as the gonads swell, and scallops remain at their peak until around June just prior to spawning, feeding on plentiful plankton. Scallop sex organs during this period are as sweet and tasty as uni, and highly prized even among those living close to their fishing grounds.

scallop

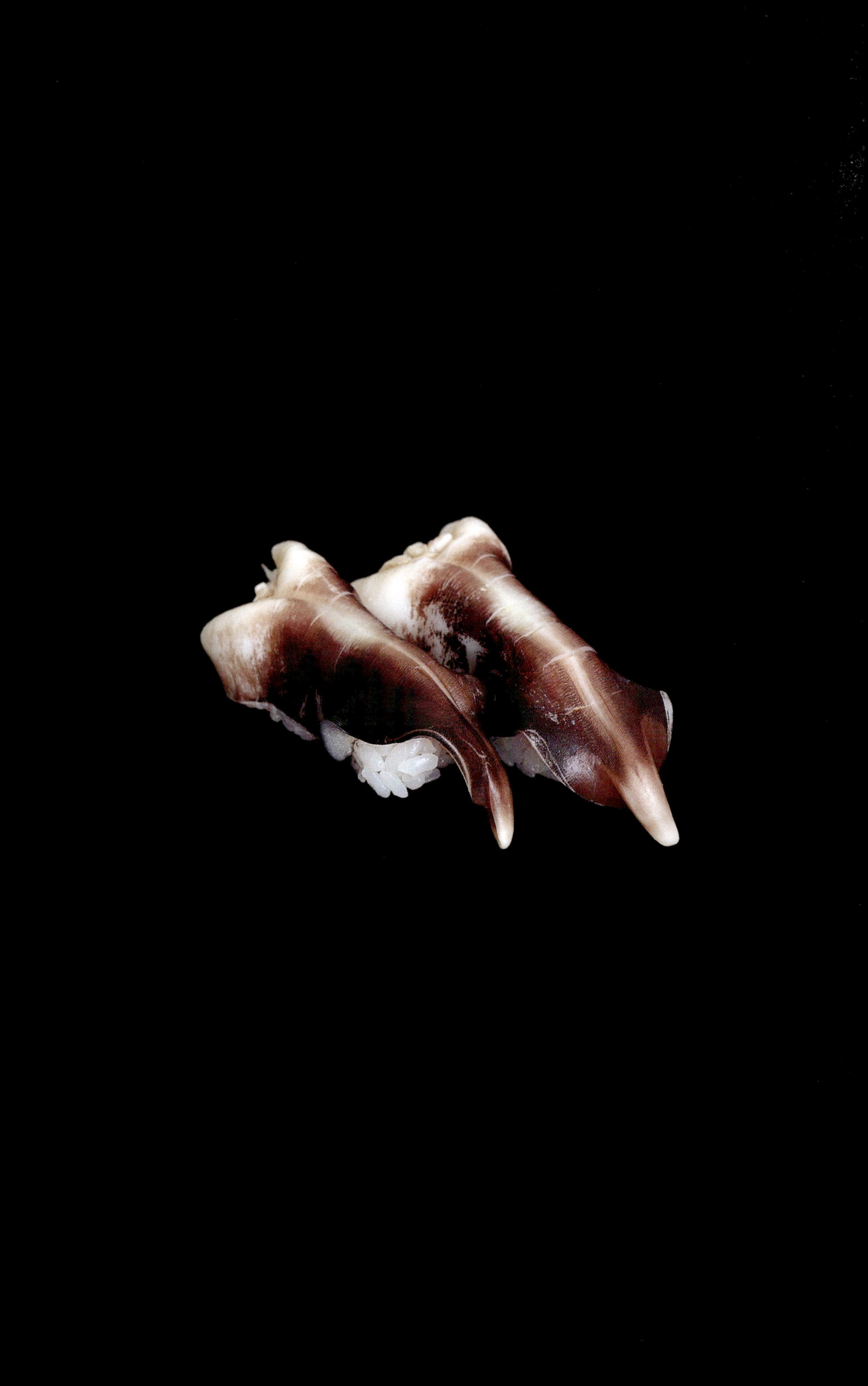

鳥貝
(torigai)

旨さの旬は３月頃から７月頃までとなるが、２年ごとにやってくる好不漁の差は激しい。鳥貝は、身肉の表面が艶やかな黒の膜に覆われる個性的な貝で、旬の到来の時期も、旨さの最高時の状況も他の貝類とは大きな違いを見せている。殻つきの活きた状態で入荷するたっぷりと太った身肉には、程よい食感がある。旬の最盛期、強い甘みを持つ卵巣の発育とともに、身肉は厚く大きく成長していく。白く大量に増えていく卵巣には食中毒の危険もなく、身肉の甘みをさらに濃いものにする。

Torigai are tastiest from around March to July, although catches fluctuate dramatically every couple of years. The shiny black membrane covering the flesh marks torigai out from other shellfish, as does the timing of their season and peak flavor. Sourced live in the shell, their plump, succulent flesh provides the perfect balance of tenderness and satisfying texture. Development of the intensely sweet ovaries in peak season makes the cockles even plumper, their proliferating light-colored mass adding to the rich sweetness of the flesh.

Japanese cockle

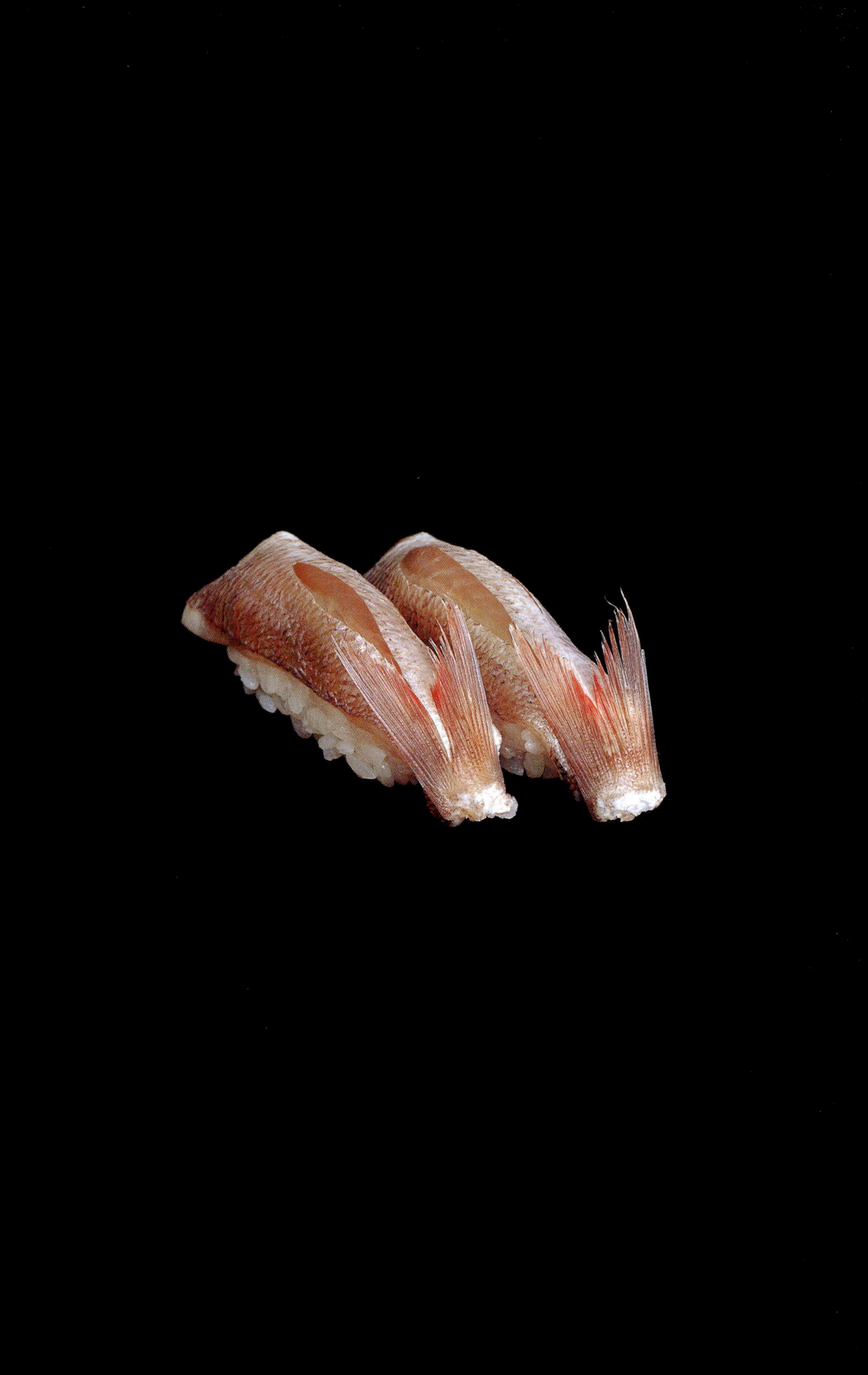

春子
(kasugo)

東京では15センチ前後の鯛の子供を"春子"と呼ぶ。表皮の鮮やかな朱色と、ピンと立つ、さらに濃い朱色の尾鰭の美しさこそが春子のすしの命となる。東京での春子の旬は、春先から夏場にかけてとされる。子供であるために、身肉が少し柔らかく、生のままでは旨みが足りない。しかし江戸前ずしの塩と酢とで締める伝統の技を施すことによって、しっかりとした新たな旨みが発揮させられる。締められた春子は、さらに昆布締めの仕事まで施すと身肉はさらにもう少し締まり、積み重ねの旨みが発揮されることになる。

In Tokyo young crimson sea bream measuring around 15cm are known as kasugo, literally 'children of spring'. The young fishes' brilliant red skin and even deeper red, upright tail fins are what give kasugo sushi its special allure. In Tokyo kasugo are deemed tastiest from early spring to early summer. Being young they are tender and somewhat bland raw, but with flesh firmed using the traditional Edo-mae sushi mix of salt and vinegar, they acquire a new, more defined flavor. Firmed again between kombu, kasugo become even more robust, the repeated firming also adding to the flavor.

sea bream fry

summer

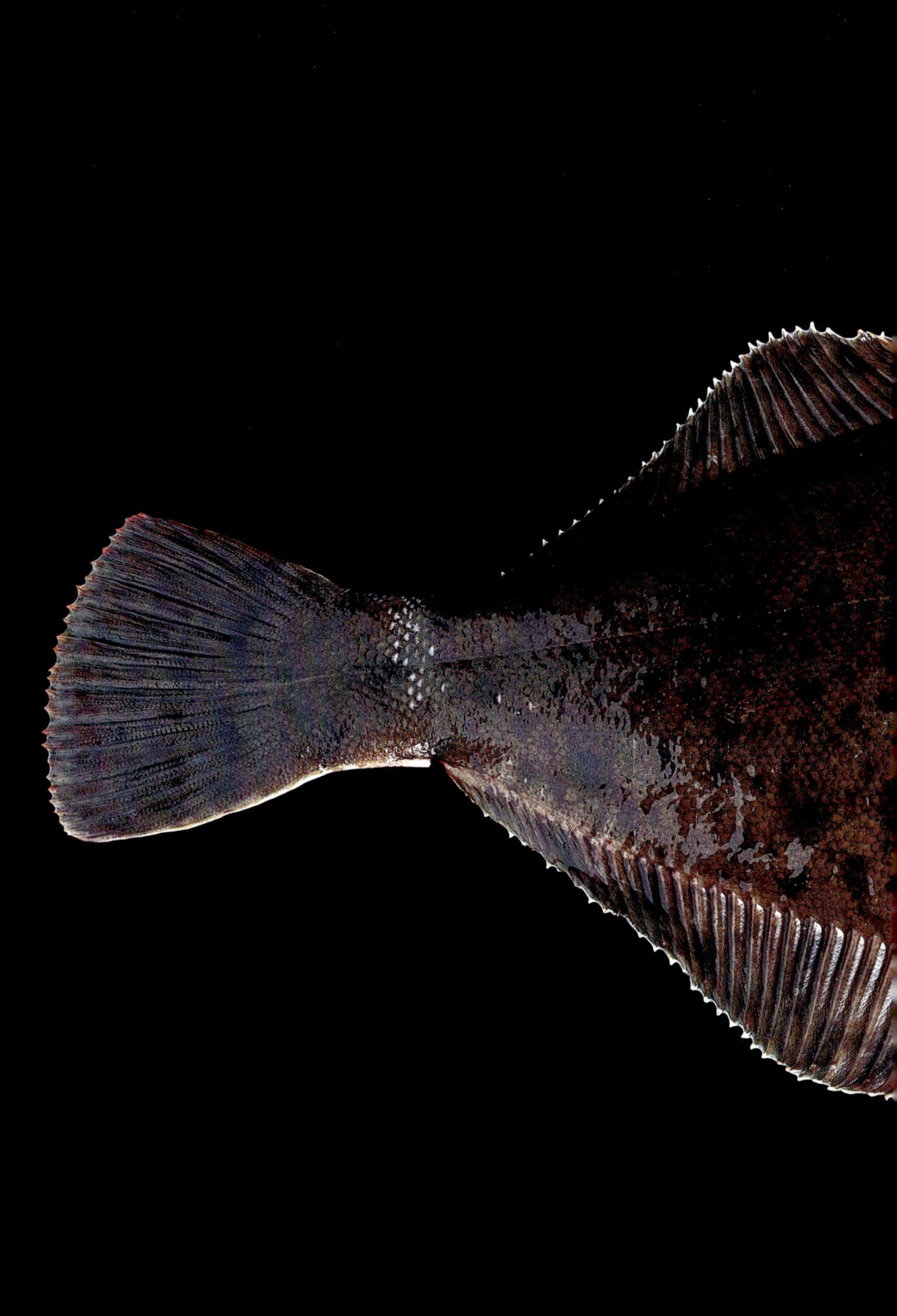

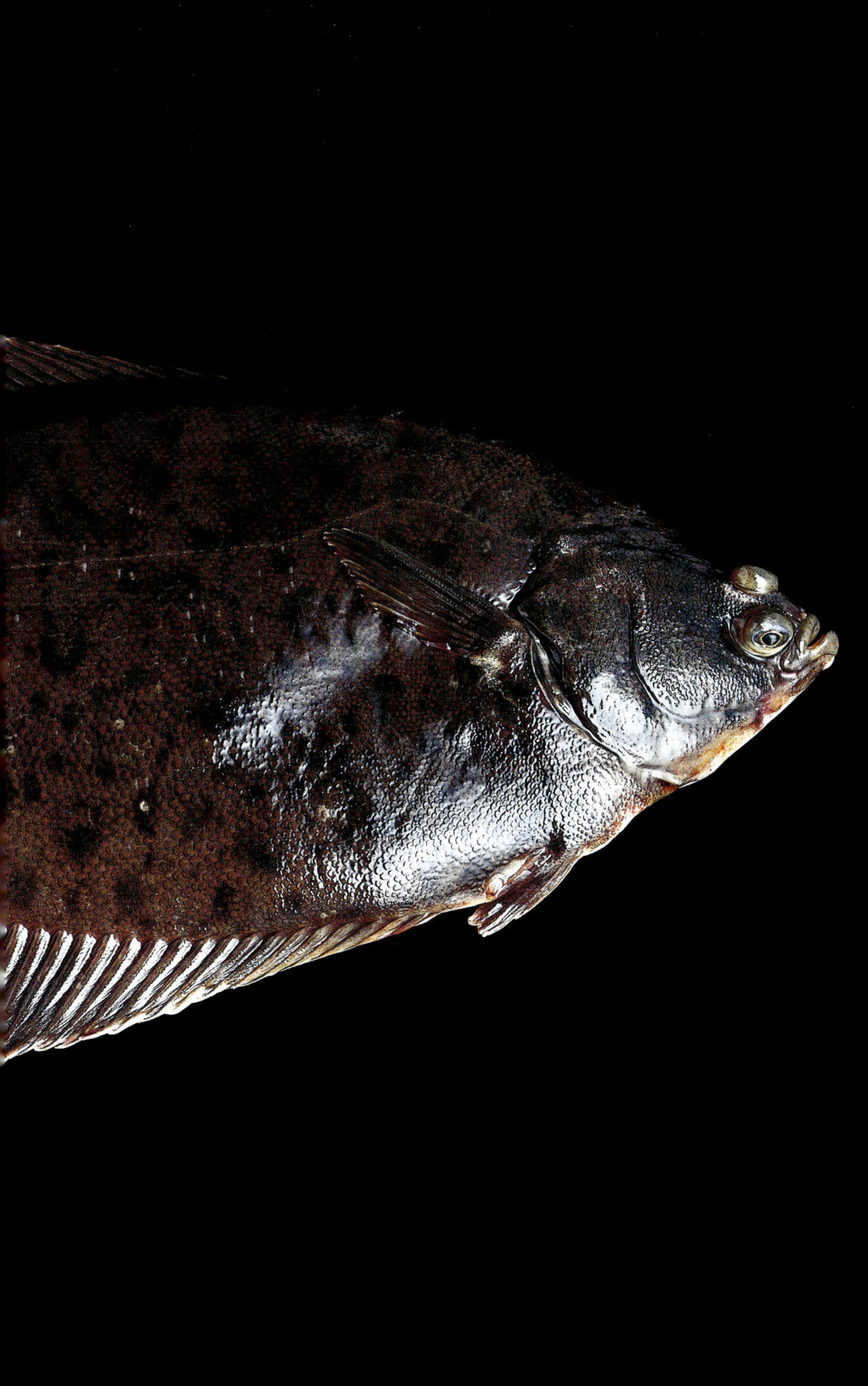

夏の魚

夏を旨さの旬とする魚たちは、水温の上昇とともに身肉を充実させ、夏の終わりから初秋の産卵に備えて旨みを増していく。冬の魚たちのような濃厚な脂の乗りの旨さではなく、淡白な味わいを持ち味とするものが多い。7月の半ば頃、江戸前ずしの伝統と誇りを背負い、江戸っ子の心意気を競い合う新子の入荷の始まりは、江戸前ずしの世界に新鮮な緊張感を走らせる。烏賊の女王とされる煽り烏賊は、強い甘みと品のよい食感を持ち味とするが、8月には産卵が始まるため、7月終わり頃までを旬とする。最高級魚の縞鯵は、皮目が金色に美しく、身を薄く白濁させ、滑らかな食感と品のよい旨味を秘めている。特大真高鮑は香り高く、豊満な甘みとゼラチン質の旨味を誇っている。真子鰈は見事な太り方を見せ、星鰈よりも身質は柔らかいのだが、品のよい脂の甘み・旨みを楽しませてくれる。夏の終わり頃には、新烏賊の入荷も少量ながら始まる。かくして夏は最高級の魚たちが勢揃いする季節となる。夏を代表する鱸も、決して過剰な脂の乗りはなく、爽やかな旨み・甘みを持っている。鯵は冬場の産卵後、水温の上昇の中で猛烈な食欲を発揮し、急激に脂を乗せていく。江戸前ずしを代表する穴子は、雨水とともに大量に流れ込む栄養分によって脂が乗り、柔らかく見事にとけていく身質と、脂の旨みを楽しむことができる。

summer fish

Species peaking in summer grow fleshier as water temperatures rise, and tastier ahead of spawning from late summer to early autumn. Their flavor is commonly milder and more subtle than the intense oily richness of winter fish. The arrival on the market of young gizzard shad around mid-July is the cue for spirited rivalry among Tokyo-ites intent on upholding the proud traditions of Edo-mae sushi, and sends a frisson of anticipation through the capital's sushi scene. Queen of squid aori-ika has an intense sweetness and refined texture, however because spawning commences in August, the season is deemed to end around late July. Premium species striped jack acquires a beautiful layer of golden fat under the skin, and a pearly whiteness to its flesh, promising smooth texture and refined flavor. Giant madaka abalone are intensely fragrant at this time of year, and boast a succulent sweetness and gelatinous mouth feel. Marbled sole grow splendidly plump, and offer a sweet, refined fattiness. By late summer, young squid appear on the market, albeit in small quantities. Thus in summer connoisseurs are spoilt for choice when it comes to premium sushi species. Sea bass, a major summer species, has just the right degree of oiliness, and an agreeable flavor and sweetness. Japanese jack mackerel exhibit a ferocious appetite as waters warm after winter spawning, and rapidly acquire fat. Conger eel, a staple of Edo-mae sushi, does likewise, thanks to the nutrients that flood in with rainwater, resulting in tender, melt-in-the-mouth flesh, and delectable fat.

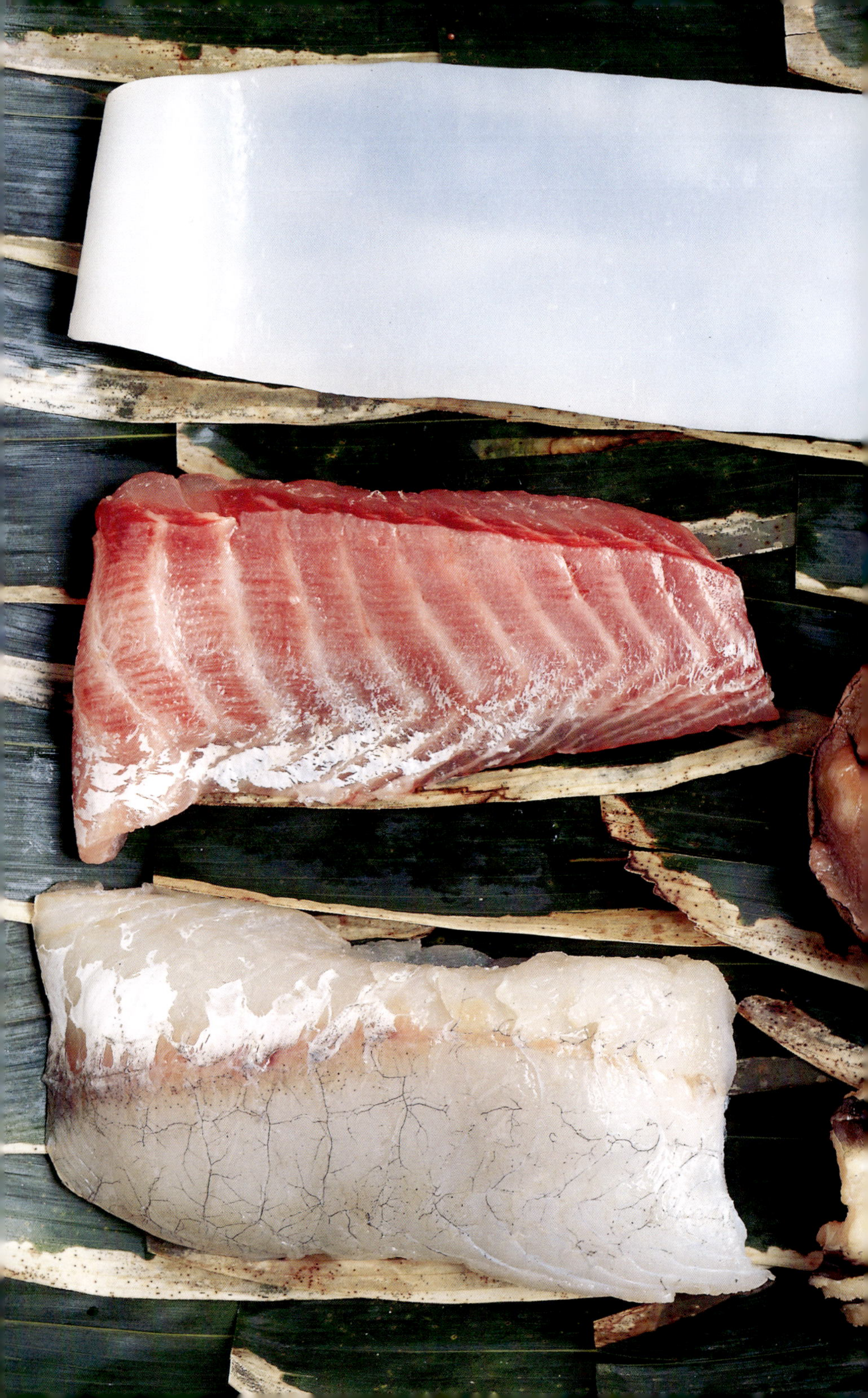

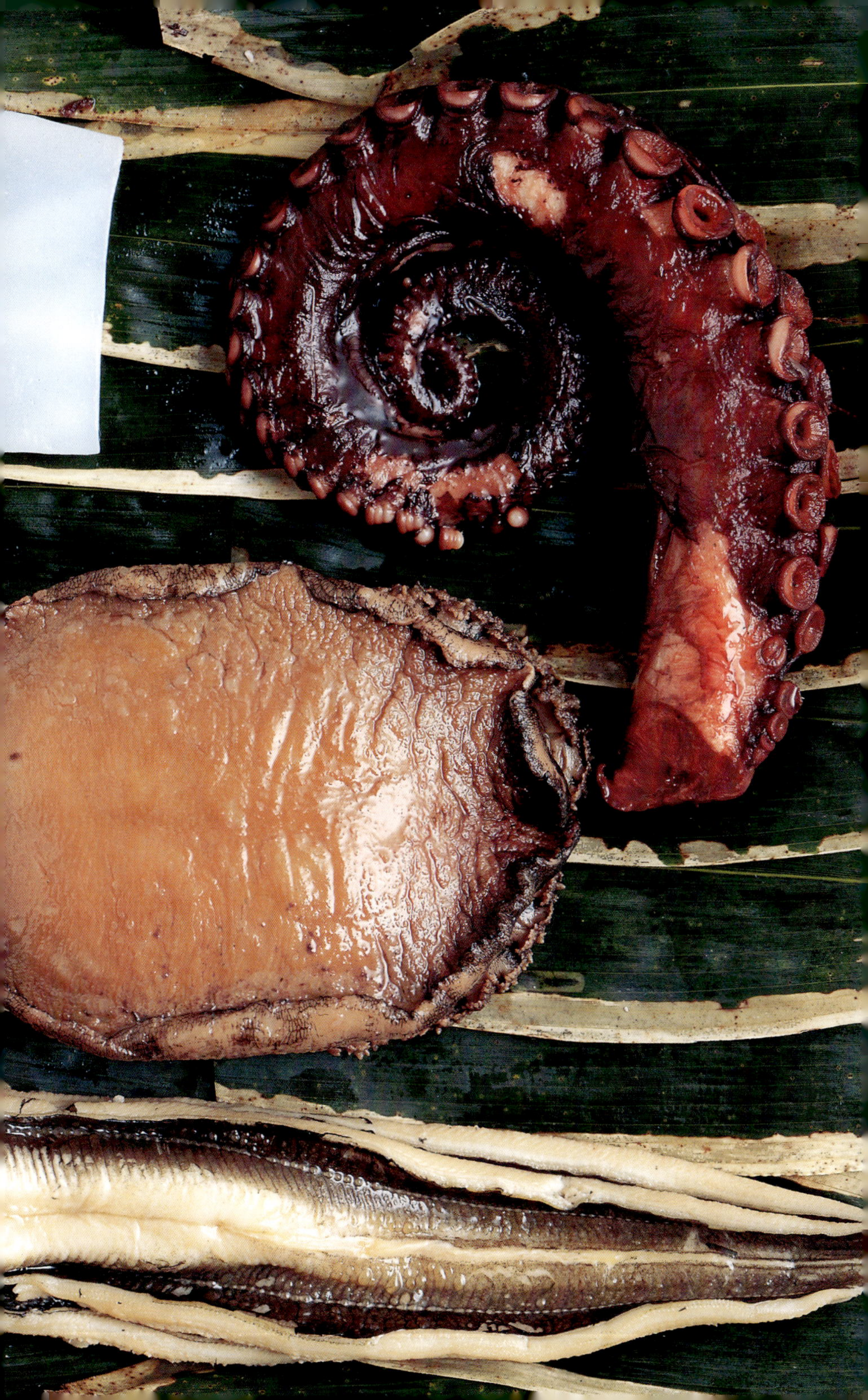

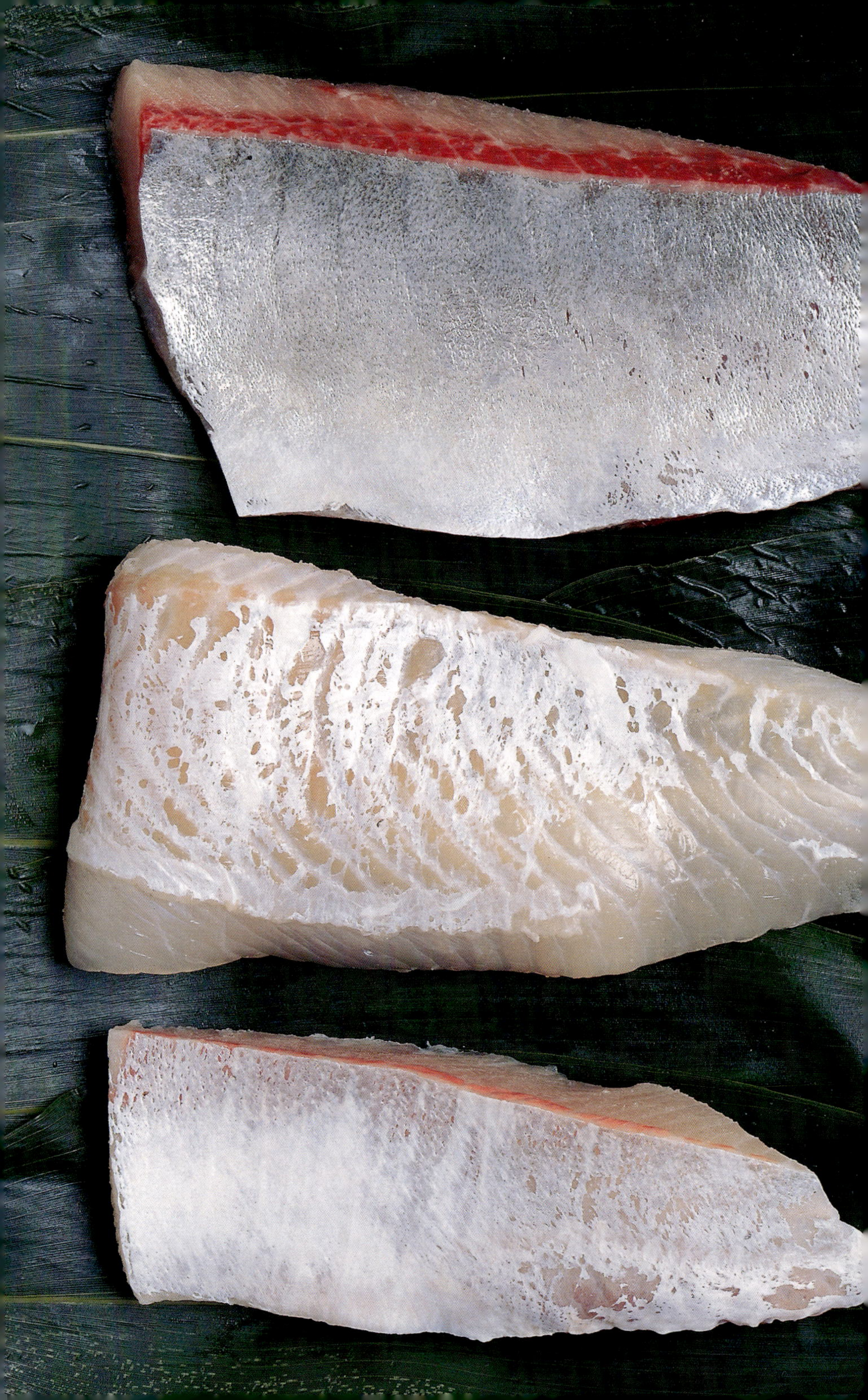

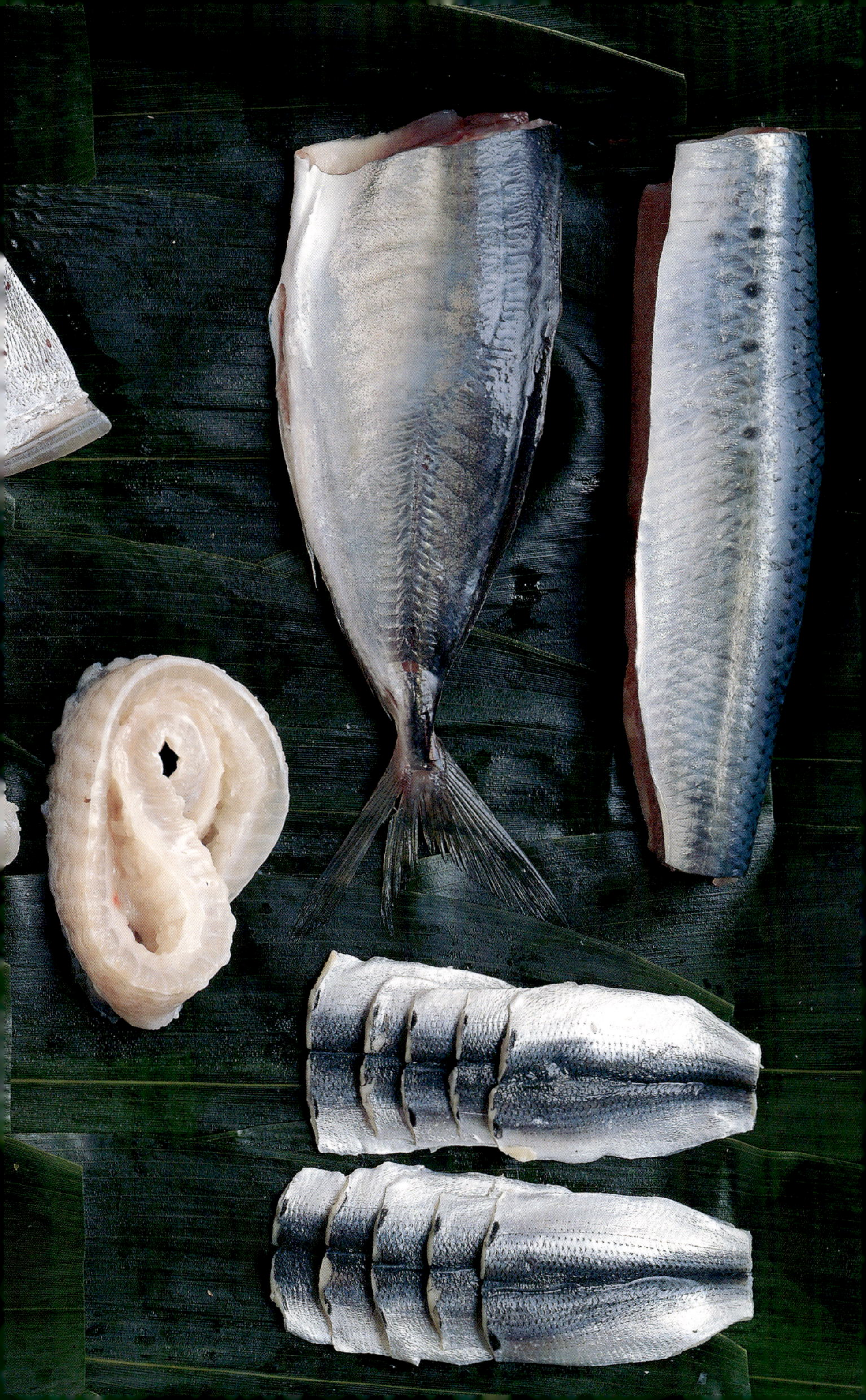

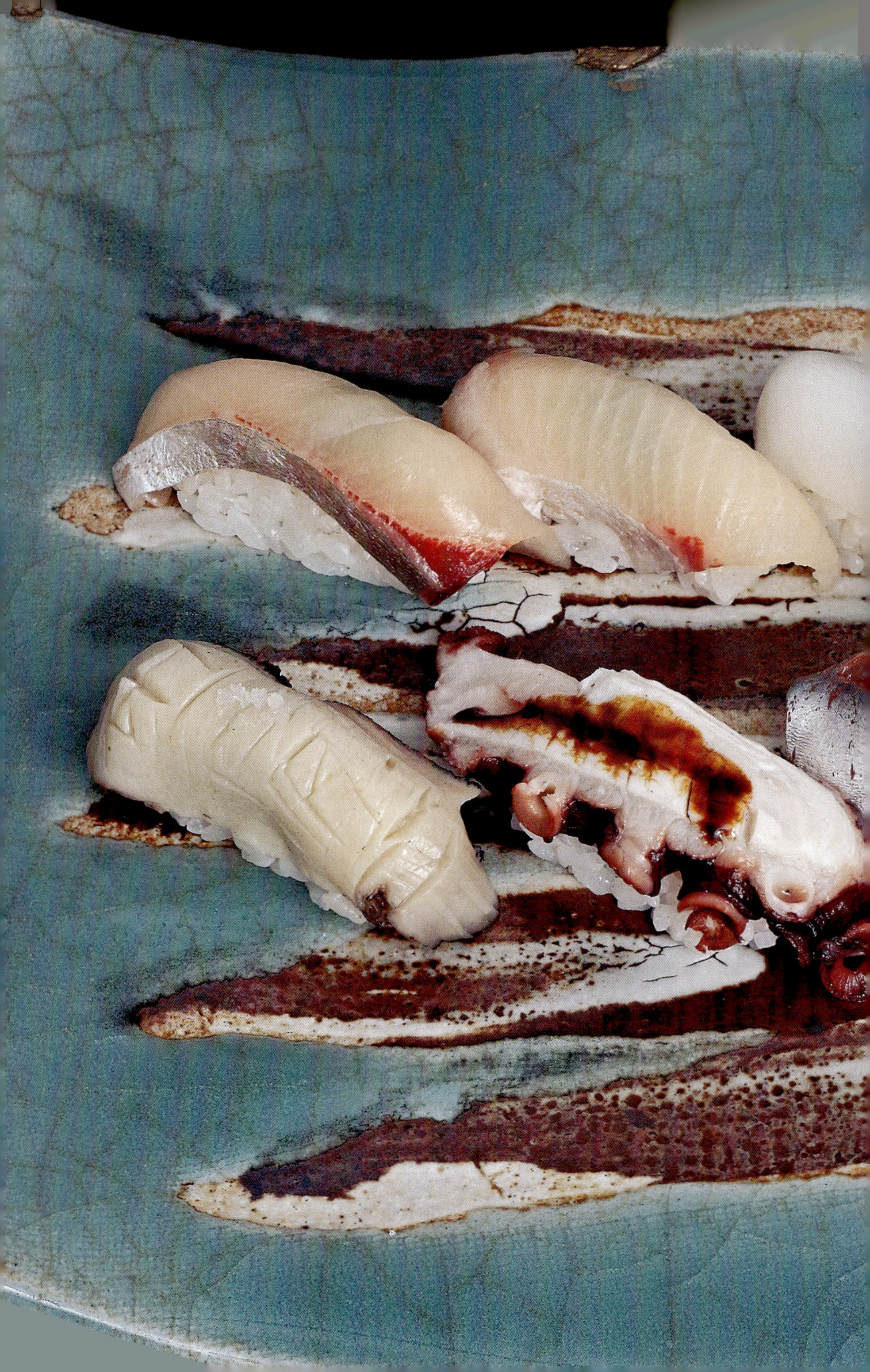

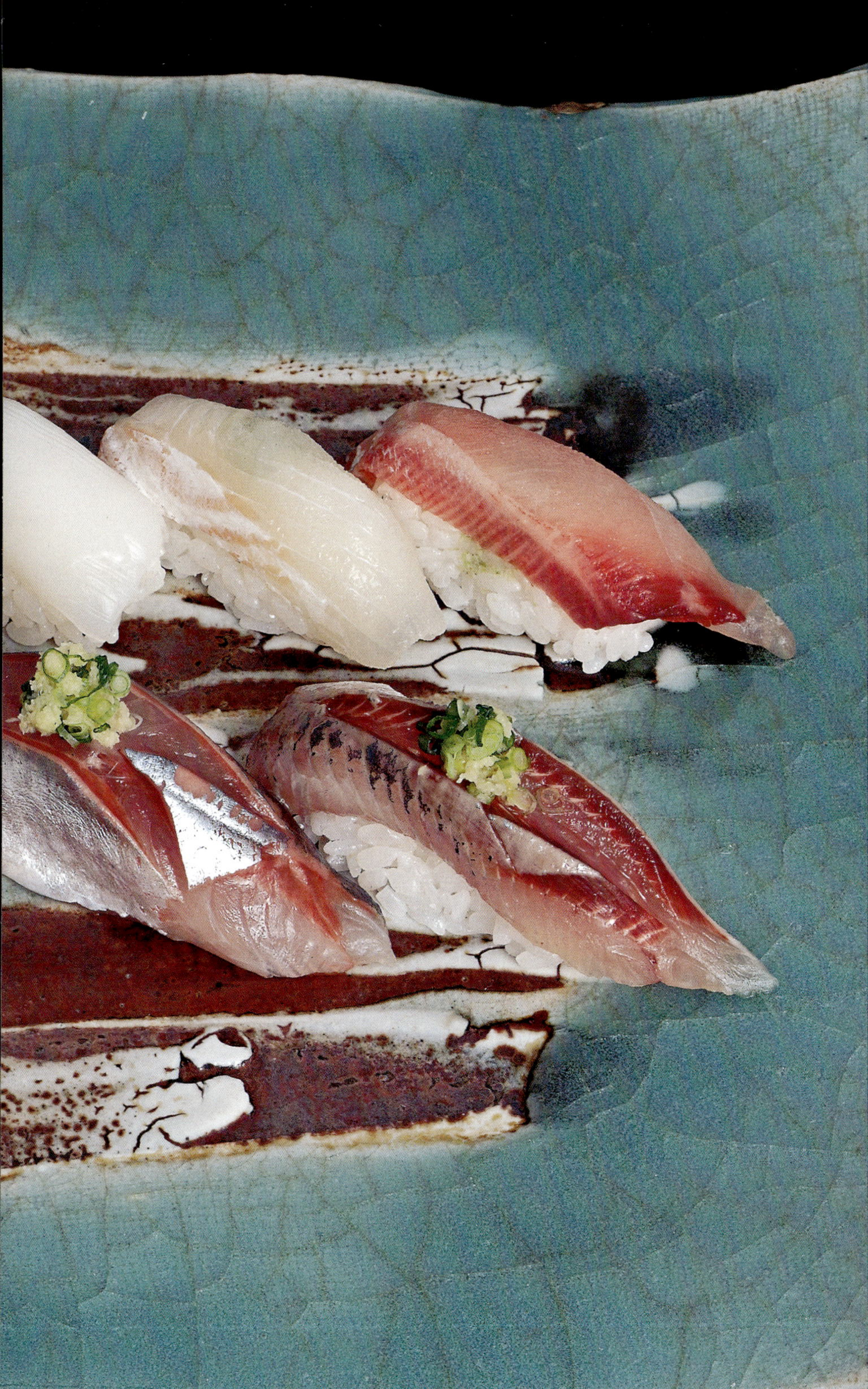

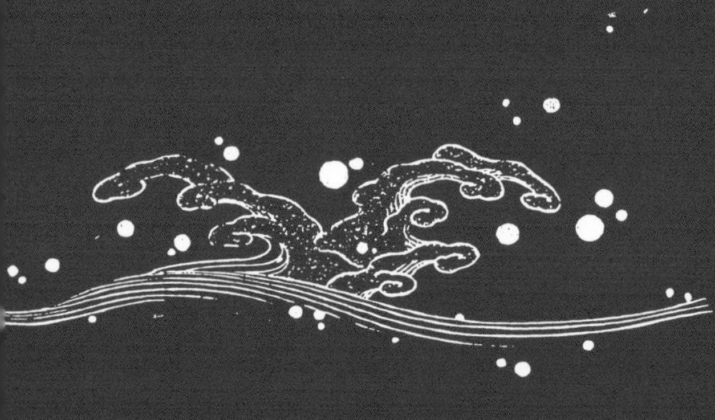

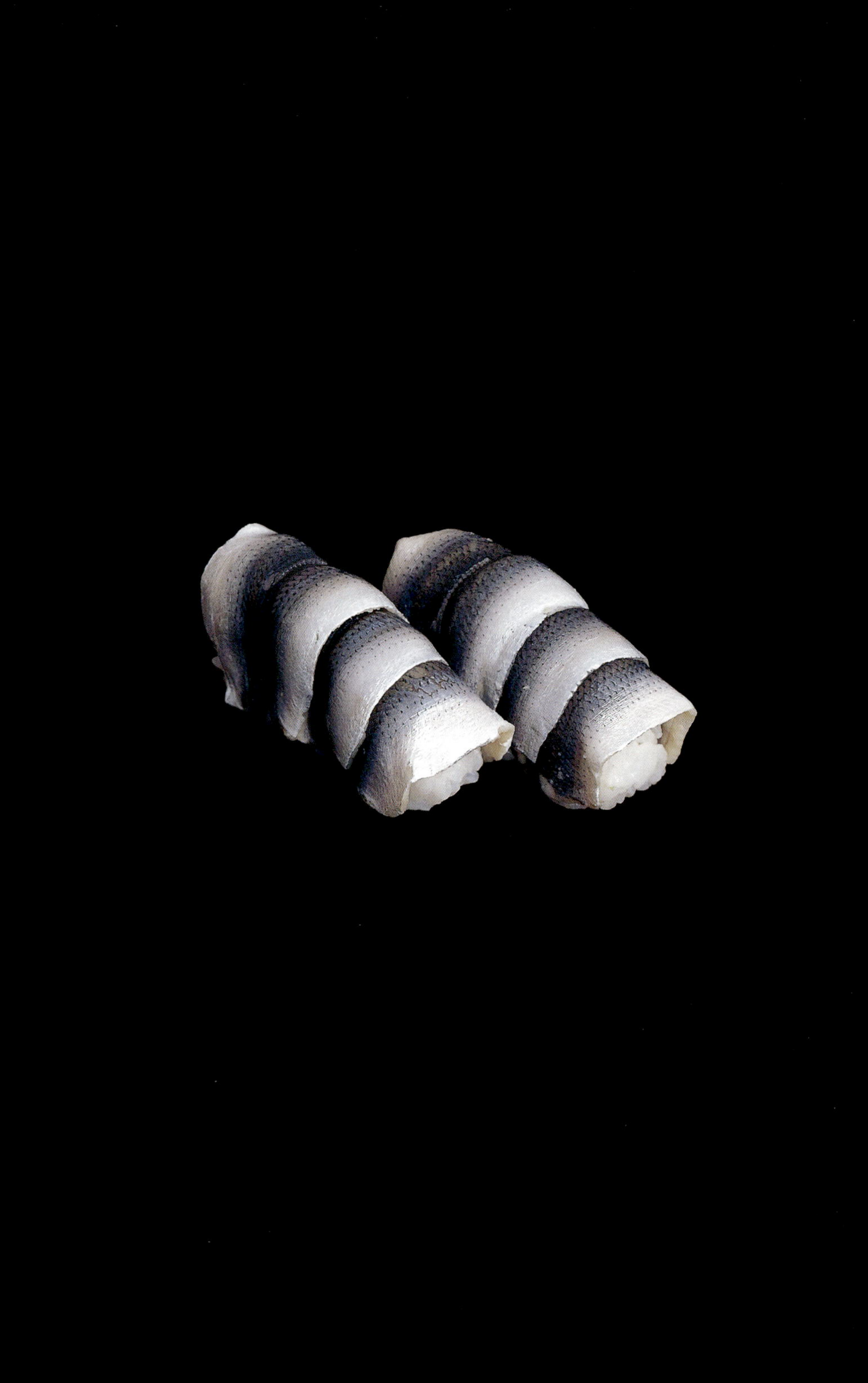

新子
(shinko)

新子は小鰭(こはだ)の幼魚の尊称だ。7月早々、極めて少量の新子が入荷してくる。この初入荷時、江戸前ずしの世界には心地よい緊張感が走る。この極少の新子を、まるで相場の暴騰を楽しむかのように東京のすし屋たちが意地と誇りと見栄をかけて奪い合うからだ。初物から10日間位、通常の小鰭の60倍ほどの値段に暴騰する。塩加減も微妙だが、酢の漬け込みも勝負どころとなる。値段や膨大な手間のことなど一切問わず、ひたすら初物の登場を愛でるのは、江戸時代の遊びを、いまだに伝承する江戸前ずしの伝統の世界を楽しむためだ。

Shinko is the honorary title for the young of the gizzard shad. Early in July a small supply of shinko becomes available, sending a delicious frisson through the world of Edo-mae sushi as the capital's sushi shops scramble to acquire the little fish in a battle of persistence, pride, and vanity, as if actually relishing the sky-high prices. For the first ten days or so after this first shipment, prices for the shad soar to about sixty times the usual level. Achieving just the right degree of saltiness is tricky, with the vinegar marinade another defining quality. This obsession with acquiring the first of the season regardless of price or effort reflects an enduring love for Edo-mae sushi tradition, with its Edo period sense of fun.

gizzard shad fry

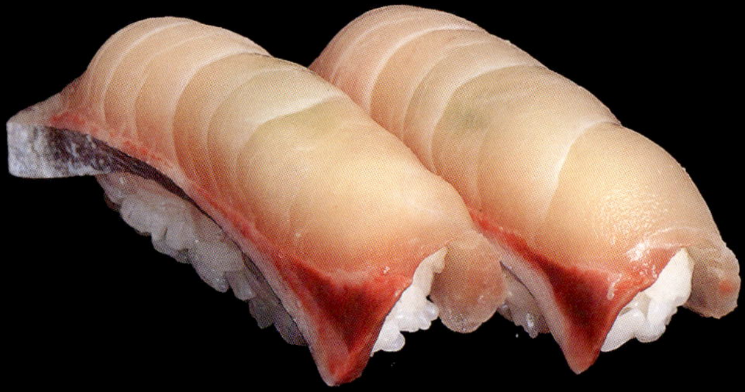

縞鯵
(shima-aji)

夏から秋にかけての旨さの旬の真っ盛りに入ると、しっとりと脂の乗った乳白色の身肉は、薄く琥珀色(こはく)を帯びてくる。脂の乗りはあくまでも程よく上品な甘みを持ち、滑らかな舌触りと、微かな乾(ほ)し藁(わら)っぽい香りが独自の旨さとなっている。2日後の熟成の旨さの最高時には、まだ微かな歯ごたえの旨さも残している。昔からの漁獲量の少なさと近年の大不漁とが重なり、純天然ものは今や幻の貴重な最高級魚となり、流通しているほとんどすべての縞鯵が、養殖ものとなってしまっている。

At the peak of the season, which stretches from summer into autumn, the succulent, milky-white flesh of the striped jack acquires a faint amber hue. The fish maintains just the right covering of fat to contribute a subtle sweetness, while its smooth texture and faint aroma of straw endow a unique taste. At its most flavorful, after two days aging, it also retains a slight, exquisite firmness. Striped jack have long been scarce, a trend compounded by a recent precipitous decline in catches, making purely wild striped jack the precious stuff of a sushi connoisseur's dreams. Almost all striped jack on the market are now farm-raised.

striped jack

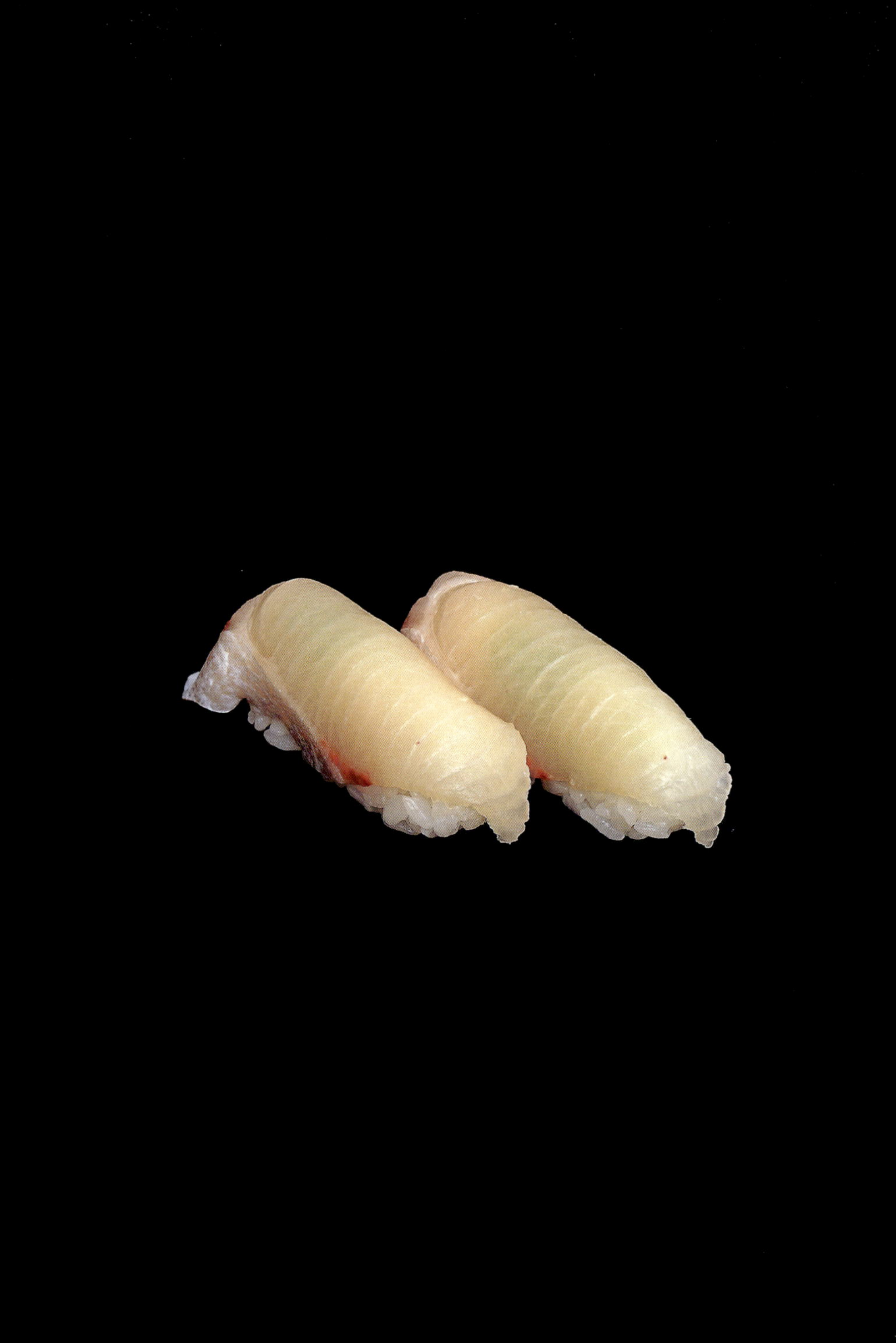

平政
(hiramasa)

初夏から夏の終わり頃を旬とする平政は、身質がしっかりと締まり、旬の最盛期でも脂の乗りは決して過剰とはならない。その淡白で上品な持ち味は夏場を代表する旨さのひとつとなっている。3キロから4キロ級の平政は、6月から7月頃が漁獲の最盛期で旨さの旬としても高く評価される。しかし最近の様々な産地からの入荷は、晩秋頃まで続くようになり、旨さの旬を不明にさせてしまっている。平政の生態系の異変は、旨さの旬のありようをまったく無視したものとなっている。

Hiramasa, best from early to around the end of summer, have firm, dense flesh, and are never too fatty even at the height of the season. Their light, subtle taste make them one of summer's supreme sushi temptations. Weighing 3 to 4kgs, most hiramasa are caught in June and July, coinciding with when the fish are believed to be at the apogee of their flavor. More recently however hiramasa from a growing number of sources have become available up to late autumn, blurring the timing of optimum flavor. Drastic changes in the hiramasa's ecosystem pay no heed to when humans deem the fish best for eating.

yellowtail amberjack

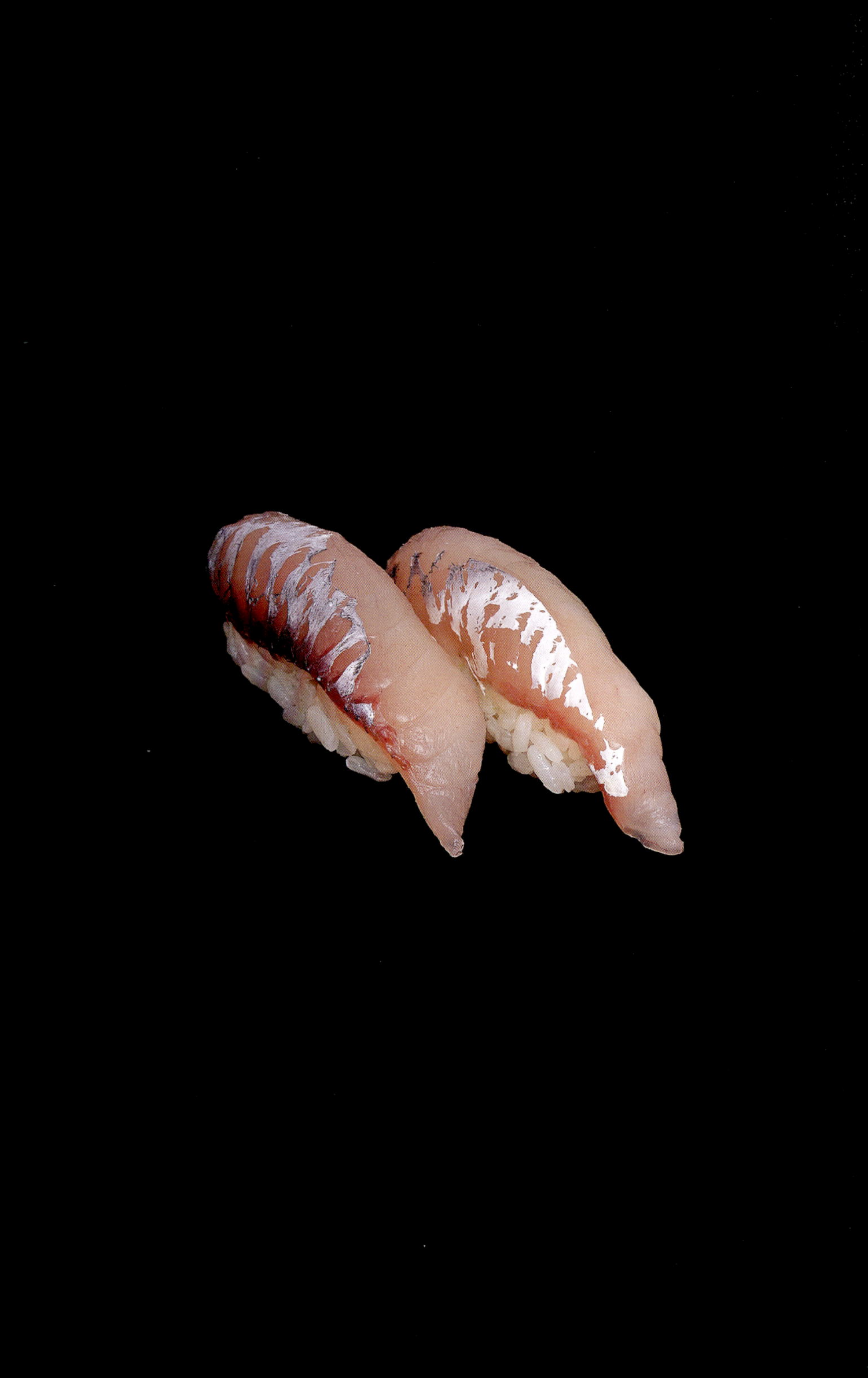

飛魚
(tobi-uo)

５月頃に入荷が始まり、２ヶ月ほどで消えていく飛魚は、やがて来る夏の訪れを、いち早く知らせてくれる季節感に富む魚だ。胸鰭(むなびれ)が飛行機の翼のように長く大きく、海面を400メートルも飛翔することがあると言われる。航行中の船に多々飛び込んでくることがあり、漁師たちはこの飛び込みの飛魚がとびきり旨いなどと言う。身質は少し柔らかく、水気の少ない淡白で癖のない味わいは夏の酷暑の中で刺身・焼き魚などの爽やかな料理に相性がよいのだが、江戸前ずしの世界では一般的には使用されない。

Appearing at markets around May and disappearing just two months later, tobi-uo are a fleeting seasonal treat, an early sign that summer is finally on the way. The fish have long, large pectoral fins resembling aircraft wings that reportedly enable them to glide up to 400m across the ocean surface. Schools of tobi-uo occasionally land on boats, fishermen voting these 'flown-in' fish the tastiest by far. Slightly soft in consistency, with a mild but not watery flavor, they make a refreshing antidote to scorching summer temperatures, whether as sashimi, dried or broiled. They are not however generally used in Edo-mae sushi.

flying fish

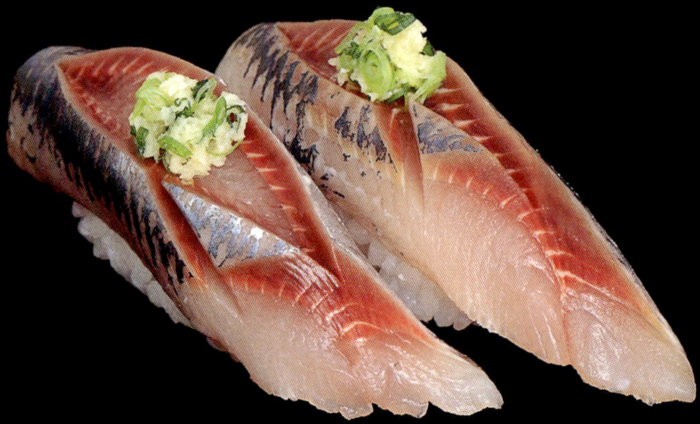

真鰯
(ma-iwashi)

鰯には、最初は春先から夏場に、さらにもう1回は晩秋の頃と、脂が乗る旨さの旬が年に2回やって来る。見事に乗った脂は皮目に白い層となり、包丁を入れると血合いの朱色とのコントラストが美しい。昔は塩と酢で締めてから、すしに握るのが通常だったが、近年では流通過程での鮮度管理が極めてよくなり、完全な生の状態でも握ることが可能となった。無数にある胸骨を完全に除去することによって、新たな旨さの登場となったのだ。生姜と浅葱と醬油の旨さによって、夏と秋の味覚を華やかに彩る握りずしとなった。

Sardines have two seasonal peaks in flavor coinciding with when they put on fat: first from early spring to summer, and then around late autumn. Cutting reveals a generous layer of white subcutaneous fat, a striking contrast to the fish's scarlet flesh. In earlier times it was usual to firm the flesh with salt and vinegar before using in sushi, but marked improvements in maintaining freshness at the distribution stage now allow consumption of even totally raw iwashi. Removing all the sardine's plethora of bones makes for a new and exciting taste experience, and teamed with ginger, chives and soy sauce, the small fish are now a big star of summer and autumn sushi menus.

sardine

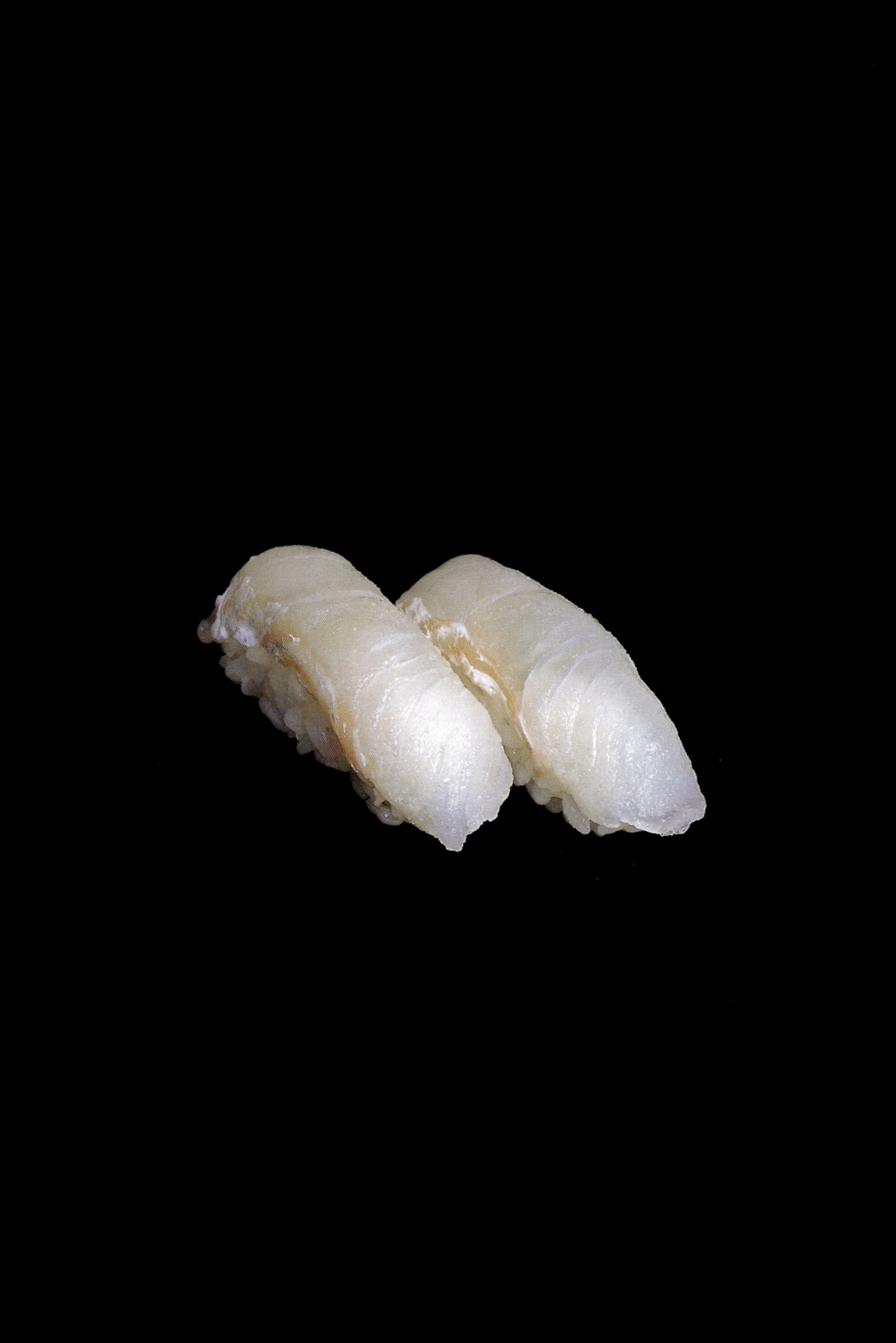

真子鰈
(makogarei)

真子鰈は、初夏から秋口までを旨さの旬とする夏場を代表する白身魚である。旨さの持ち味は異なるものの、冬場の鮃（ひらめ）にも匹敵する高級魚とされる。旬真っ盛りの絶頂期には、身肉が薄い琥珀（こはく）色をたたえ、しっとりとした脂をにじませている。鮃よりも少し水気が多いのだが、柔らかく心地よい歯ごたえとともに甘みと旨みを充分に楽しませてくれる。さらに熟成された翌日の昼には、身肉の締まりをもう少し緩めながらも、まだ程よい歯ごたえを保持している。噛めば噛むほどにじませてくるたっぷりとした甘み・旨みを、前夜よりもさらに強く主張しながら、旨さの最盛時となっている。

Makogarei is the white-fleshed fish synonymous with summer, peaking from early summer to the start of autumn. It is a luxury species rivaling winter olive flounder (hirame), albeit with a distinctively different taste. At the height of the season, the flesh acquires an amber hue, and is shot through with succulent fat. Although slightly more watery than hirame, its tender, pleasant consistency combined with sweetness and flavor make it a gourmet delight. Aged, by lunchtime the next day the flesh is a little slacker, but still retains its exquisite texture. Generous sweetness and flavor that intensify with chewing dominate even more than the night before, making this the prime time to savor the fish.

marbled sole

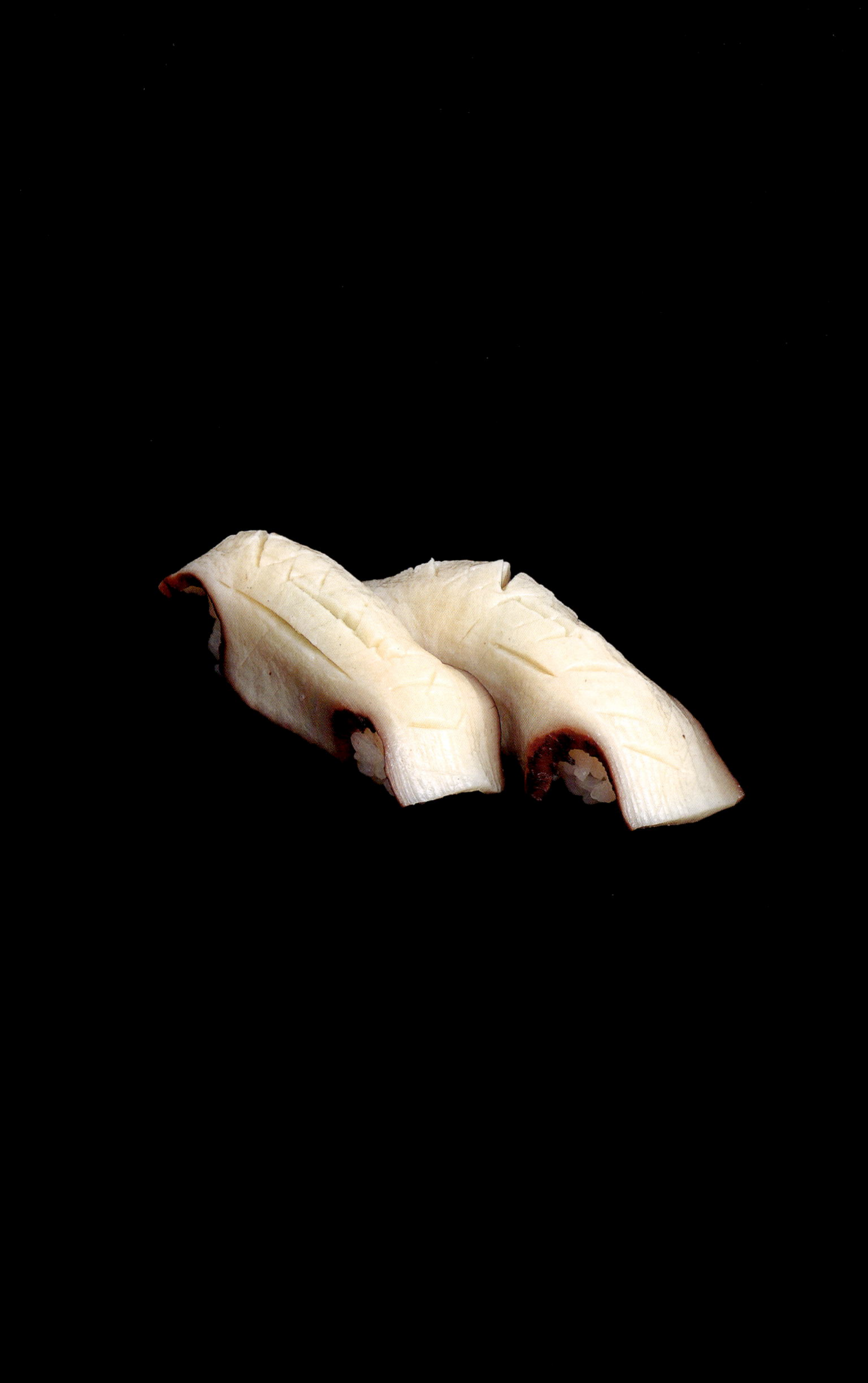

鮑
(awabi)

<ruby>黒鮑<rt>くろあわび</rt></ruby>、<ruby>真高鮑<rt>まだかあわび</rt></ruby>、<ruby>雌貝鮑<rt>めがいあわび</rt></ruby>は初夏から秋口を旨さの旬とし、<ruby>蝦夷鮑<rt>えぞあわび</rt></ruby>は晩秋から春先までを旬とする。黒鮑と蝦夷鮑は生のまま食すことによって磯の香りのする心地よい硬めの食感と、生の鮑特有の旨み・甘みを味わう。真高鮑と雌貝鮑は火を通すことによって身肉を柔らかくさせ、生の状態とは別種の新たに立ちのぼる香りと甘み・旨みを味わうことができる。1キロ以上の特大真高鮑はミルクっぽい芳醇な香りとゼラチン質の濃厚な旨みを持っている。大きく太った黒鮑は、わざと硬く締めず、まだ活きている柔軟な状態の間に、素早く食すと意外にも深遠な美味を楽しめる。

Black abalone, madaka abalone, and giant abalone are tastiest from early summer to the start of autumn, while Ezo abalone peak from late autumn to early spring. Consumed raw, black and Ezo abalone have a pleasant, slightly chewy consistency and salty tang, and the distinctive flavor and sweetness of raw abalone. Madaka and giant abalone are cooked to tenderize the flesh, giving them a different aroma, flavor and sweetness to when raw. Giant madaka abalone weighing over 1kg have a mellow, slightly milky aroma and rich, gelatinous taste. When eaten swiftly while still living and pliable, rather than deliberately firmed, large, fat black abalone are an unexpectedly tasty treat.

abalone

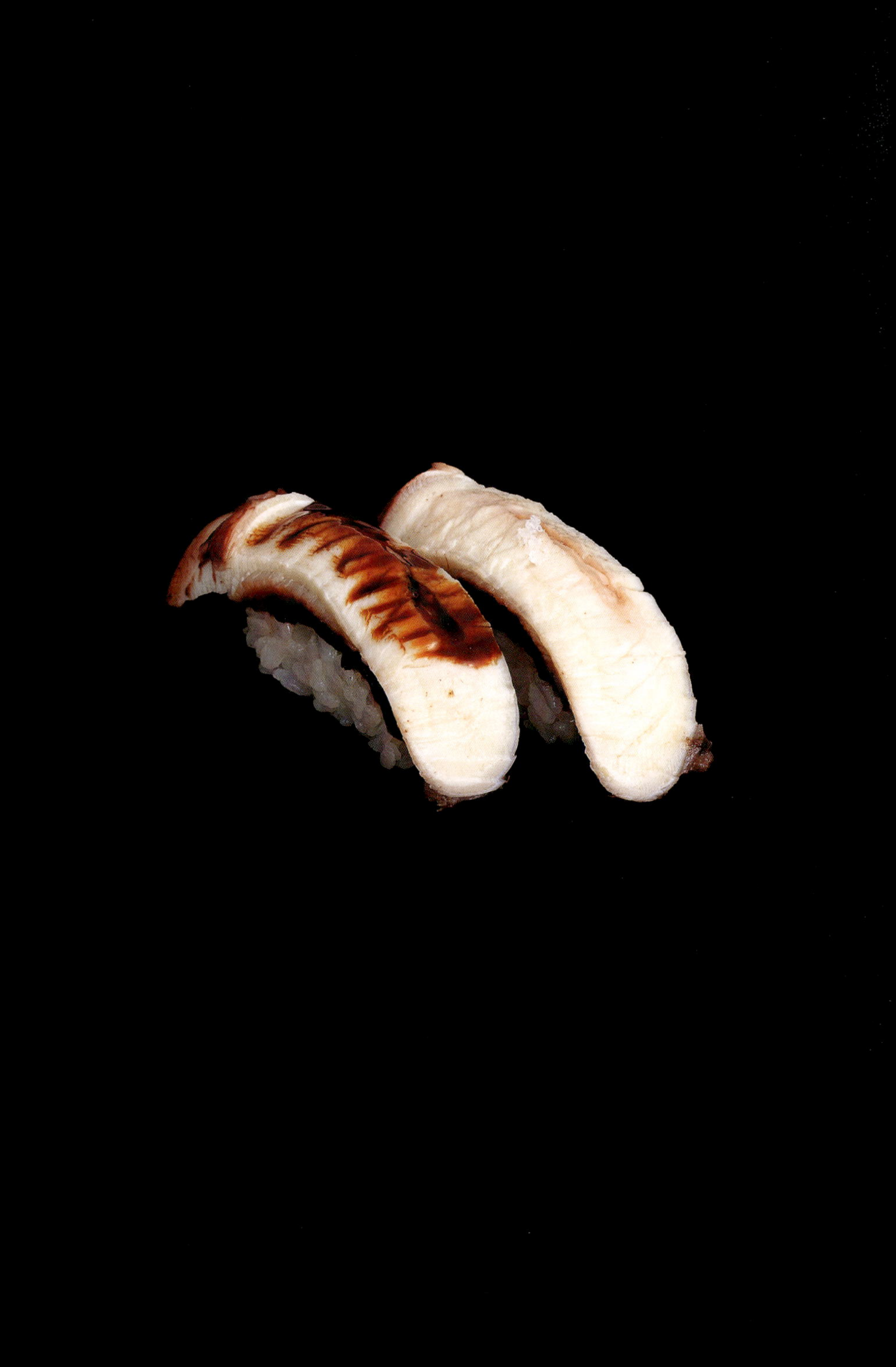

蛸
(tako)

蛸は寿命が1年半で、産卵とともに命を終えていくのだが、産卵を基準にすると、2つの旨さの旬を見ることができる。夏場の産卵の準備の過程で、旺盛な食欲のもとに急激に成長し、身肉が充分に太った6月から7月頃を旬とする夏蛸の時期と、水温の低下とともに餌を豊富に食い込み、水温低下の影響の少ない深場に、産卵の準備のために移動をする11月から12月頃の秋蛸の時期とがある。旬の時期には、ゼラチン質の旨みをたっぷりと蓄えた蛸の足は、はち切れるほどに太っている。特に活きているうちに煮たものは、動物の持つ肉感的な旨みと高い香りを放ち、高く評価されることになる。

Octopus live just 18 months, dying after they spawn, and have two peak periods for flavor, both based around spawning. Summer octopus feed ravenously and grow dramatically in preparation for summer spawning, their flavor peaking in June-July when they are sufficiently fattened, while autumn octopus are caught in November-December, when they consume more food as the water temperature drops and dive deeper ahead of spawning, to avoid the effects of these cooler temperatures. At their tastiest, octopus legs are swollen with gelatinous goodness. Those cooked alive are especially prized for their sensual animal flavor and intense aroma.

octopus

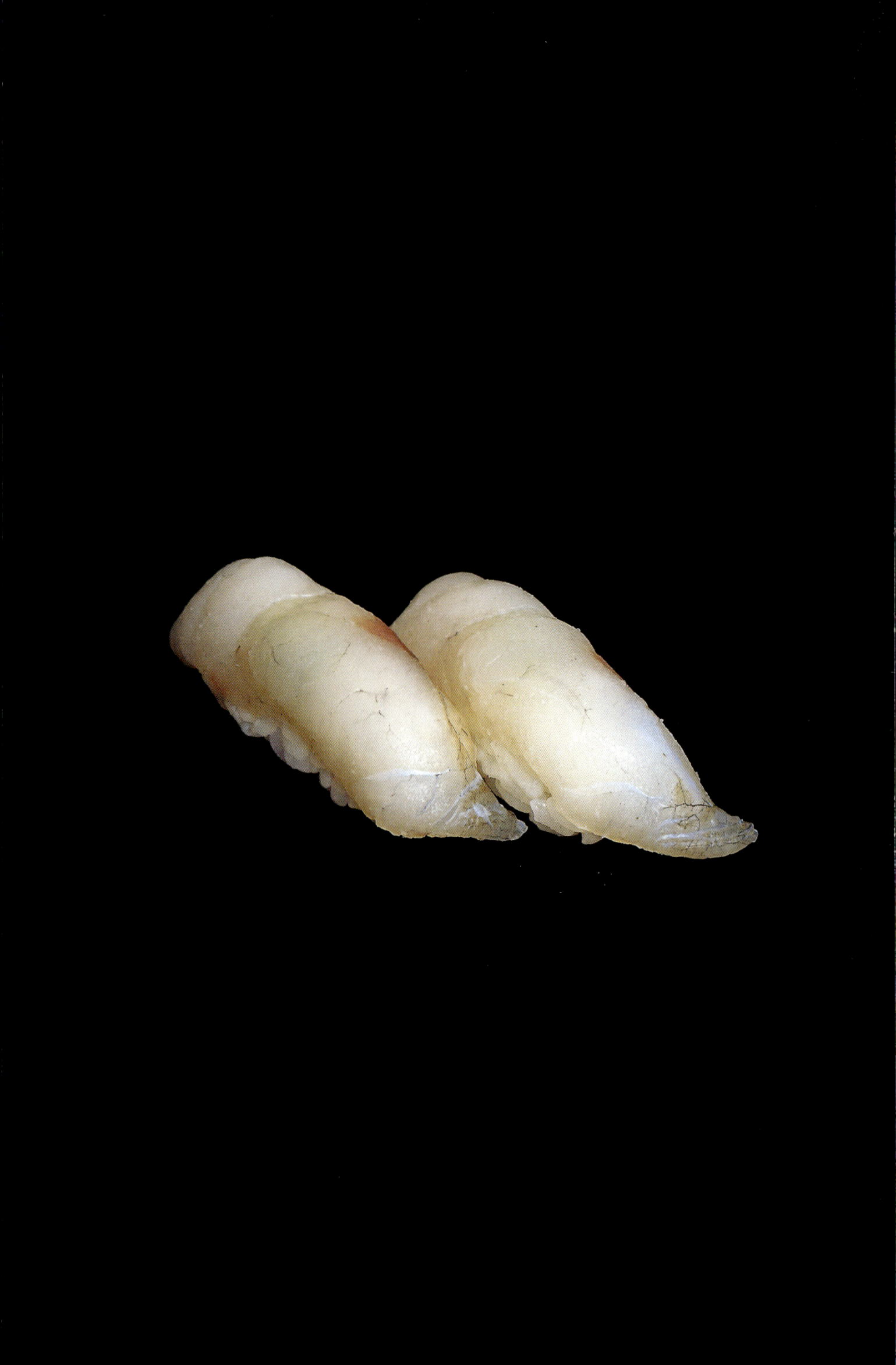

真鯉
(magochi)

初夏から夏場を旨さの旬とする真鯉は、よく冬場の河豚と比較される。河豚同様に、無味に近い淡白さを持ち味とするが、咀嚼するほどにゼラチン質を有する魚特有の旨みがにじみ出し、微かな香りも味わうことができる。河豚に近いほどにしっかりと締まった身質には、水っぽさはほとんどなく、半透明の美しい刺身となる。握りずしでは、身肉を薄く大きく切りつけると、淡白でしっかりと締まった身肉の旨みを充分に味わい楽しむことができる。翌日、旨さのための熟成時間と身肉の緩みを計算し、少し厚めに切りつけて握ると、真鯉のすしの旨さの真髄を楽しむことができる。

A premium summer species, magochi are often compared to winter's fugu. Like fugu, their pale flesh appears to be almost tasteless, but with each bite that peculiarly piscine gelatinous flavor begins to penetrate the palate, accompanied by a subtle fragrance. Their firm, dense, almost fugu-like flesh is not at all watery, and makes attractive, translucent sashimi. In nigiri, cutting the fish into large, thin pieces ensures maximum delight in its pale, firm flesh. The following day, the optimal aging time and slackening of texture are calculated and the flesh cut slightly thickly for sushi, allowing diners to enjoy magochi at its finest.

flathead

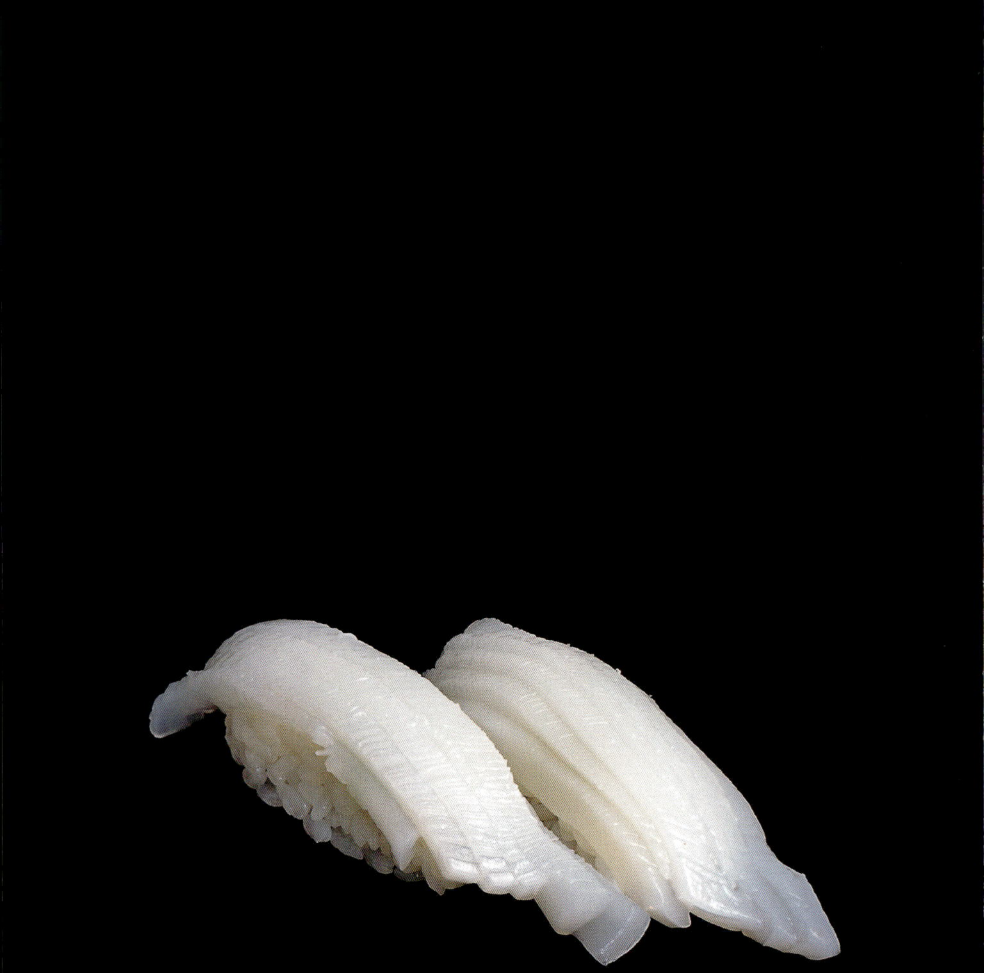

煽り烏賊
(aori-ika)

5月から7月頃までが、旨さの旬の最盛期となる煽り烏賊は、最高の旨さと少ない漁獲量のせいもあって、最高級の烏賊として格付けされている。その厚みのある身肉には、濃い甘みと柔らかな食感の旨さが秘められている。しかしこの旨さは、外側の身肉の中に半分埋まるように張りついている分厚く硬い皮を、力を込めて完全に剥ぎ取らないと、充分に味わいつくすことはできない。そして半日から1日の時間をかけて身肉の旨さを熟成させ、糸のように細く長く切りつけてから握ることによって、煽り烏賊の極上のすしの旨さを満喫することができる。

A combination of outstanding taste and scarcity has resulted in aori-ika, which peaks in flavor from May to about July, being ranked highest of all squid species. Their robust flesh belies an intense sweetness and melt-in-the-mouth texture. To fully appreciate aori-ika requires completely peeling away the thick, hard skin half-buried in the outer flesh: no small effort. The squid is then aged a half-day to a day to develop optimal flavor, and cut in long threads for the ultimate aori-ika sushi experience.

bigfin reef squid

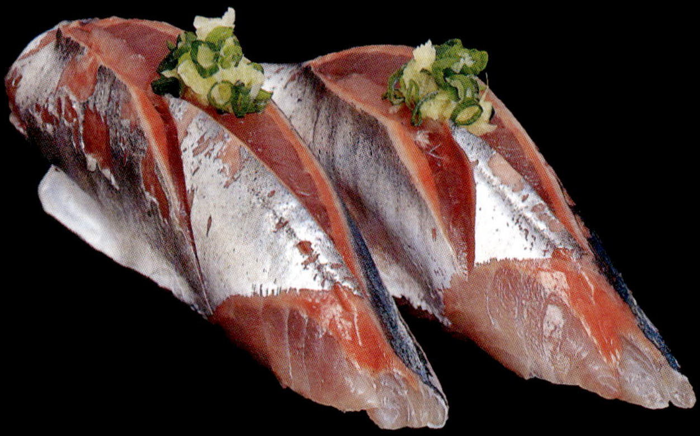

真鯵
(ma-aji)

真鯵は夏から秋にかけてが旨さの旬となる。昔は塩と酢で締め、皮付きのまま握るのを常としたが、最近では最高の鮮度のものが入荷するようになったために、皮を剥き生のままを握るのが主流となってきている。絶妙な鮮度の保持と熟成によって、本来は柔らかめの身質なのに、微かに残る食感の心地よさが加わり、新たな旨さの要素となっている。旬への移行とともに濃くなってくる脂は、滑らかだが、強い旨みを持っている。鮮度落ちと臭みの発生を防ぐためにも使用される新生姜と浅葱は、爽やかな色彩を添えて美しく、その芳香と辛みは真鯵の握りの旨さを一層引き立たせている。

Ma-aji are in their prime from summer to early autumn. They were once treated with salt and vinegar to firm and made into sushi with skin on, but now being available very fresh, are generally skinned and used raw. An exquisite balance of freshness and deliberate aging adds a pleasant hint of texture to what is in fact quite a soft fish, adding a new dimension to its enjoyment. The fat, which grows more succulent moving into the peak season, is smooth but flavorful. The new ginger and chives also used to guard against spoiling and odor add a vivid dash of color, their fragrance and zing serving to further showcase the wonderful flavor of ma-aji sushi.

Japanese jack mackerel

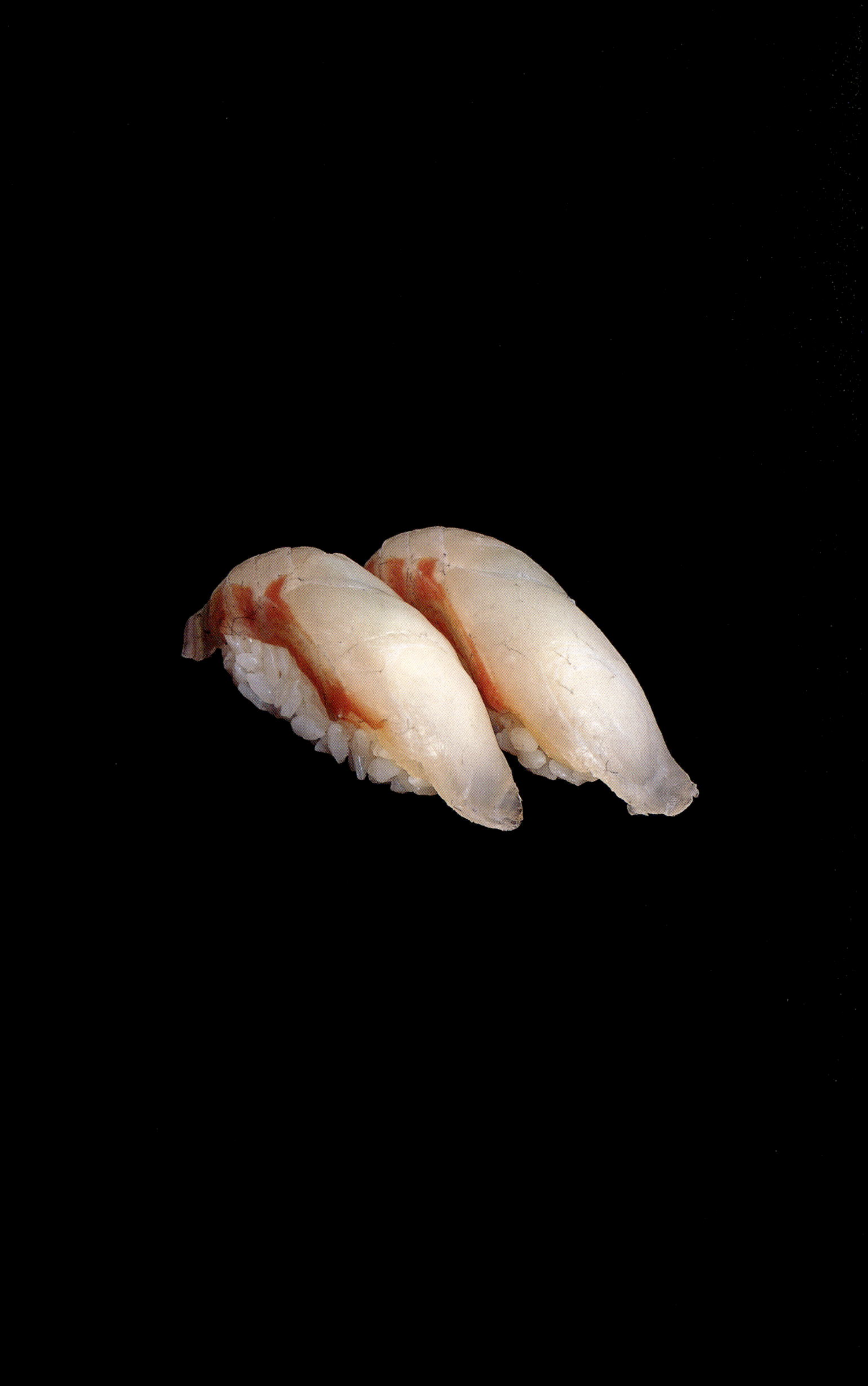

鱸
(suzuki)

鱸は鯎(せいご)、フッコ、鱸と成長しながら名前を変えていく。盛夏に入り、腹太に丸々と太った鱸の最高品は、身肉を薄い琥珀(こはく)色に染め、旨みたっぷりの脂を強くにじませている。噛むほどに広がってくる脂の甘み・旨みの中に、鱸特有の個性のある香りが混じる。各地への分布は広く漁獲量も多い。比較的安価なために、江戸前ずしの世界では、夏場の最もポピュラーな魚として愛され、賞味される。東京湾内では、食物ピラミッドの頂点にいるため、環境汚染の犠牲になることが多い。身肉の食感の旨さと、適切な熟成の時間の取り方が難しい。

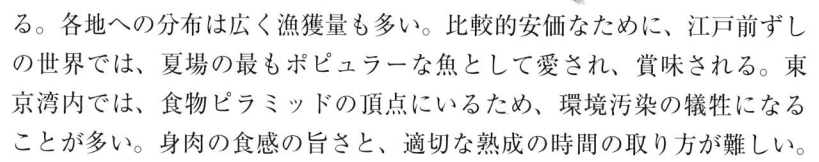

In Japanese sea bass change names as they mature, progressing from seigo, to fukko, and finally suzuki. In midsummer, the highest-quality specimens are plump with flesh of a light amber tinge, and full of flavorsome fat. The delectable sweetness of this fat, which mesmerizes the palate more with each bite, is mingled with a distinctive fragrance. The species is widely distributed, and catches plentiful. Its comparative cheapness makes suzuki the most popular, and most savored, summer fish in the world of Edo-mae sushi. In Tokyo Bay, suzuki is at the top of the food chain, and as such often a victim of pollution. The trick to serving perfect suzuki is to obtain the texture, and allow the right aging time.

sea bass

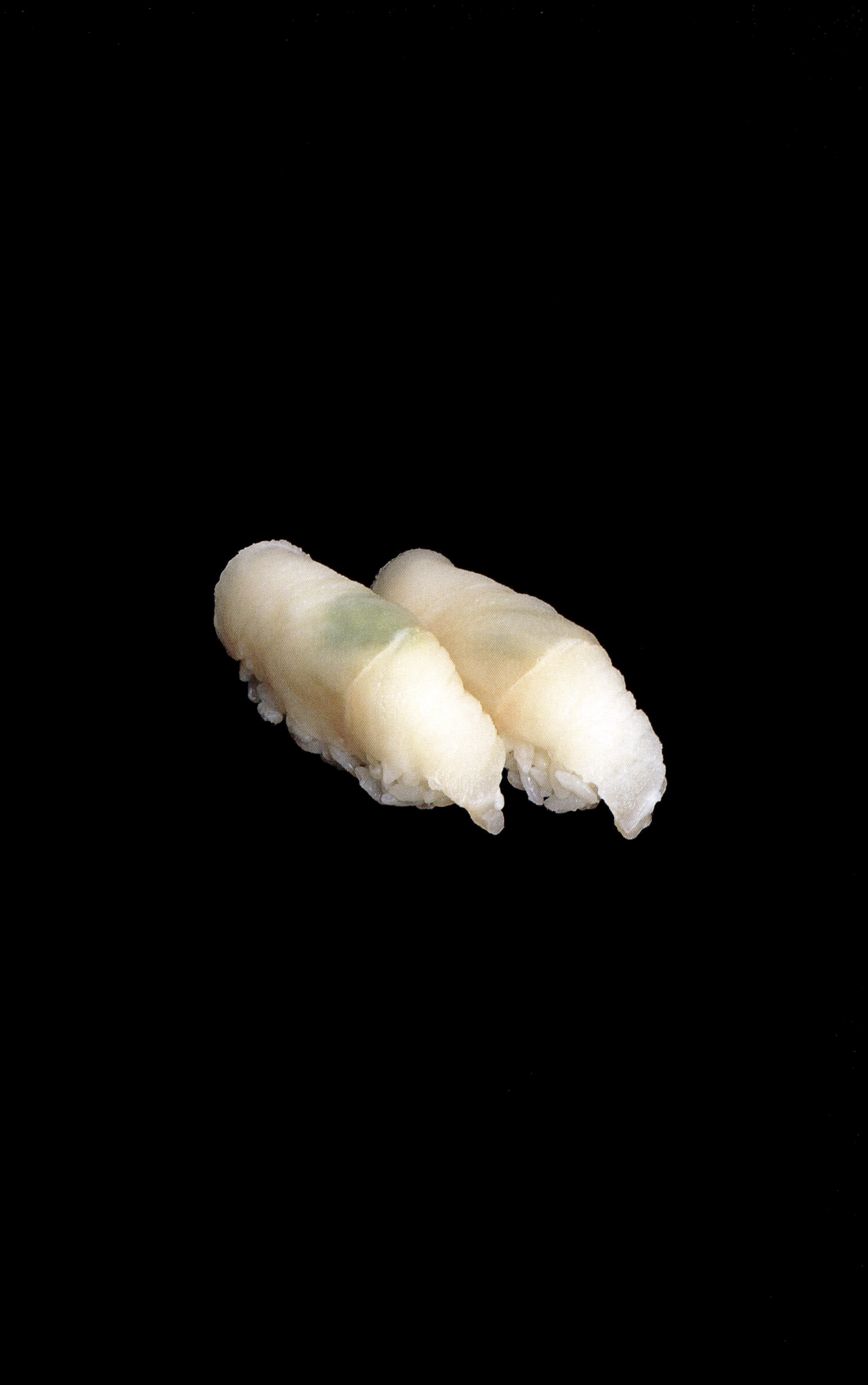

鮎魚女
(ainame)

夏場の旬真っ盛りに入った、１キロ級の鮎魚女の身肉からにじみ出てくるような緻密な脂は、充分な甘みと旨みをたたえている。密度のある身質なのだが、柔らかい食感で、噛むほどに旨みが出てくる。脂とゼラチン質に富んだ焦げ茶色の皮を炙ってすしに握ると、香ばしい皮目の旨みも加わり、さらに新たな味わいを楽しめる。鮎魚女は、初夏を代表する魚で、ゼラチン質に富んだ身肉は、煮魚にするとさらに本領を発揮し、歯にねちっと絡みつくような身質と脂の旨みは上物の煮魚の風格を持っている。

The delicate fat virtually oozing out of ainame of around 1kg caught during the fish's summer prime is sweet and tasty. Ainame has dense flesh, but is surprisingly soft, and more flavor is extracted with each bite. When the dark-brown skin, fatty and gelatinous, is seared and the fish made into sushi, the fragrant aroma of the subcutaneous flesh adds another taste dimension. A popular boiled dish in early summer, ainame really comes into its own here, the gelatinous flesh and lip-smacking fat elevating it to a class of its own.

fat greenling

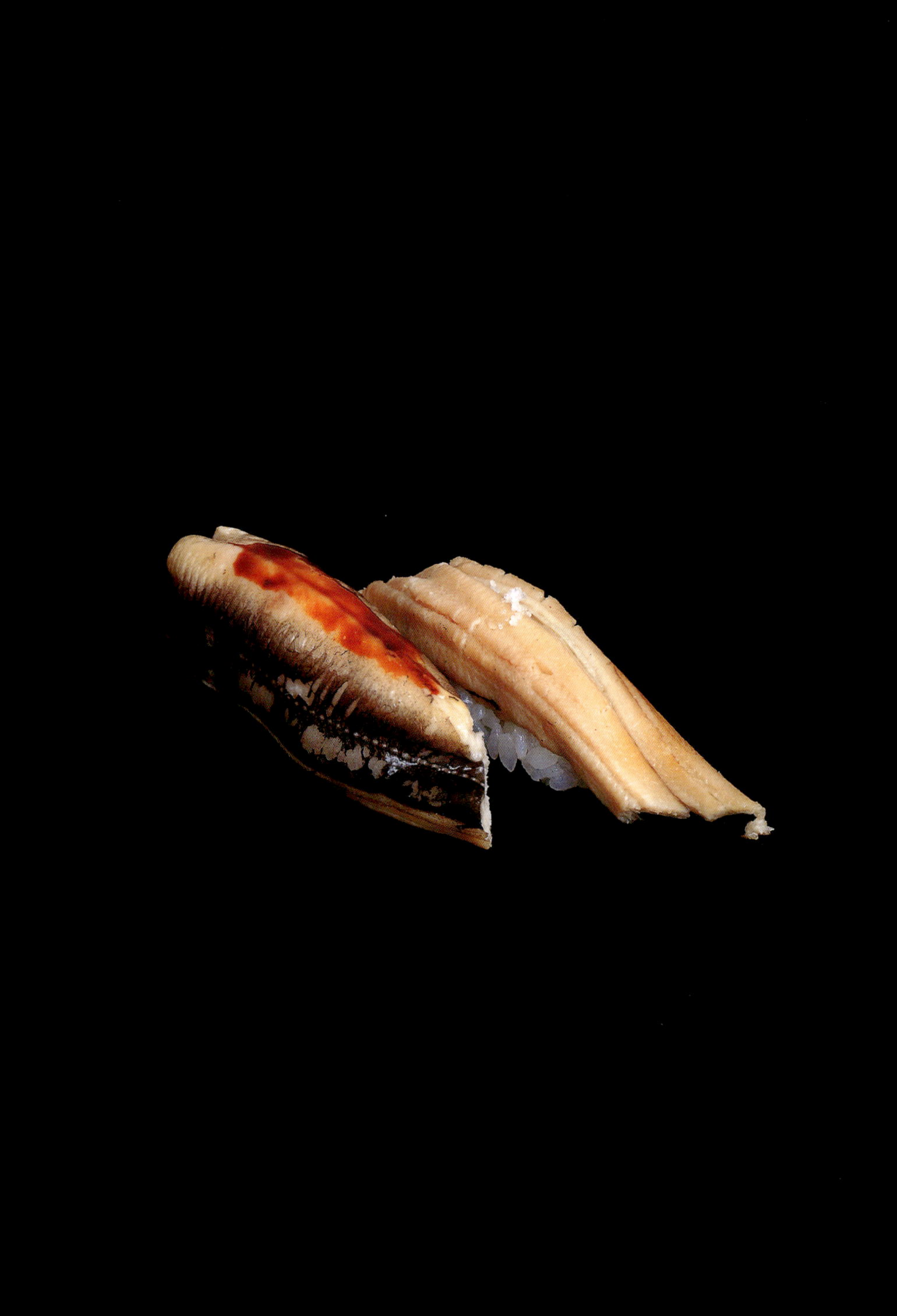

穴子
(anago)

5月、穴子の腹鰭は、もうすっかり黄色味を帯びている。身肉はうっすらと美しい琥珀色に染まり、密度の濃い脂がしっかりとにじみ出している。6月、梅雨に入り、流れ込む川水を飲みはじめると、さらに脂が乗り旨くなる。身肉がまだ活きているうちに沸騰した煮汁に入れると急激に収縮し、この収縮が身肉の厚みと膨らみの旨さとなる。満々の脂を乗せた煮上がりの穴子は、熱々の豊かな香りと、意外なほどにさっぱりとした脂の旨さとともに、柔らかく、跡形もなく口中にとろけていく。いよいよ旬の最盛期に入ったのだ。冷めた穴子は炙り戻すと、新たな旨さが再現されることになる。

By May, the pelvic fin of the conger eel takes on a distinctly yellow tinge. The attractive amber flesh oozes rich, dense fat. By June, the eels start to drink the river water that flows in during the rainy season, and acquire even more fat and flavor. Placed into boiling stock, the fresh eel flesh contracts dramatically, adding a delectable density and plumpness. Freshly boiled anago, fat-suffused and piping hot, has a rich aroma and fat of surprisingly subtle taste, and is also tender, melting in the mouth without a trace. Anago like this has finally reached its seasonal peak. Cooled and seared, the eel takes on yet another delectable flavor.

conger

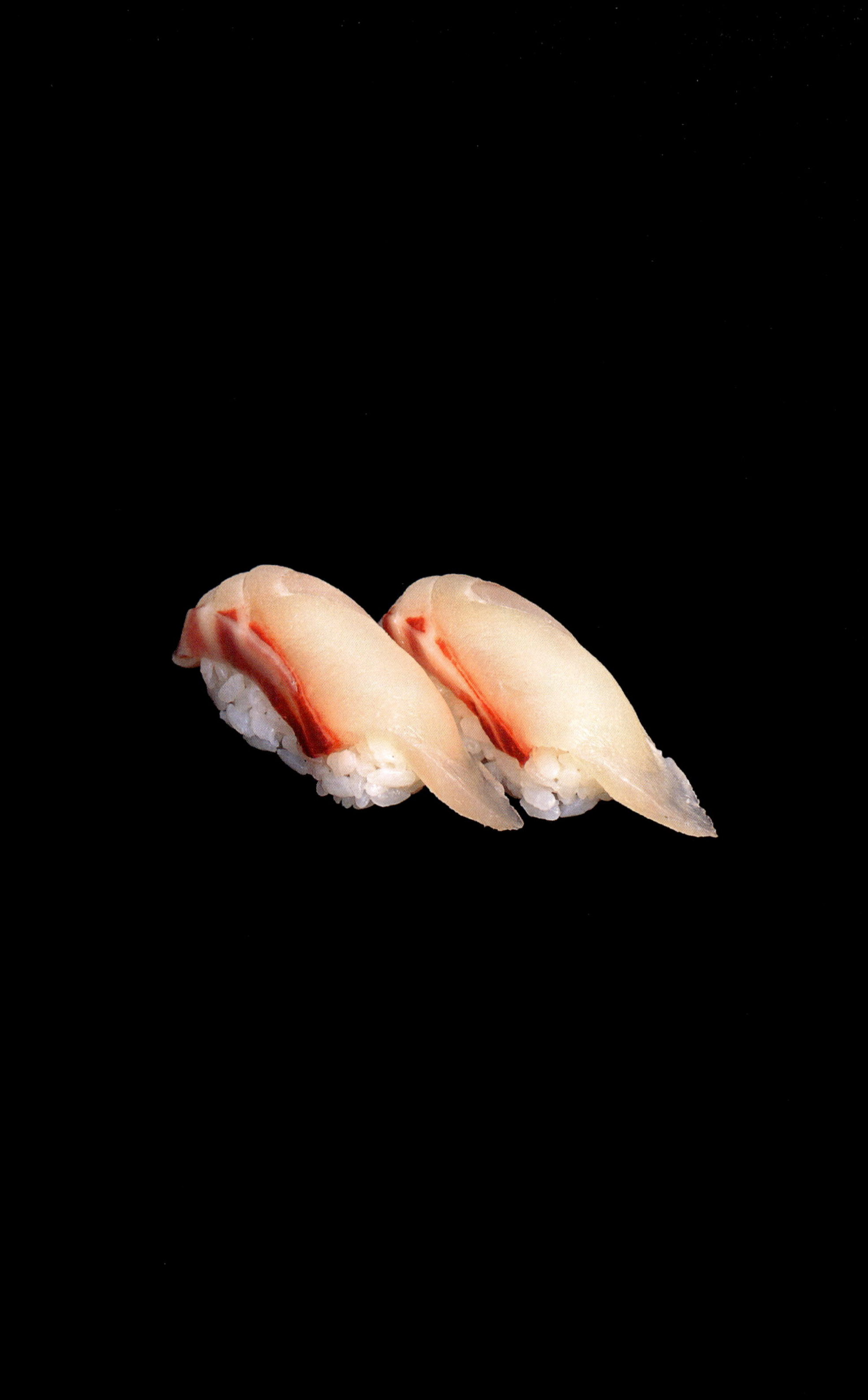

伊佐木
(isaki)

伊佐木は、5月に入ると、初夏の訪れを待っていたかのように現れはじめ、夏場に向かって、旨さを濃いものにしていく。皮を剥いだ皮目の身肉は真鯛のように見事に朱く美しく、その上にうっすらと乳白色の脂肪をまとっている。6月、旨さの最盛期を迎えた伊佐木は、成熟した身肉と、白濁した脂の中に、夏場の魚特有の、決して強すぎない甘みと旨みを味わうことができる。伊佐木は、締めてから2日間位の熟成の時間を経過させることによって、さらに最高の旨さの瞬間を楽しむことができるようになる。

Isaki begin to appear in May, as if longing for the start of summer, and acquire an increasingly strong flavor moving into the hottest part of the year. Just below the skin isaki flesh is a beautiful red, like that of madai (red sea bream), with a delicate, milky white coating of fat. Peaking in June, the now mature flesh and opaque fat offer that never-too-intense sweetness and flavor peculiar to summer fish. Aging for about two days after firming results in even better flavor.

chicken grunt

autumn

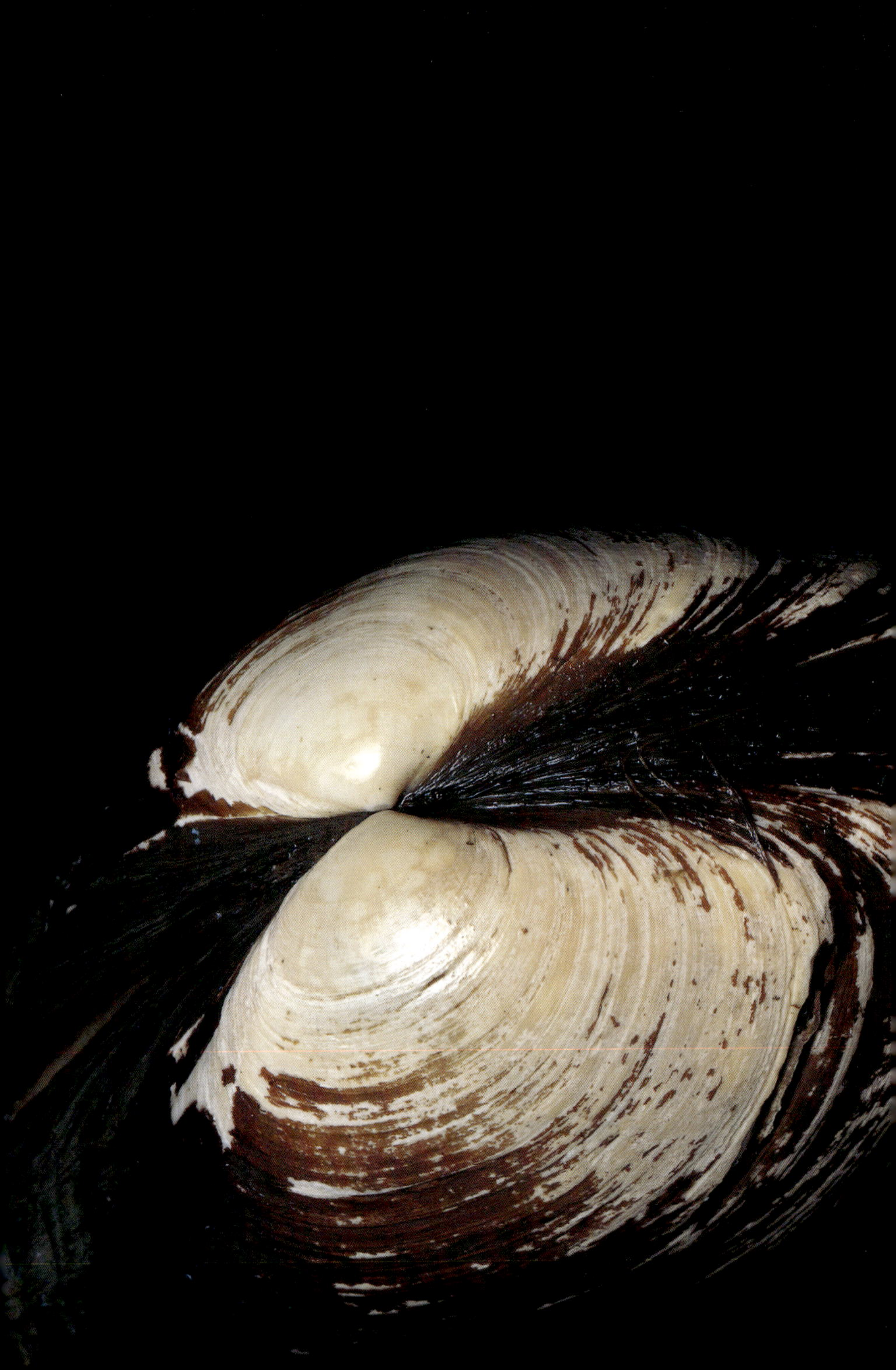

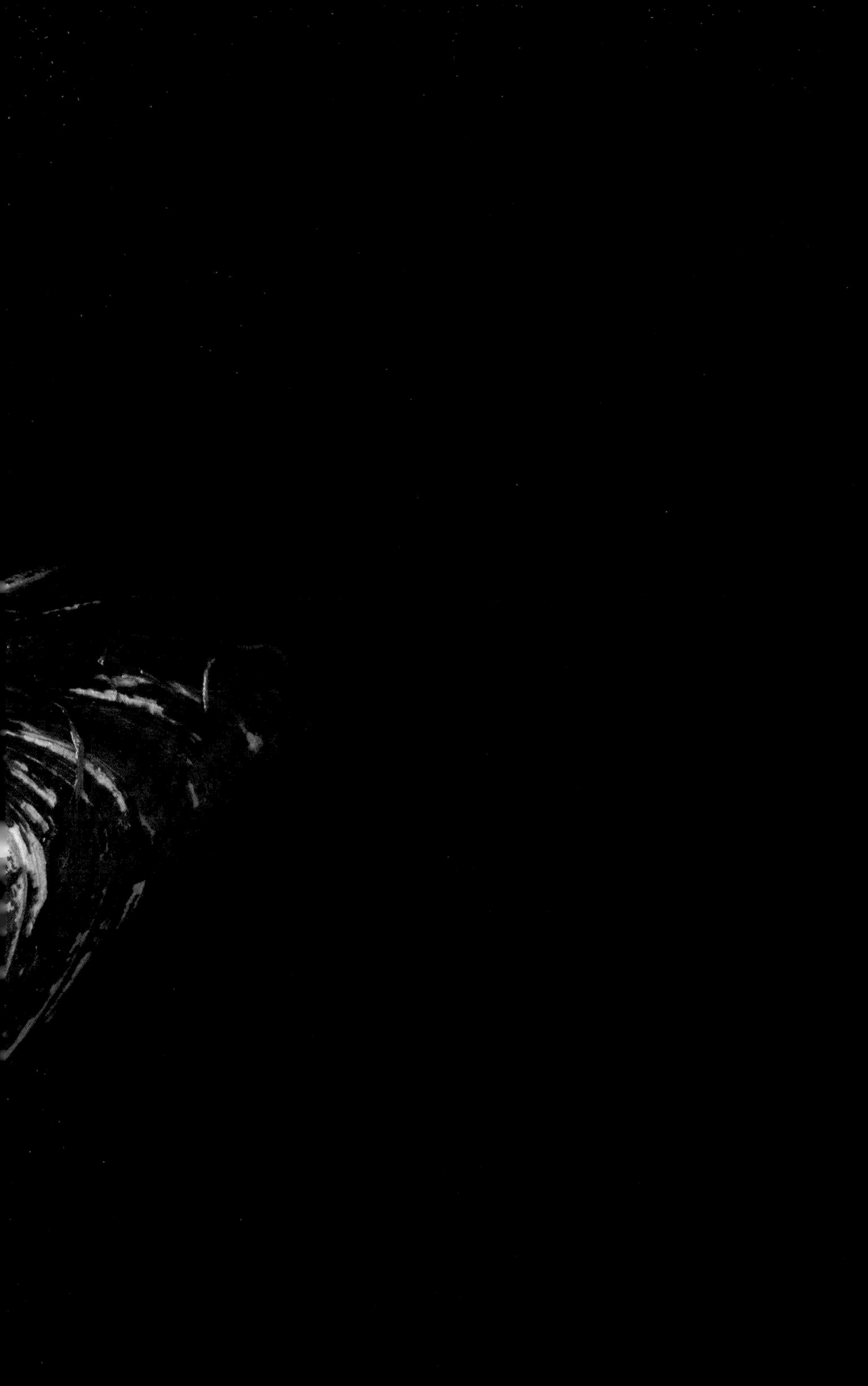

秋の魚

秋を旨さの最盛期とする魚介類は、一般に言われるほどに多くはない。白身の魚はほとんどないに等しい。晩秋から冬場を旬とする皮剥（かわはぎ）は、最近では少し旬が早まり、10月頃にはたっぷりとした肝を抱きはじめる。皮剥の肝はすべての魚介類の中で最も旨いとされ、身よりも肝が旨さの主役となる。脂を充分に乗せた鰹（かつお）は、北海道沖から南下を始め、南下とともにさらに脂と旨味を強くしていく。高い鮮度による真っ赤な身肉の色は鮮度の落ちとともに瞬く間に褪色（たいしょく）し、旨みも抜けてしまうのだが、その瞬間性と濃い脂の香りの旨さゆえに、昔から人気の高いものとなっている。8月の終わりに始まる新烏賊（しんいか）は10月に入ると最適の旨さの大きさに成長し、繊細で微妙な食感の旨さを、軽い緊張感を持って食すことになる。鯖（さば）は、晩秋の最盛期に向けてさらに充分な脂の旨みを増していく。脂と旨みを乗せたイクラ、醤油イクラに加工される鮭（さけ）の卵のイクラは、10月から11月頃に最高の旨さとなる。年に2回の旬を持つと言われる海松貝（みるがい）は、10月頃に再度、卵を大きく成長させ、水管も充分な甘みを持ち、見事な食感を楽しませてくれる。道東の甘海老（あまえび）漁が解禁となる。北海道から南下する秋刀魚（さんま）は、鰹と同じように南下とともにたっぷりとした脂を乗せ、江戸前ずしの新しい種の仲間入りとなった。

autumn fish

Not many varieties of seafood are generally said to reach peak flavor in autumn. White fish are almost nonexistent. Kawahagi (thread-sail filefish), best for eating from late autumn into winter, have recently started to come into season a little earlier, acquiring a sizeable liver around October. The liver of kawahagi is considered the tastiest of all sea creatures, and plays the main role in flavor terms, above that of the fish's flesh. Bonito with a generous layer of fat starts migrating south from the seas off Hokkaido, growing in fattiness and flavor on the journey. The bright red flesh discolors and loses freshness very quickly, along with its flavor, but the very transience of this freshness and the fragrant flavor of the rich fat make it a perennial favorite. Young squid arriving in late August have grown to their tastiest size by October, their subtle, delicate texture savored with a slight thrill of anticipation. Chub mackerel acquire a fatty succulence heading into their late autumn prime. Lustrously oily, tasty ikura and the salmon roe processed into soy sauce ikura reach their peak from October to November. Geoduck, said to have two seasons annually, grow luscious roe again around October, their siphons also sweet and succulent, with a splendid texture. Ama-ebi (pink shrimp) fishing opens off the east coast of Hokkaido. Pacific saury (sanma) migrating south from Hokkaido acquire a rich layer of fat in the same manner as bonito, and in recent years have become another new option on the Edo-mae sushi menu.

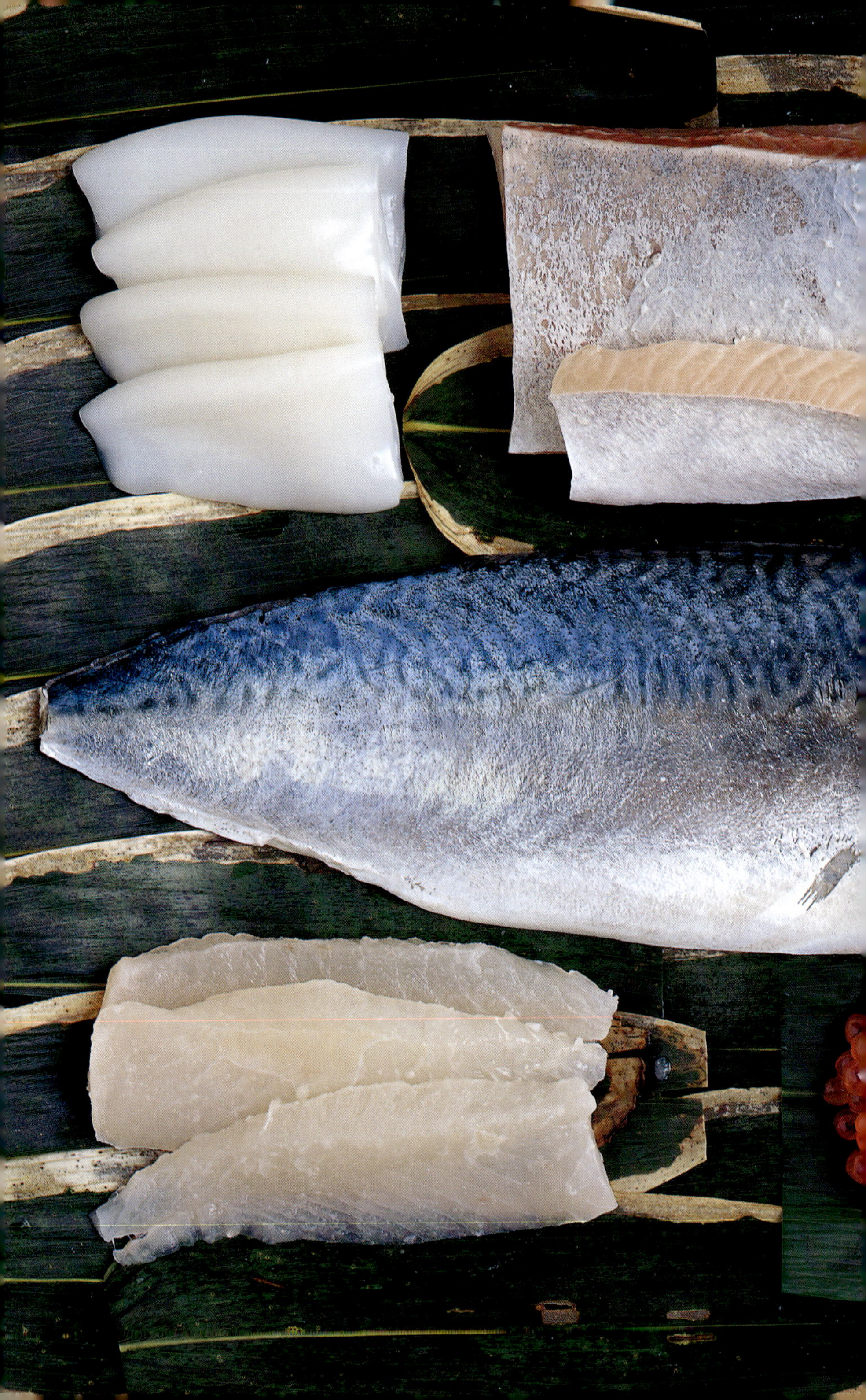

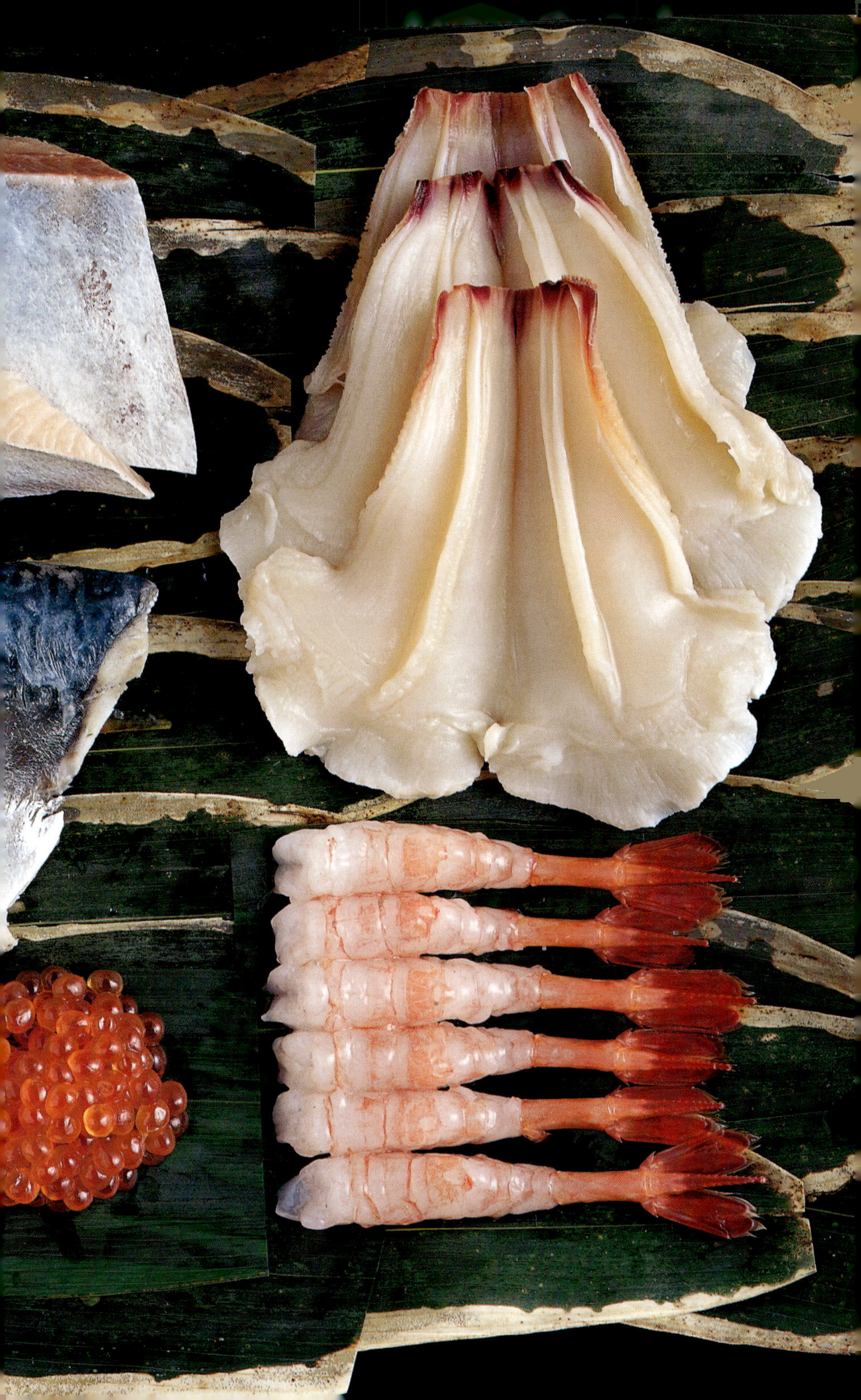

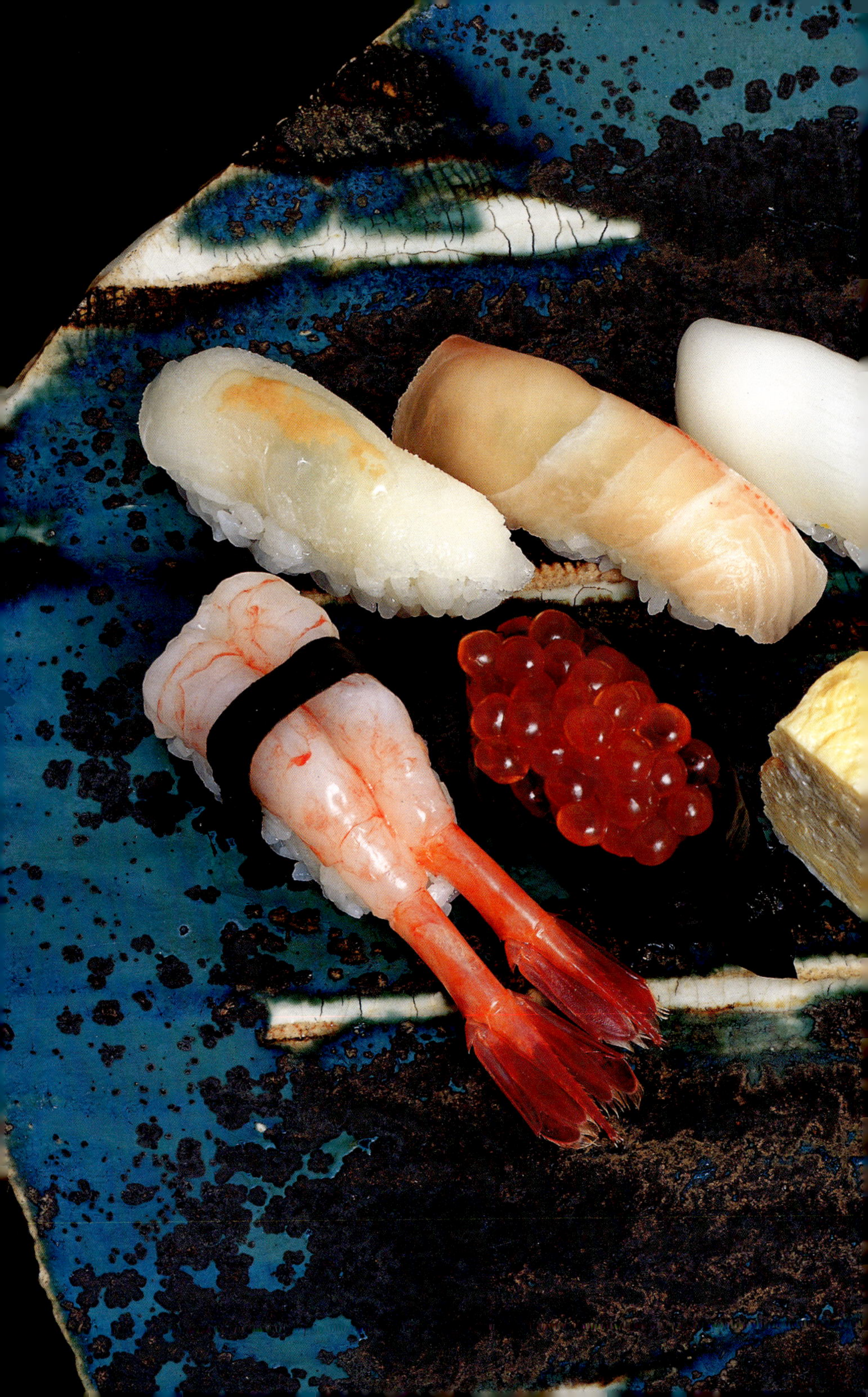

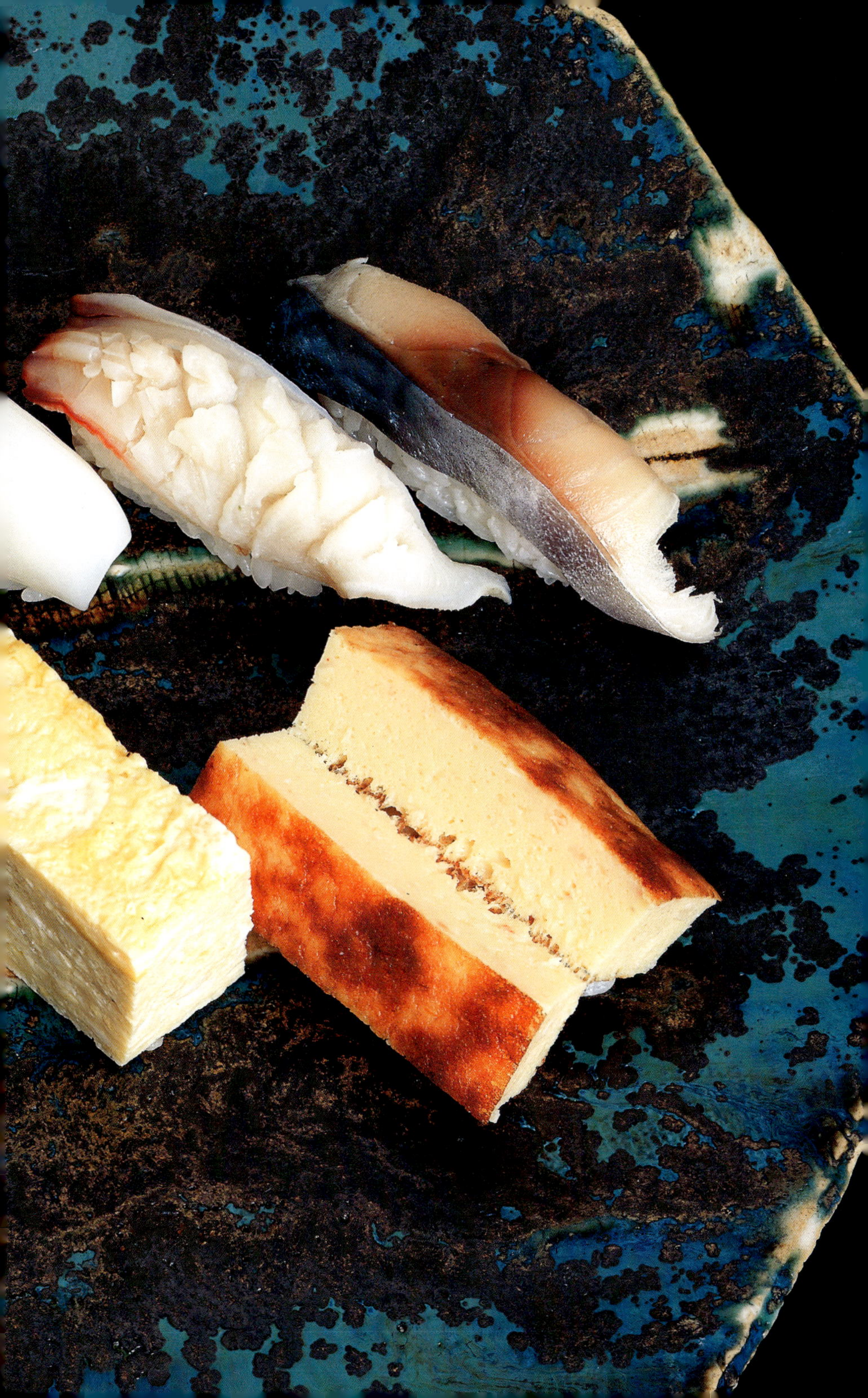

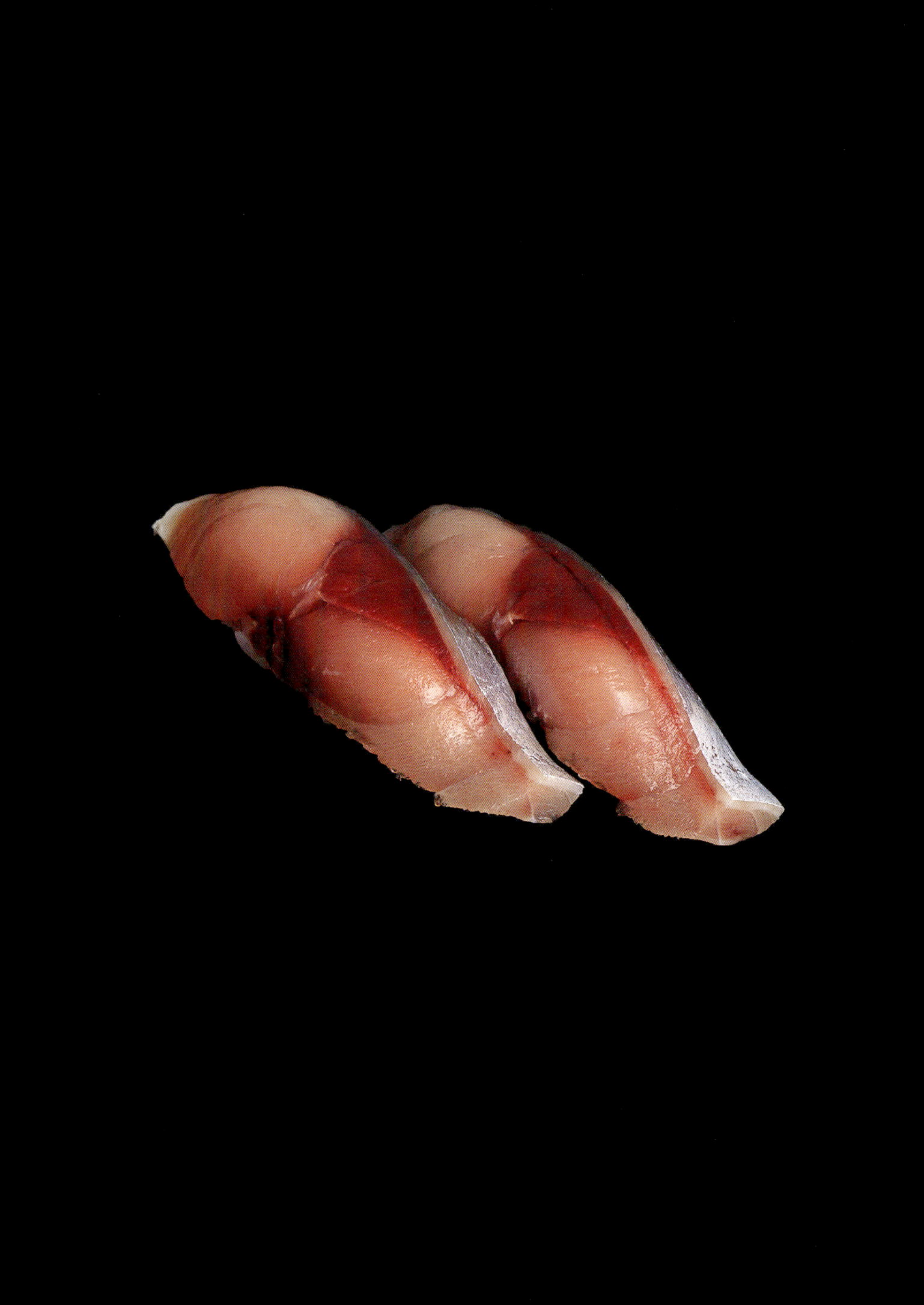

鯖
(saba)

初秋から晩秋にかけて旨さの最盛期となっていく真鯖は、秋鯖と呼ばれる。鮮度落ちが早く、身割れしやすいために、鯖は必ず塩と酢とで締めて使われる。旬真っ盛りの脂の乗った鯖の身肉は、口中で簡単に崩れて、濃い旨みとともにとろけていく。小鯖とともに、シャリとの相性が抜群に良く、江戸前ずしを代表する人気の高い魚のひとつとなっている。寄生虫や、ヒスタミンの生成によるじんましんの発生等、鮮度に関係なく危険性の多々ある魚なのだが、それを承知で旨さの冒険をするファンが多い。

Chub mackerel (masaba/*Scomber japonicus*) are known as autumn mackerel, autumn being when the fish are at their tastiest. Because mackerel go off quickly and disintegrate easily, they are always lightly cured with salt and vinegar before use. The oily flesh of prime mackerel dissolves in the mouth with a rich, oleaginous sensation. Mackerel, like gizzard shad, makes a sublime match for vinegared rice and ranks among the most popular fish in Edo-mae sushi. The possibility of parasites, or a rash due to histamine poisoning, makes the species a risky choice raw regardless of freshness, but this does not deter adventurous gourmets.

mackerel

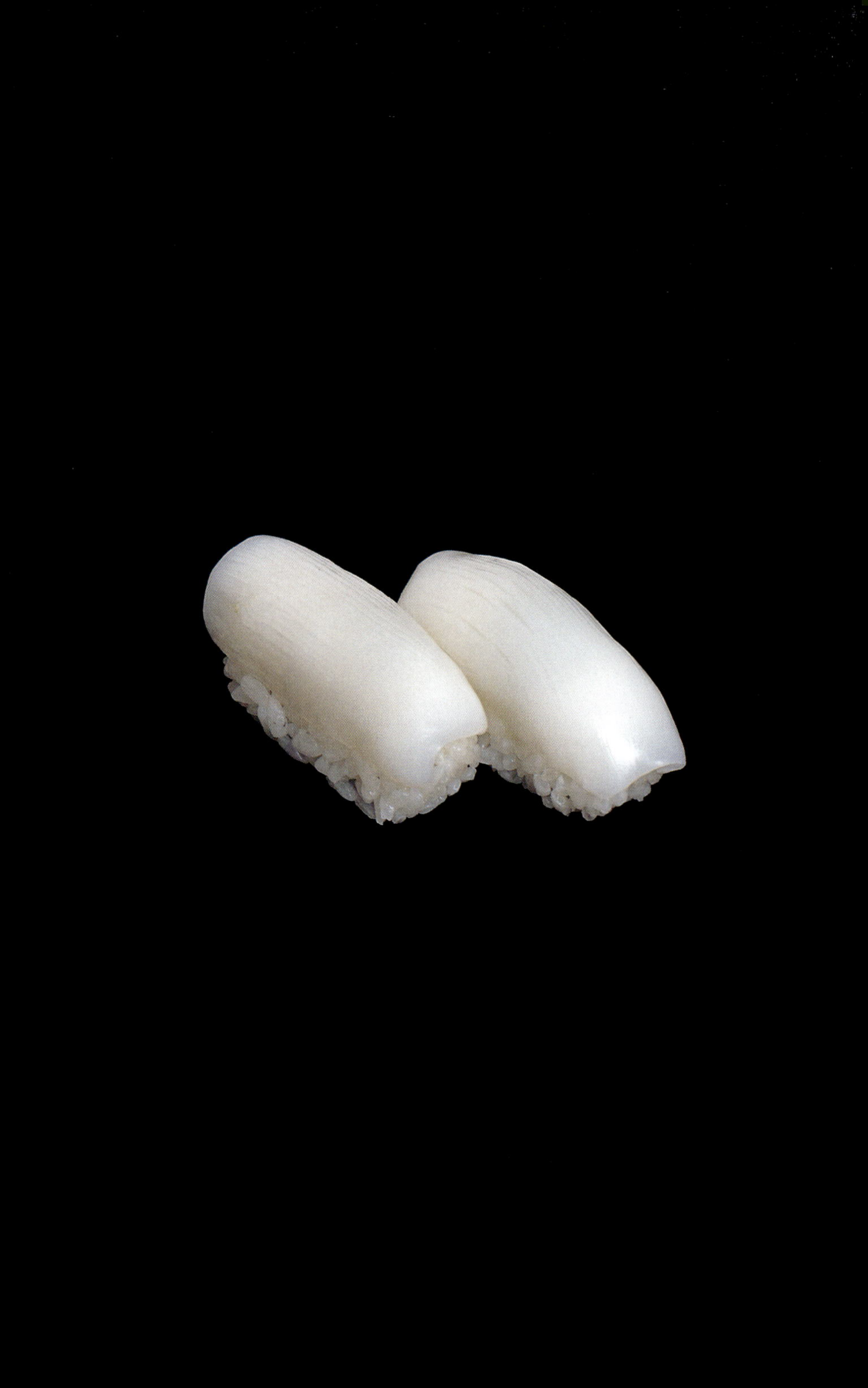

新烏賊
(shin ika)

8月上旬、1パイでやっと1貫のすしが握れる大きさの墨烏賊(すみいか)の子供が入荷しはじめる。この初物には驚異的な高値がつけられていく。初物好きの伝統を今でもしっかりと受け継ぐ東京のすし屋たちの間で、意地と誇りと見栄をかけて、誰が最初に使うかの戦いが始まるからだ。やがて2貫握れる大きさに成長すると、新烏賊の真髄となる。そして初冬の頃には片手を超える大きさに成長し、食感はさらに強いものとなっていく。

Early August marks the arrival of young sumi-ika finally grown large enough to make one nigiri each. Even now a traditional Tokyo preference for the first of the season sees these early specimens selling for astounding sums, as a battle of wills prompted by pride and vanity leads sushi shops to compete to acquire the squid first. When eventually the young squid grow large enough to make two nigiri, they truly come into their own in terms of flavor, the pleasing texture of their tender flesh the very essence of what makes shin ika so delectable. By early winter they grow to slightly larger than a hand and acquire an even more robust texture.

young cuttlefish

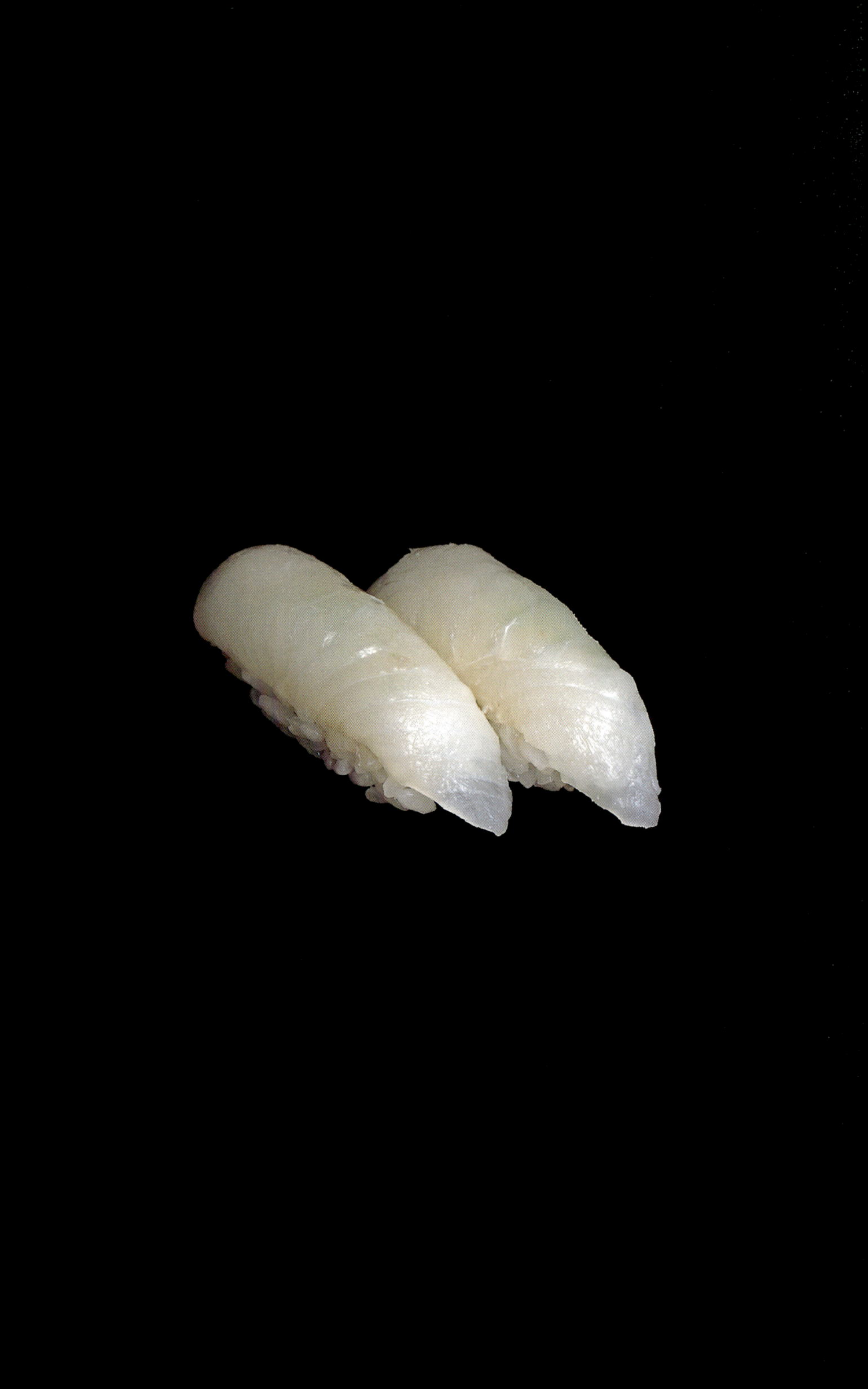

皮剥
(kawahagi)

10月から11月頃になると、皮剥の肝は見事に肥大し、旨さの旬に入っていく。肝はとろけるように甘く、密度の高い脂肪は滑らかな旨みをたたえている。透明感の高い身肉を切りつけると、薄くしっかりと伸びて美しい。皮剥を握るときは、この肝の旨さを最大限に利用することになる。肝をポン酢で和える。薄く大きめに切りつけた身を、山葵をきかせて握り、身の上にドロリと濃厚な肝を乗せる。すしの世界では変則的な旨さの取り方だが、皮剥の肝の、旨さを引き出す最良のやりようとなる。

In October–November, the liver of the kawahagi swells superbly and peaks in flavor. Meltingly sweet, the liver's dense, rich fat gives it a silky smooth flavor. The translucent flesh stretches thinly to stunning effect when cut. The exquisite flavor of the liver maximizes the appeal of kawahagi nigiri. A liberal dose of wasabi is added to the fish's flesh, which is cut into thin, slightly large pieces, and topped with the rich, succulent liver, dressed in ponzu sauce. Breaking all the rules of sushi style, this remains the best way to savor the superlative taste sensation of kawahagi liver.

thread-sail filefish

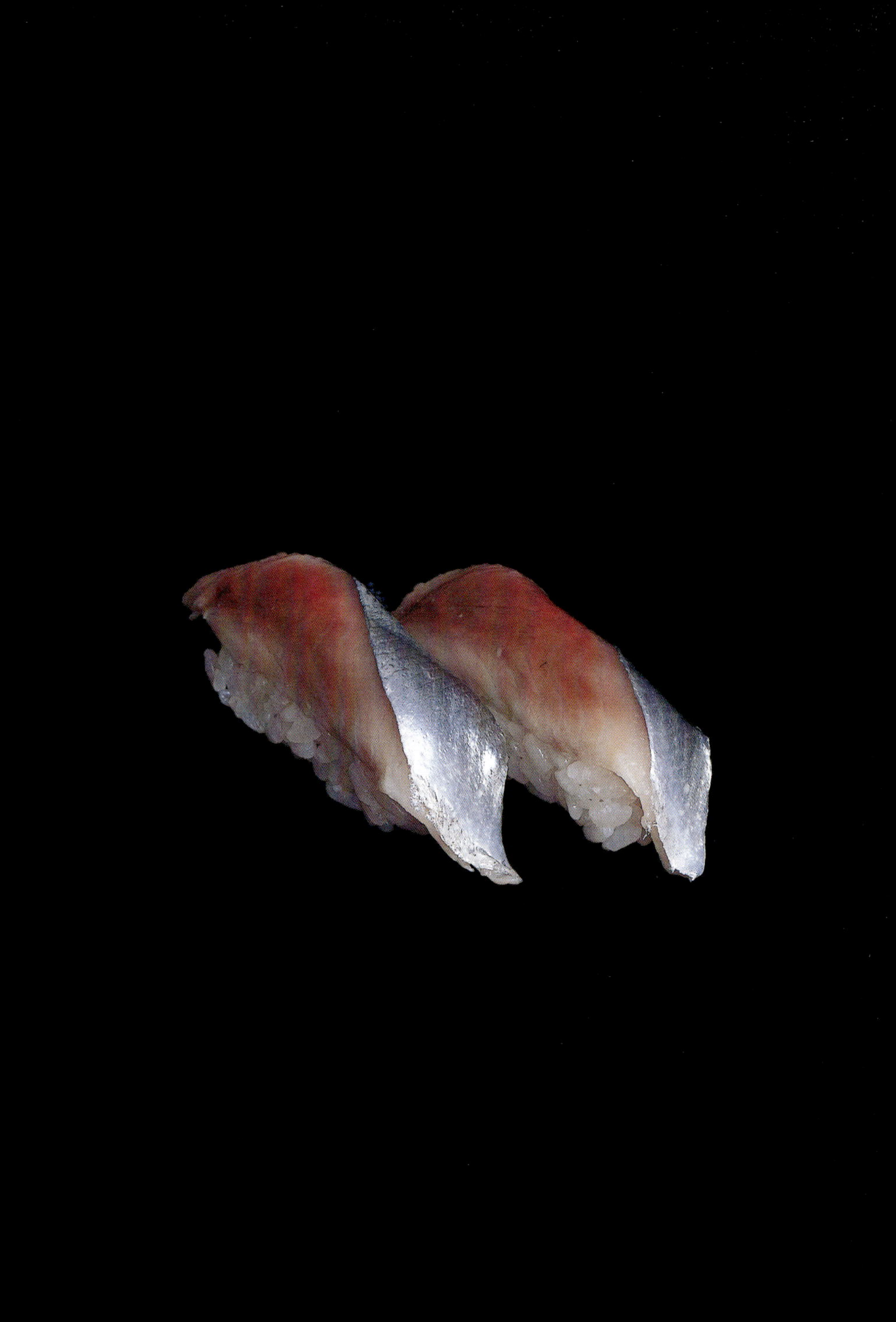

秋刀魚
(sanma)

秋刀魚は大量に漁獲されるために安価で、たっぷりと乗った脂の旨みとともに秋の味覚を代表する大衆魚として人気が高い。そして流通の画期的な進歩に伴い、鮮度のよい秋刀魚がただちに入荷するようになった。たっぷりと脂の乗った秋刀魚を生のままずしに握ると、さすがに旨い。しかし、東京のすし職人たちの、魚を塩と酢で締める技術を秋刀魚に応用すると、過剰なほどに脂の乗った秋刀魚は、別種の魚かと思われるほどの、独自の抑制された旨さの世界をもたらすことになる。

Large catches of sanma make this an accessible species, which added to its tasty, oily flesh, makes it a widely enjoyed autumn favorite. Revolutionary advances in transport and distribution mean that fresh sanma is now available soon after catching. And used raw in sushi, its fat-suffused flavor does indeed delight. But when the sushi chefs of Tokyo apply their skill at curing fish with salt and vinegar, the almost excessively fatty sanma enters an entirely different league of distinctive, understated flavor, to the extent one cannot quite believe it is the same fish.

Pacific saury

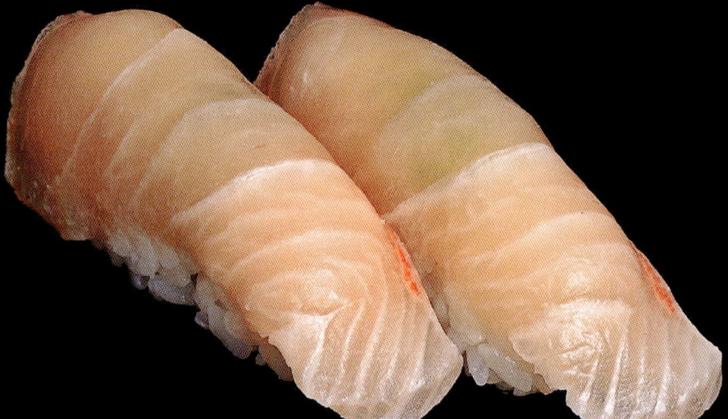

間八
(kanpachi)

秋の初めから中秋頃、間八はもうすでに旨さの旬に入っている。比較的漁獲量も多く、身質は全体的に赤みを帯びているが、しっかりと締まって美しい。最盛期に濃厚な脂が乗ってくると身は白濁し、甘みも強くなる。３キロから４キロ前後のものが使い勝手がよく、脂の乗りも程よい品の良さを見せる。間八の旨さを位の熟成の時間を高級魚として高値になる。堪能するには、丸２日間必要とする。まだ活きている身肉の食感の旨さを優先させるか、それぞれの魚の個性を醸しだす、熟成された豊潤な旨さを取るか、選択の余地は充分にあるはずだ。

From early to around mid-autumn, kanpachi are already at their best. Comparatively plentiful, their flesh is distinguished by an overall redness, but is beautifully firm. A generous laying down of fat in their prime brings a cloudiness to the flesh, and a more intense sweetness. Specimens of around 3–4kgs are most versatile, the fat also having a refined quality that helps drive up prices for this high-class fish. Kanpachi is best savored after a full two days or so of aging. The delectable texture of the still-living flesh, or the succulent flavor of fish aged to draw out its individual flavor: the choice is yours.

greater amberjack

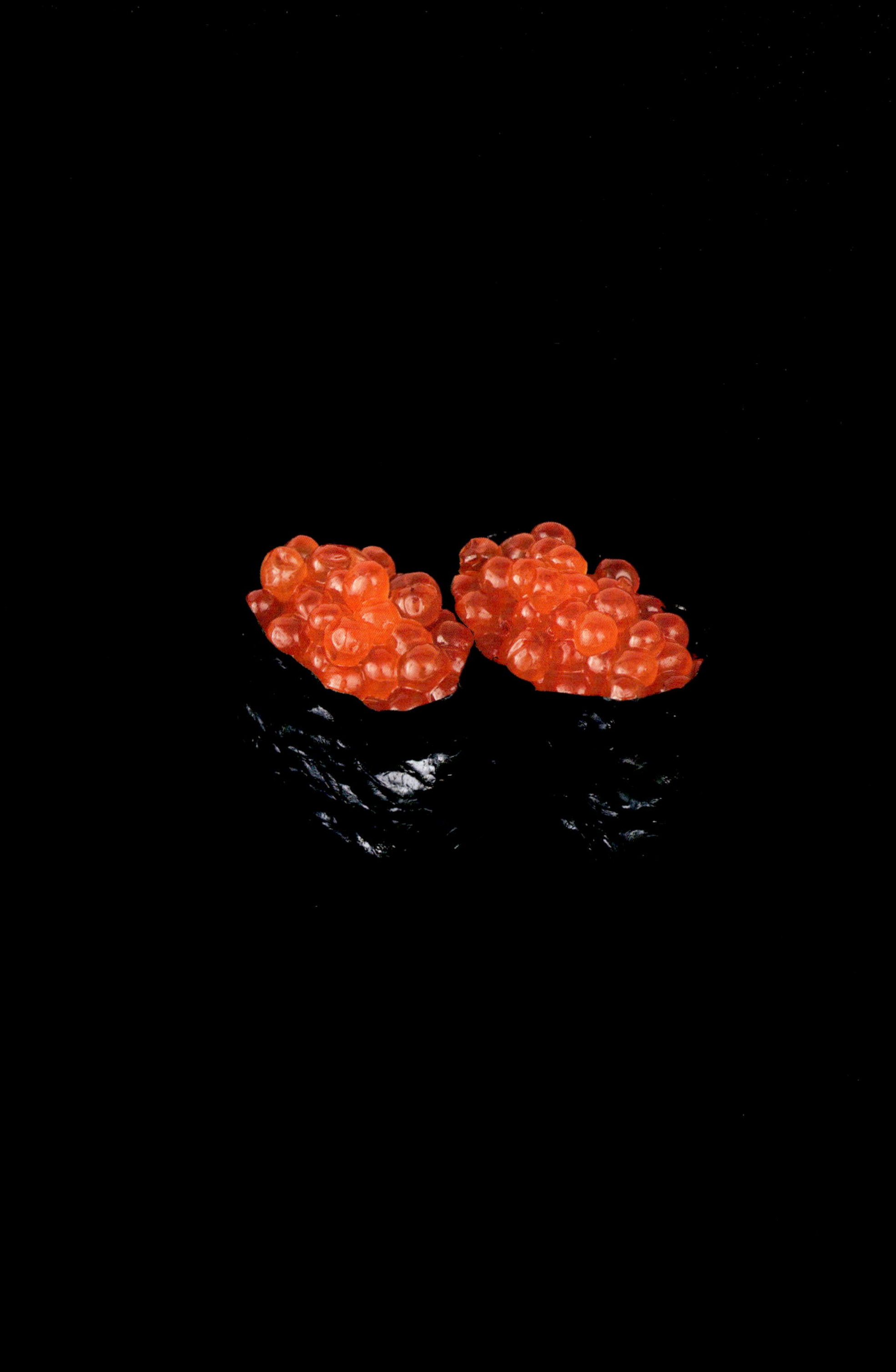

イクラ
(ikura)

鮭の腹子(卵)をロシア語でイクラと言う。すしに使われるイクラには塩漬けにされた塩イクラと、醬油に漬け込まれた醬油イクラとがある。10月中旬から11月中旬頃の旨さの最盛期の鮭の卵で加工されたイクラを最高級品とする。脂の乗った朱色のイクラの粒は、美しく大きく膨らんでいる。歯に絡みつくような濃厚な脂は、卵の表皮までも程よいネットリとした旨みに変えてしまう。すし種としては海胆とともに新参の部類に入るのだが、その旨さゆえに高級品として圧倒的な人気を持っている。加工されたイクラは冷凍保存され、一年中使用される。

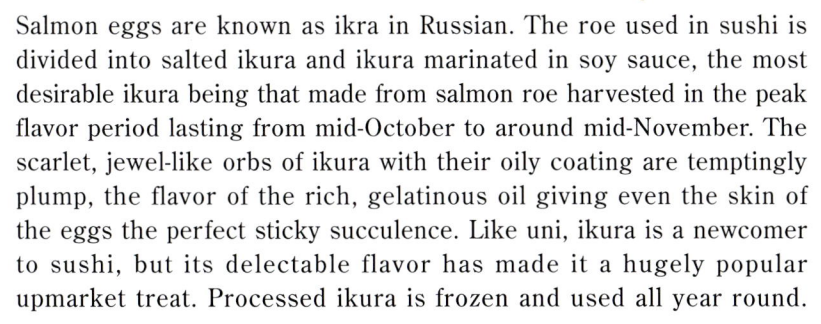

Salmon eggs are known as ikra in Russian. The roe used in sushi is divided into salted ikura and ikura marinated in soy sauce, the most desirable ikura being that made from salmon roe harvested in the peak flavor period lasting from mid-October to around mid-November. The scarlet, jewel-like orbs of ikura with their oily coating are temptingly plump, the flavor of the rich, gelatinous oil giving even the skin of the eggs the perfect sticky succulence. Like uni, ikura is a newcomer to sushi, but its delectable flavor has made it a hugely popular upmarket treat. Processed ikura is frozen and used all year round.

salmon roe

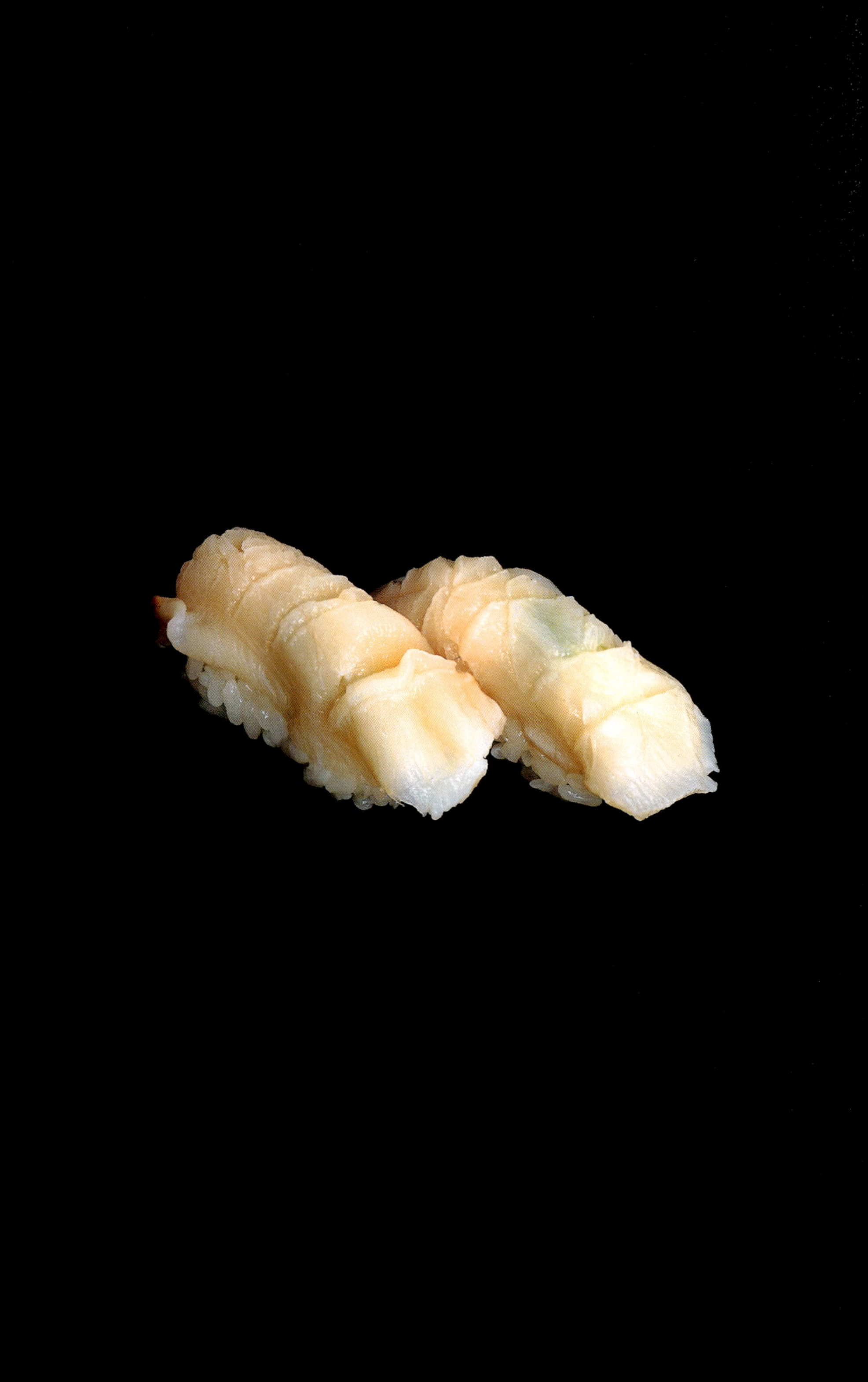

海松貝
(mirugai)

海松貝は、3月と10月の産卵を中心に年に2回、旨さの旬を持っている。卵の肥大とともに旨さが増し、こりこりとする歯ごたえと、個性的な香りと強い甘みを持ってくる。しかし鮮度の劣化とともに、これらの特徴は最悪の状態に変化してゆく。身肉は緩み、香りは悪臭に変化し、甘みも消されていく。だから海松貝の旨さは鮮度こそがすべての勝負どころとなる。海松貝は軽く焼いてやると香ばしさの中に、さらに強い甘みが立ちのぼり旨い。近年では漁獲量が激減し、鮑(あわび)・赤貝(あかがい)と同格の高価な値をつけるようになった。

Geoduck have semi-annual flavor peaks around spawning in March and October. Growing tastier as their roe swells, they have a crunchy texture, distinctive fragrance and intense sweetness. As time passes after harvesting however these characteristics take a dramatic turn for the worse; the flesh slackening, fragrance turning to odor, and all trace of sweet flavor vanishing. Thus when it comes to geoduck, freshness is all. Light grilling further highlights the element of sweetness amid the fragrance. Recent years have seen a precipitous decline in geoduck harvests, making this odd-looking mollusk a luxury to rival abalone and blood cockle.

geoduck

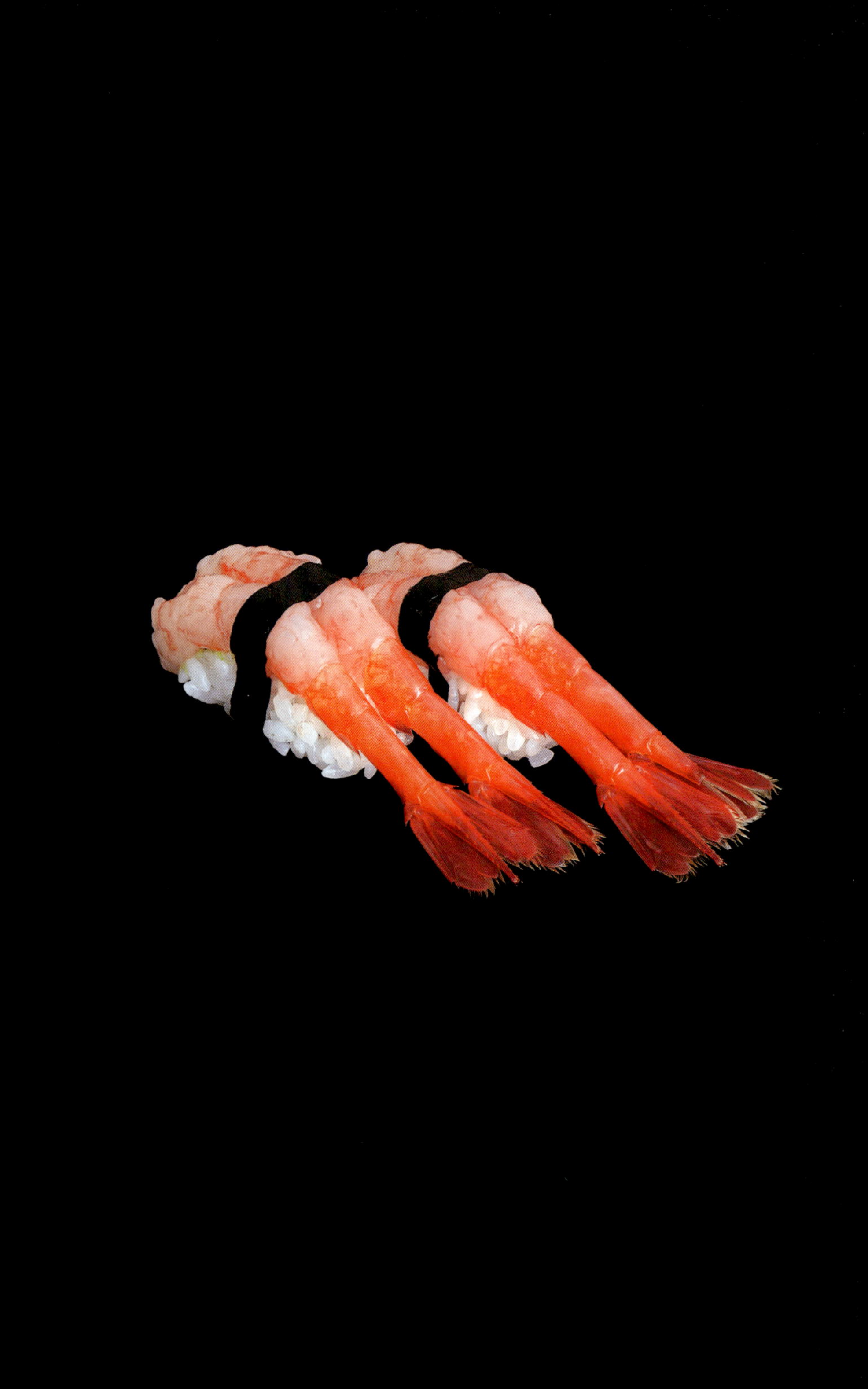

甘海老
(ama-ebi)

甘海老は生鮮の生食が旨い。透明感のある身質は、べっとりと舌にまとわりつくような食感と強い甘みを持っている。体色は美しく、鮮やかな紅朱色をしているのだが、処理が悪く、鮮度が落ちるとすぐに剥落し、変色する。活きている甘海老は、ぷりぷりとした食感を持っているが、鮮度が良過ぎると、身肉の表面の鮮やかな紅朱色がまだ発色できず、舌にとろけていく強い熟成の甘みも醸しだされていない。だから甘海老の旨さを充分に味わうためには、死んでから丸1日ほどの時間の経過が必要とされる。

Amaebi is best consumed fresh and raw. The deliciously sweet, translucent flesh clings to the tongue. The shrimps are a vibrant red, but do not handle well, and when no longer fresh drop their shells and discolor. Live amaebi are crisp and succulent, but a little *too* fresh, that is lacking the scarlet surface color, and the intense, melt-in-the-mouth sweet sensation acquired on aging. Thus to really get the most out of amaebi, it should be left about a day before consuming.

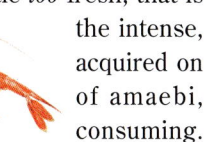

pink shrimp

winter

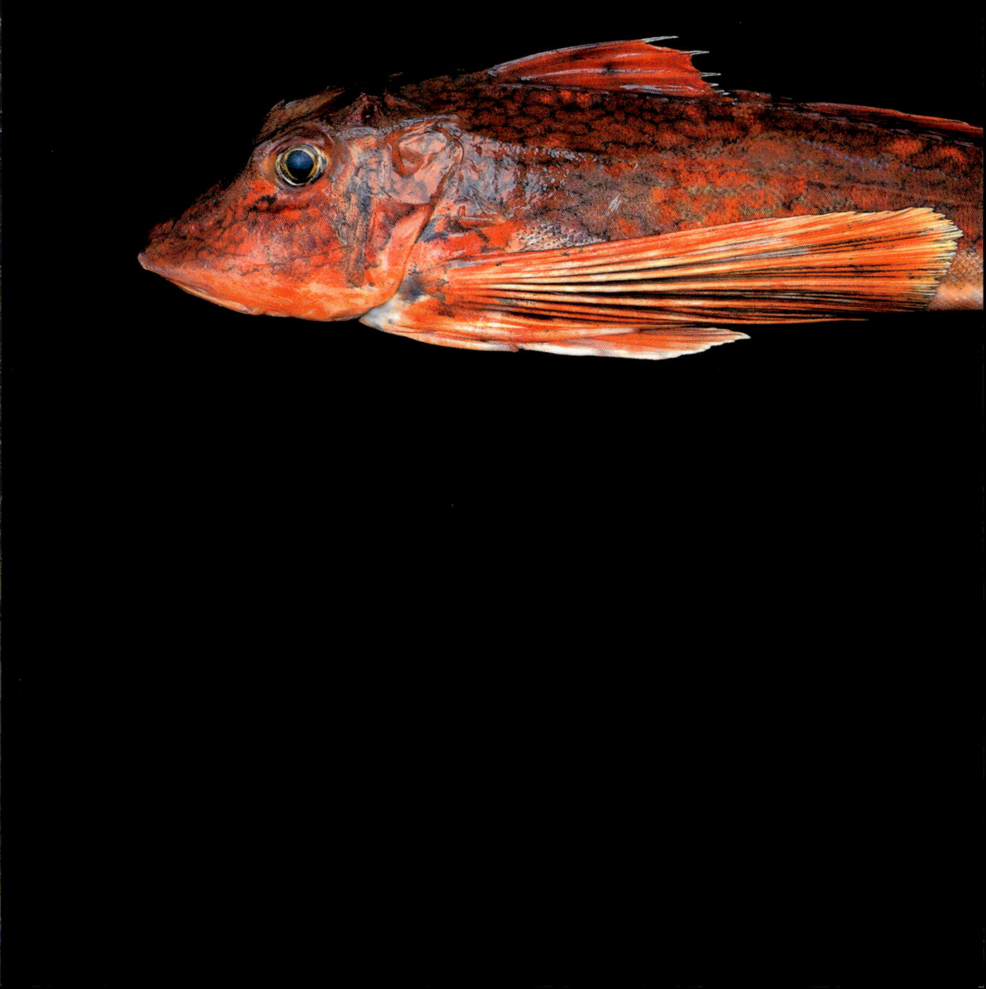

冬の魚

冬を旬とする魚たちは、たっぷりと乗った脂の旨さを持ち味とするものが多く、淡白な旨さを特徴とする夏場の魚とは対照的となる。本鮪(ほんまぐろ)は、晩秋から冬にかけて濃厚な脂を乗せていき、旨さの最盛期となるが、あまりにも少ない漁獲量と、圧倒的な人気ゆえに驚異的な価格の暴騰を見ることになる。一本釣りの勇姿と色の濃い朱色の身肉の美しさ、血の香りと強い旨みは、江戸前ずしの象徴的な魚となっている。12月に入ると、10キロ以上の見事な旨みを持つ鰤(ぶり)が登場してくるが、時期は短い。鮃(ひらめ)も、年明けとともに俄然身肉が充実し、旨さの最盛期となる。漁獲量の少ない平鱸(ひらすずき)は、緻密な身質に良質な脂をたたえ、心地よい食感を楽しませてくれる。水温が下がりきった時期の鮄鮄(ほうぼう)は、華やかな外見からは想像もつかない滑らかな食感と豊かな甘みと旨みを持っている。下顎(かがく)の先端を朱で染めている細魚(さより)は、繊細な食感と旨みを持っている。水温の低下とともに深場へ移行しはじめる車海老は、身肉を太らせ、充実した強い甘みと旨みを発揮する。赤貝、平貝、蝦夷鮑(えぞあわび)は色艶が美しく、太って甘みを増してくる。江戸前ずしの元祖であり、握りずしの旨さを代表する小鰭(こはだ)は、晩秋から冬の初め頃に最高の脂の乗りを見せ、旨さの最盛期となる。

winter fish

Many winter species are prized for their fatty quality, in contrast to summer fish characterized by subtle flavor. Bluefin tuna acquire an intense lipidity from late autumn into winter, reaching their prime, however the scarcity and overwhelming popularity of the species make for astoundingly high prices. The gallant fighting spirit of the pole-fished tuna, its attractive deep scarlet flesh, bloody aroma and intense flavor make it emblematic of Edo-mae sushi. By December, flavorsome amberjack weighing over 10kg start to appear, but only for a shortlived season. Olive flounder (hirame) also suddenly pack on weight with the new year, and are deemed to be at peak flavor. Scarce blackfin (hira-suzuki) acquire good-quality fat on their delicate flesh, for an agreeable texture. Gurnard in the period when sea temperatures are lowest have a smoothness and intense sweetness and flavor belied by their gaudy looks. Japanese halfbeak, notable for the scarlet tip of their lower jaw, have a delicate texture and flavor. Tiger prawns, which move to deeper waters as temperatures drop, gain weight and exhibit a satisfying intensity of sweetness and flavor. Blood cockle, pen shell and Ezo abalone take on a lustrous sheen, and grow sleek and sweet. Gizzard shad, one of the original ingredients in Edo-mae sushi and a fish typifying the delectable appeal of nigiri-zushi, is at its succulent best from late autumn to around early winter, when sushi fans can enjoy the flavor of shad at its fat-suffused finest.

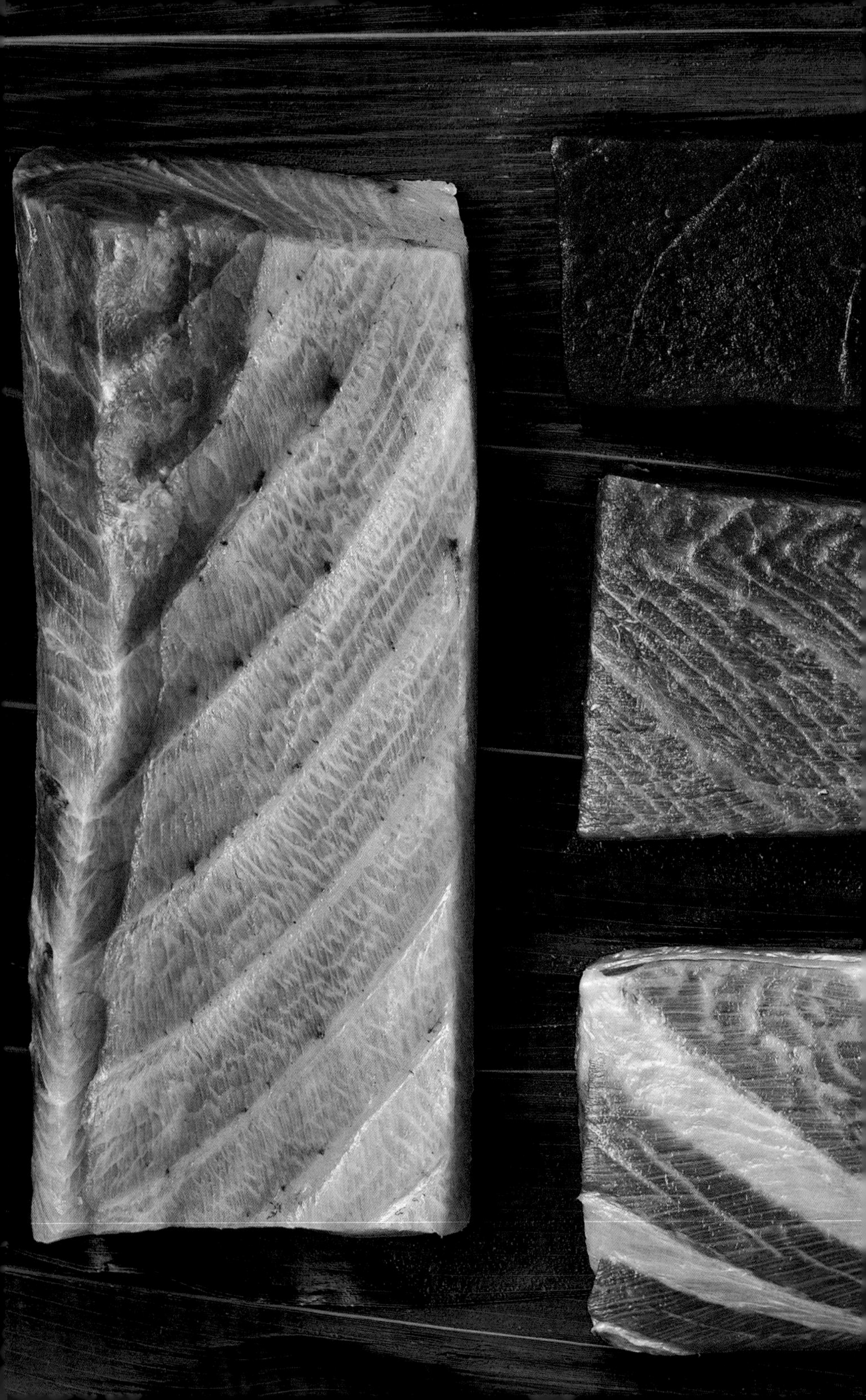

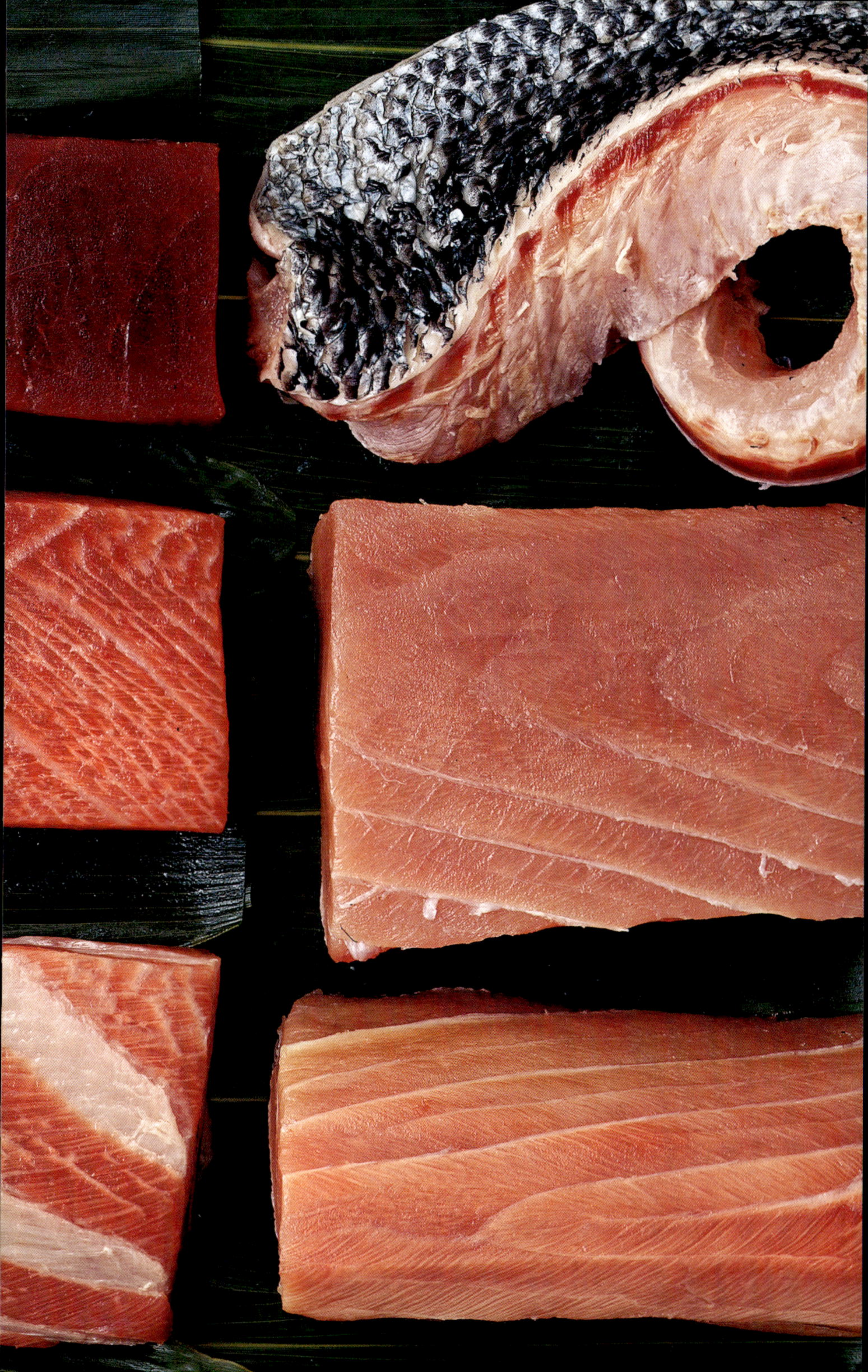

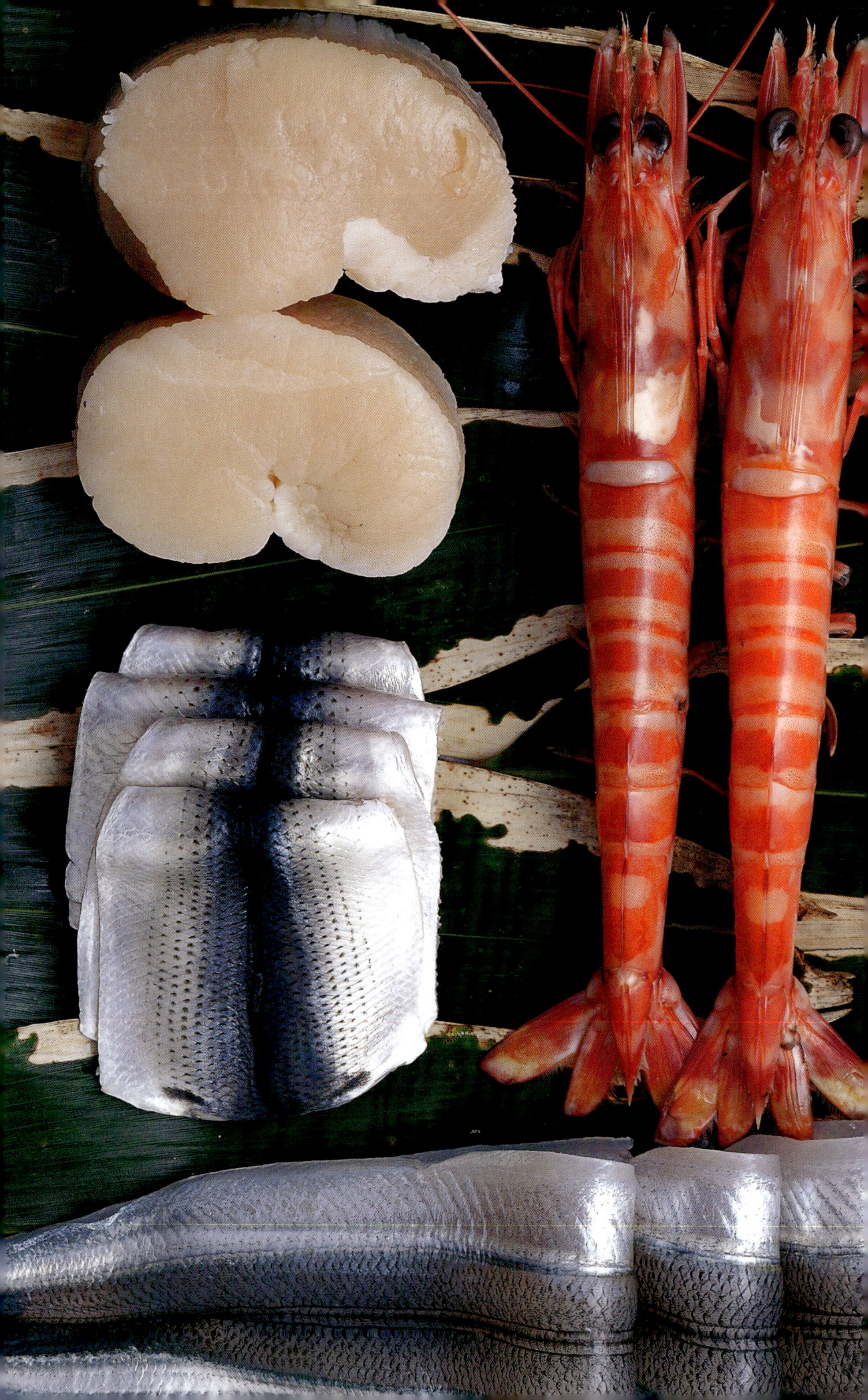

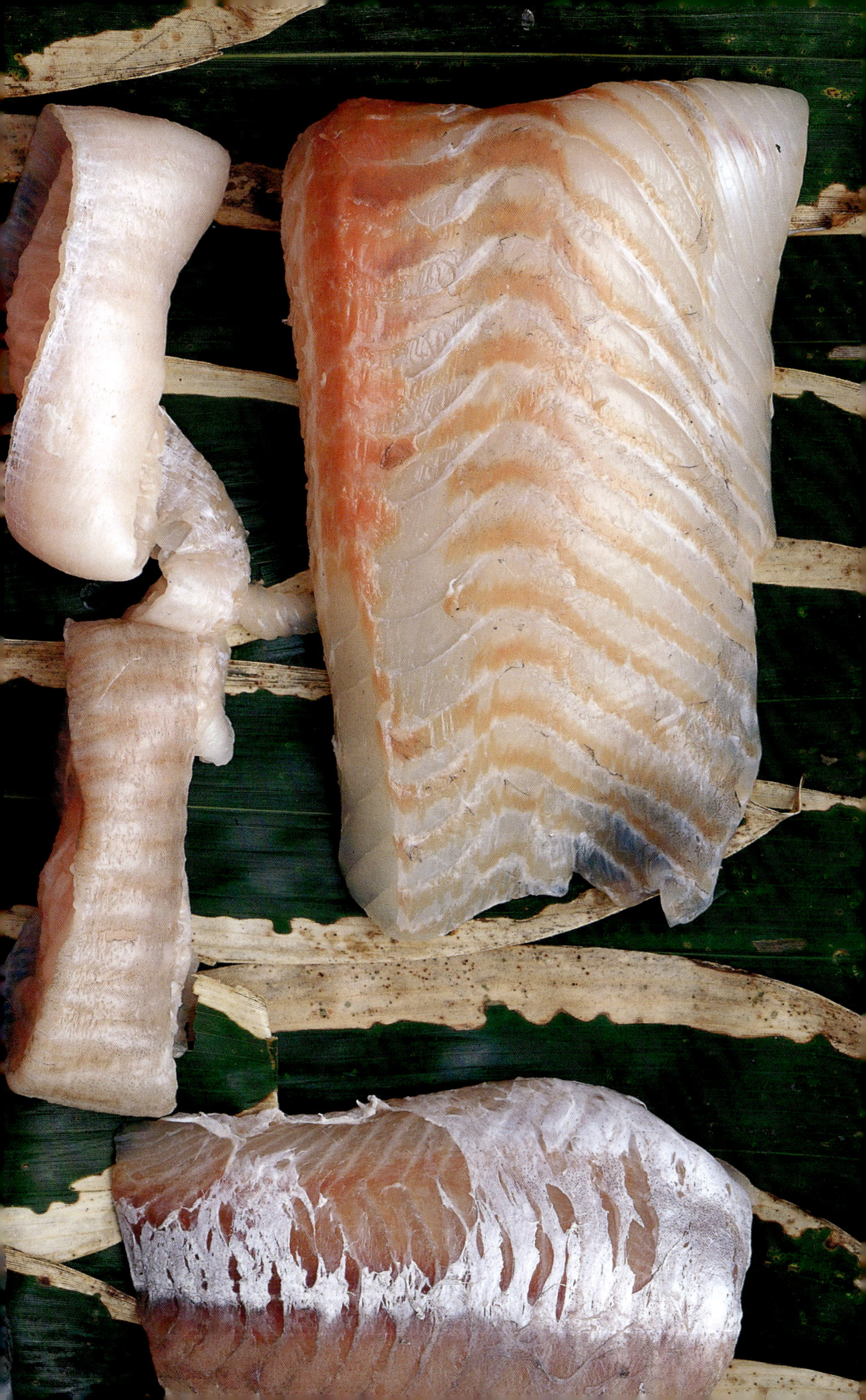

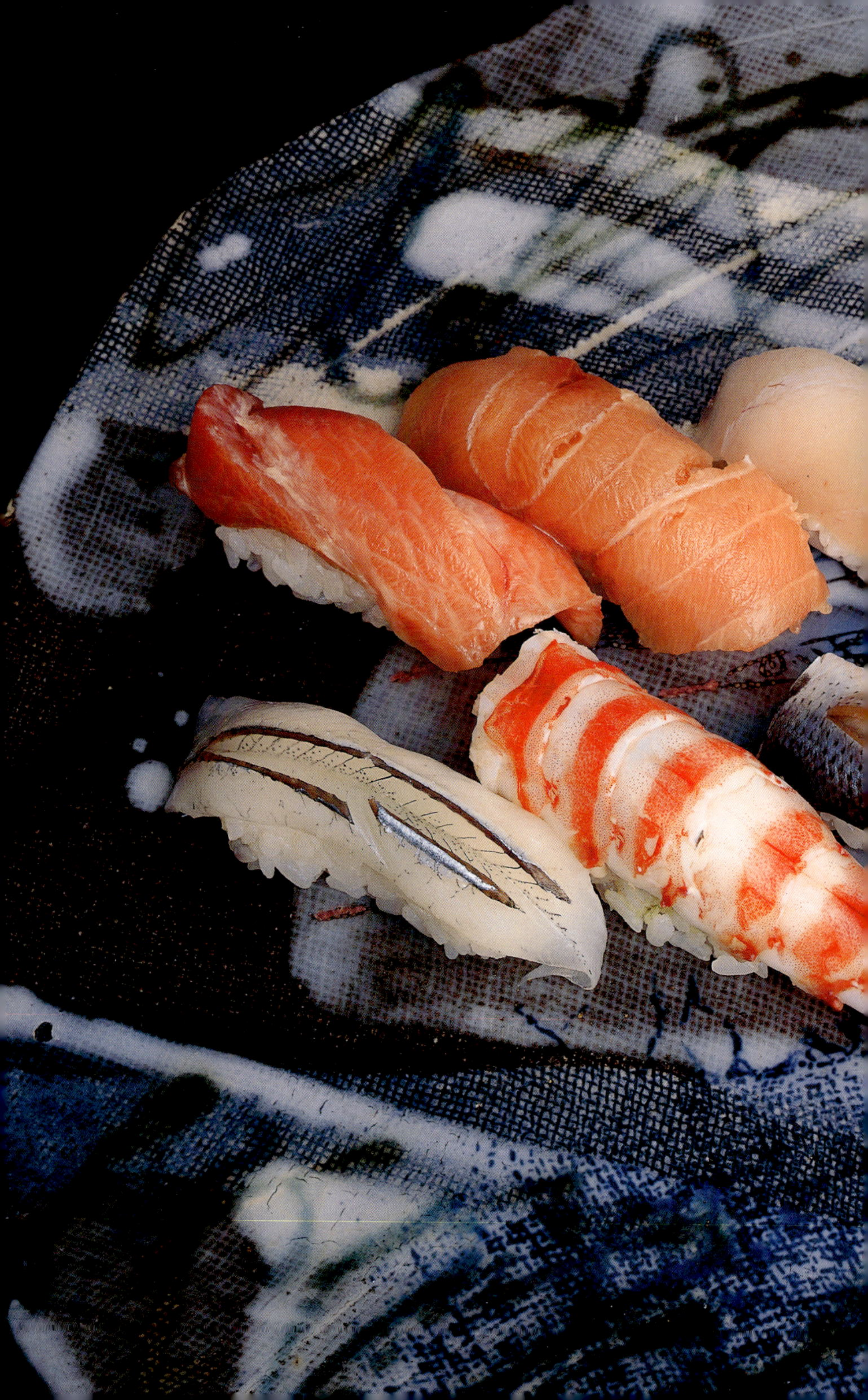

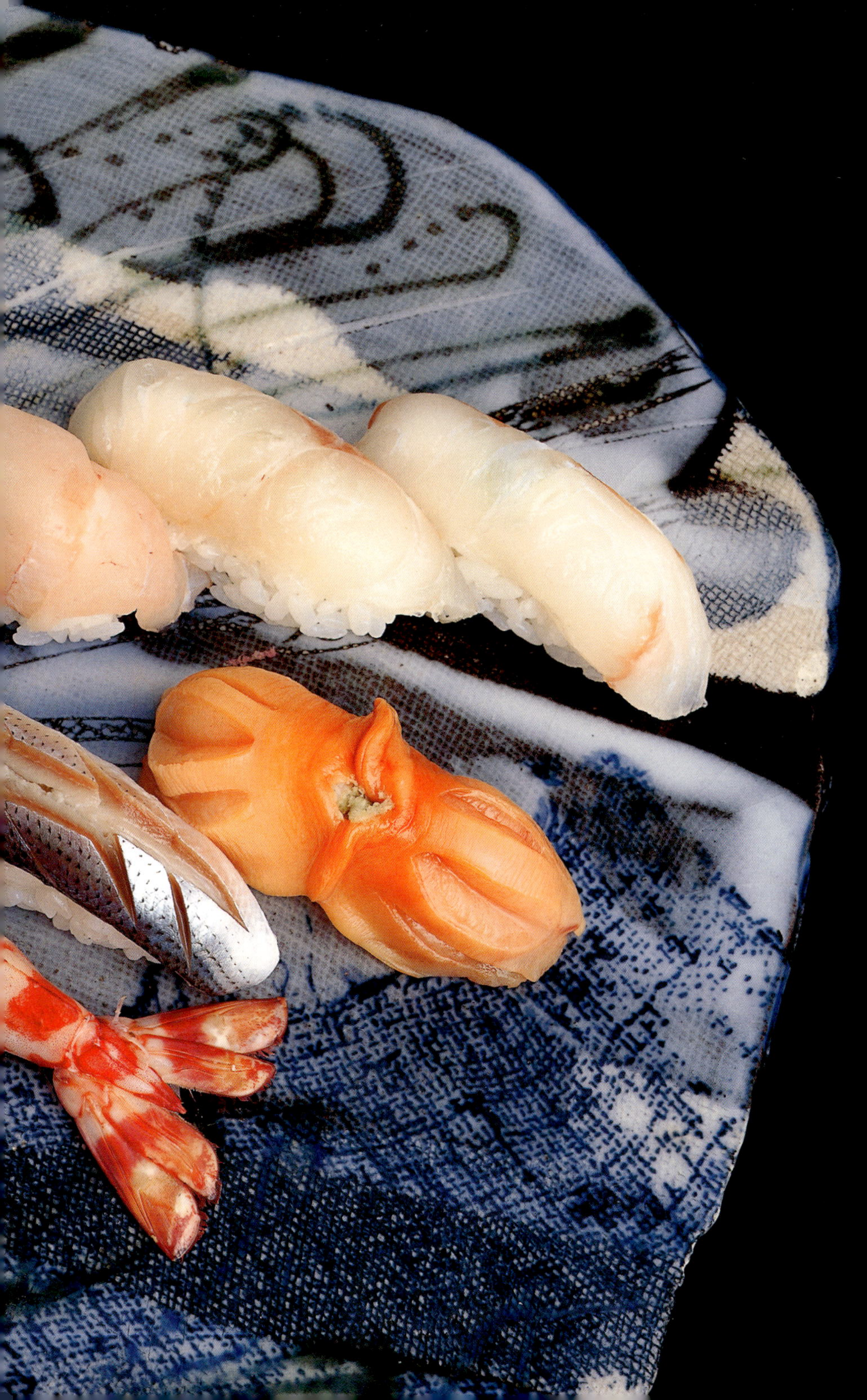

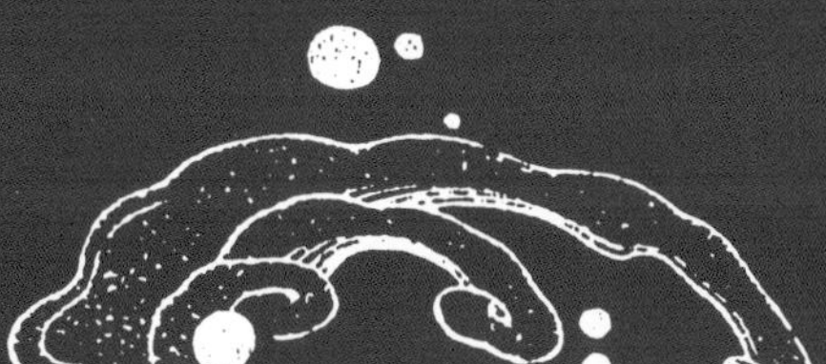

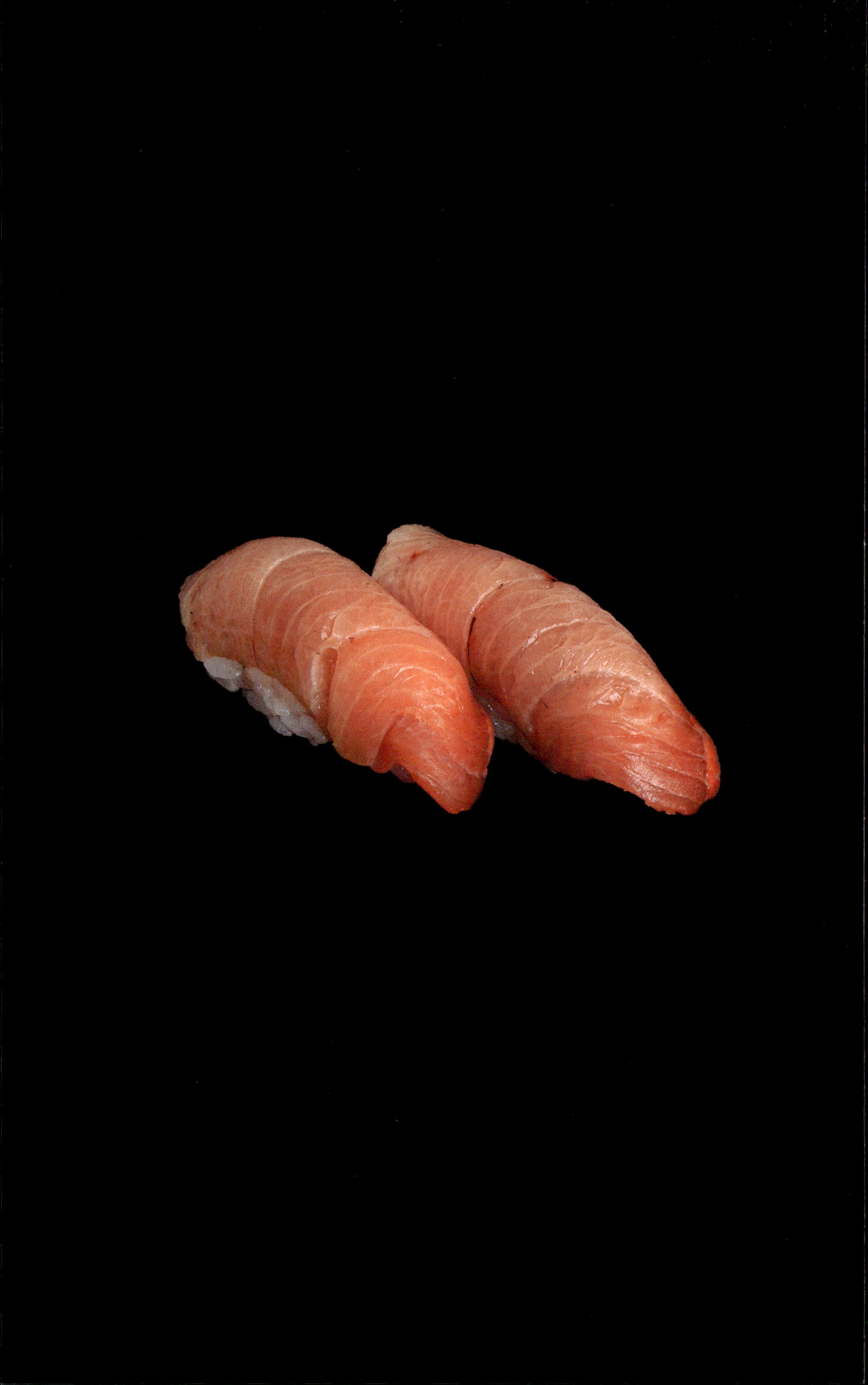

鰤
(buri)

鰤は10キロ以上の大きさに成長した稚鰤(わらさ)に与えられる名称で、最大16キロ前後にまで成長する。晩秋から冬場にかけての鰤は"寒(かん)"鰤(ぶり)と尊称される。しかし12月上旬から下旬にかけての頃、富山湾から佐渡島に達する回遊の群れは、別格のものとして評価される。旨さが違うのだ。この成熟した鰤たちは本鮪(ほんまぐろ)の旨さに通じるものを持っている。血の香りと鉄分が持つ絶妙な酸味に、まろやかな脂の甘みと、豊潤な香りが加わっている。この香りこそが、厳冬の雷と荒波の中から到来する寒鰤たちの最高の旨さの魅力となっている。

Buri is the name given to amberjack of 10kg or more, with some fish growing to around 16kg. Late autumn and winter specimens are given the honorary title of 'kan' or 'cold-weather' buri. The schools migrating from Toyama Bay to Sadogashima during December are deemed in a class of their own; that is, offering a taste experience of an entirely different dimension. These mature buri boast flavor to rival bluefin tuna, the scent of blood and slight tartness of iron supplemented by the sweetness and succulent aroma of their silky-smooth fat. This aroma is precisely what makes cold-weather buri arriving from harsh winter storms and high seas so appealing.

Japanese amberjack

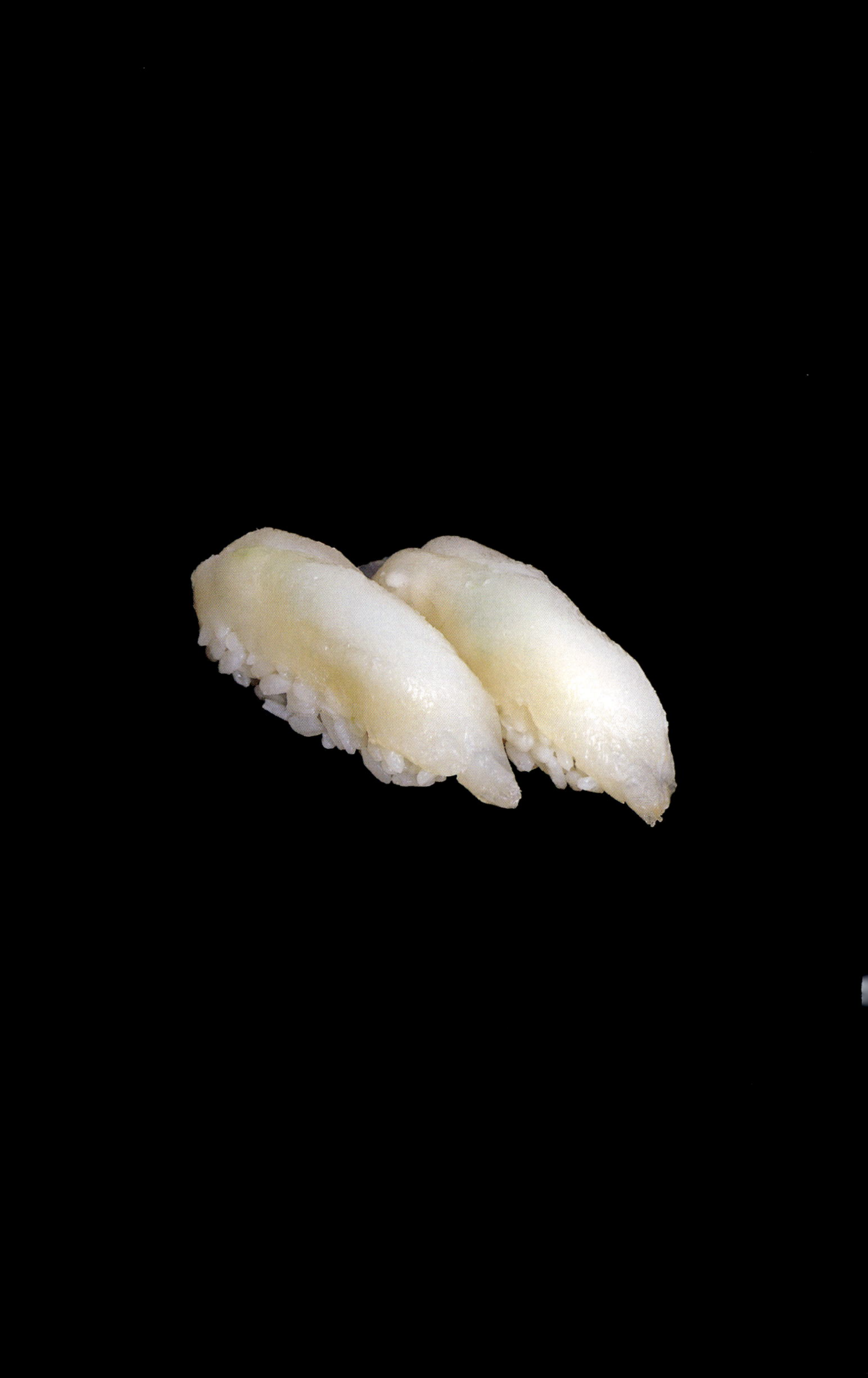

真鱈
(madara)

冬の寒気の到来とともに、真鱈は旨さの旬に入っていく。精巣である白子が特に旨く、この時期にはトロリとした食感とともに、甘み旨みが強くなってくる。真鱈をすしに用いるときには、昆布締めにする。身には水分が多く、淡白で甘みが足りず、鮮度の落ちとともに軟化してしまうからだ。昆布で締めることにより、水分を脱水し、昆布の旨みも添加することができる。真鱈に薄く塩を打つ。しっとりとにじみ出てきた水分を拭き取り、昆布に挟む。少し押しをして１日、身にはもう充分な昆布の旨みが添加されている。真鱈は昆布締めすることによって、上質なすし種の一品に変貌する。

Madara peak with the arrival of winter chill. Cod semen is a gourmet treat, and particularly sweet and creamy at this time. Cod for sushi is kombu-cured, due to the fish's watery, somewhat flavorless flesh, which also slackens over time. Curing with kombu removes excess moisture, and adds flavor. The fish is sprinkled lightly with salt, the moisture oozing out as a result wiped away, the fish placed between two sheets of kombu and lightly weighted. After a day the flesh has acquired enough of the kombu's flavor, transforming madara into one of the choicest sushi varieties.

Pacific cod

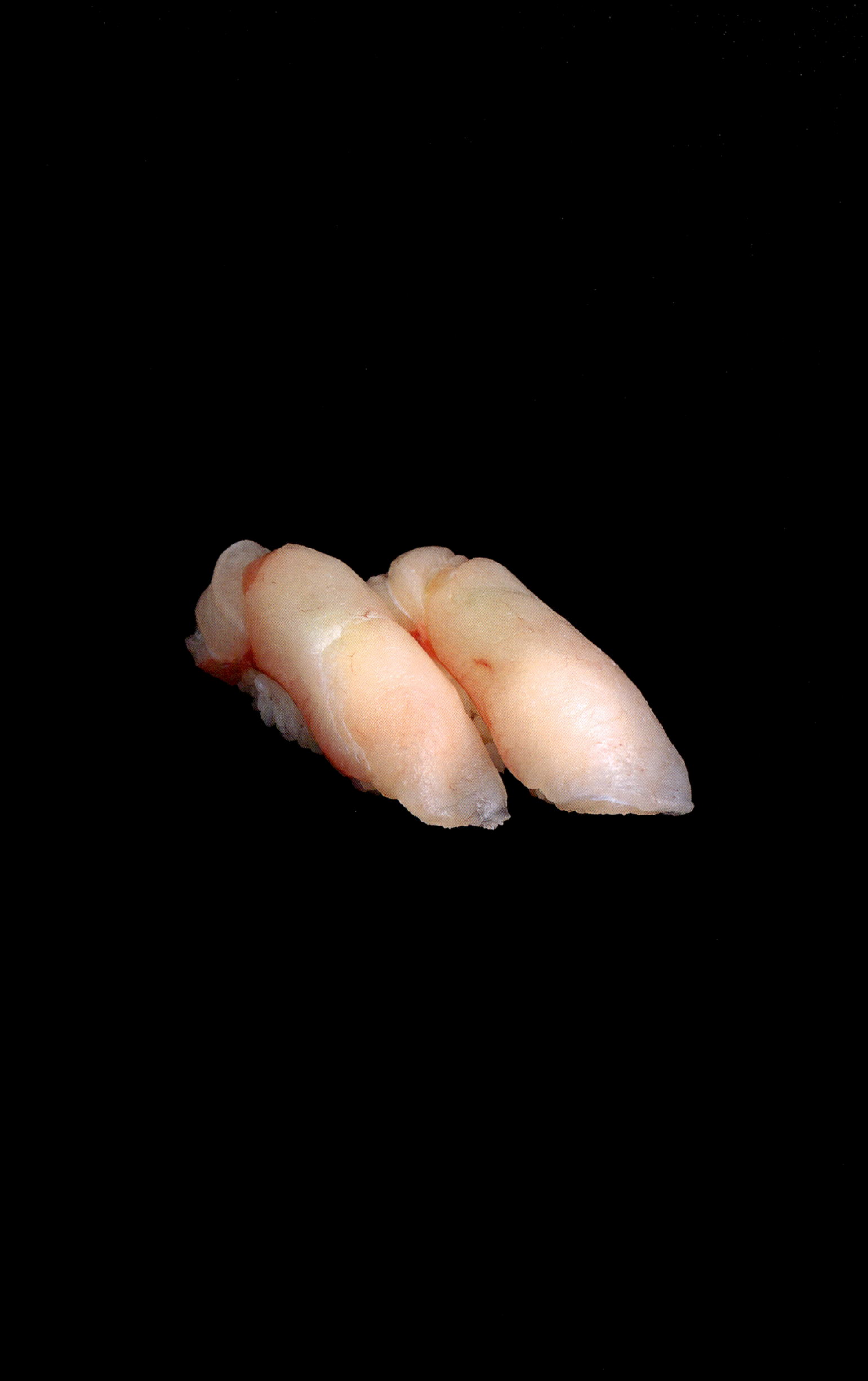

𩺊
(ara)

晩秋から冬にかけて旨さの旬となっていく𩺊は、20キロから30キロに達する大型の魚で、刺身でも、煮ても焼いても、鍋にしても、どんな料理にも合う旨みのある魚だ。大型魚にしては、身肉はしっかりと締まり、時間の経過とともに身質が緩んだり、水っぽくなるということもなく、変色も少ない。大ぶりの身肉は、3日目位に熟成の旨さの頂点に達する。深場に生息する魚特有の、脂の乗りは濃く、他の繊細さを身上とする白身の魚たちとは異なり、噛みしめるにつれて強い甘みと旨みの世界を醸し出してくる。

Reaching their prime in late autumn-winter, and weighing up to 20-30kg, ara are large fish, with a flavor suited to sashimi, simmering, broiling, or in *nabe* (one-pot) dishes. Firm-fleshed for its size, ara does not lose this firmness or become watery over time, and suffers minimal discoloring. The large chunk of meat reaches its pinnacle of flavor after about three days' aging. Like other deep-sea species it contains a generous proportion of fat, but unlike other white fish, in which delicacy is deemed a merit, ara offers greater sweetness and flavor with each successive bite.

saw-edged perch

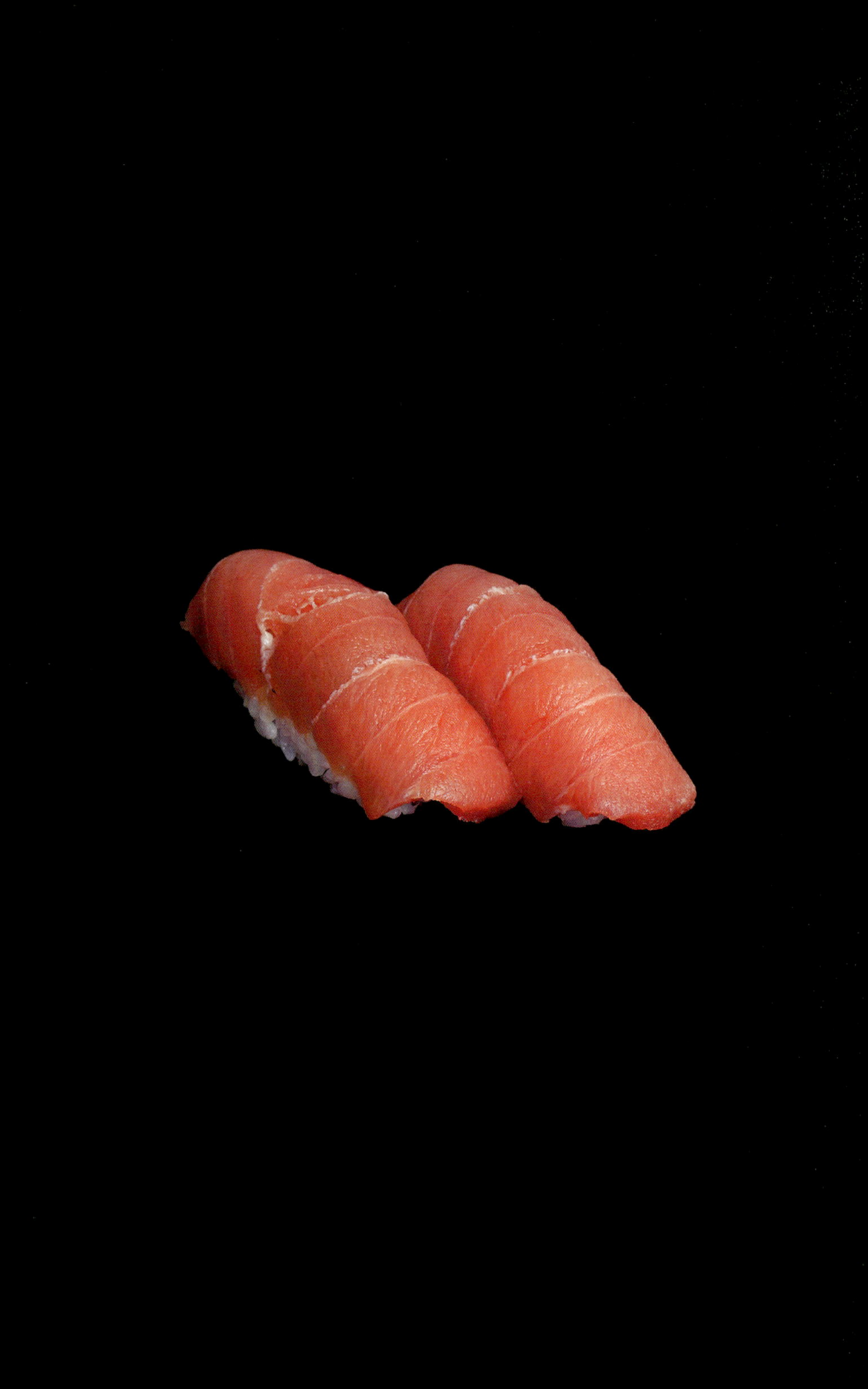

真梶木
(makajiki)

真梶木は晩秋頃から充分な脂を乗せはじめ、旨さの旬に入っていく。本鮪(ほんまぐろ)ほどの強い旨みと香りのある魚ではないが、薄い桃色をした淡白な味わいの身は、色目が薄く色変わりが遅いために、宴会などで重宝される。腹身には充分な脂が乗らず、筋も残り、商品価値が少ない。背の真ん中の皮側の身には程よい脂が乗り、特に珍重される。脂の乗りのために、うっすらと白濁しながらも、黄土色に染め上げられた身は美しい。この時期には本鮪の鉄分っぽい酸味と血潮の香りを含んだ旨みを、微かに程よく楽しむことができる。

Striped marlin acquire extra fat from late autumn, heralding their peak season for flavor. While lacking the intensity and aroma of bluefin tuna, the mild, pale pink flesh retains color well, making it a favorite banquet dish. The belly is sinewy and short on fat, giving it little market value. The subcutaneous meat on the center back has a good covering of fat and is especially prized, while the flesh has an attractive ochre tinge, albeit slightly cloudy due to the fat. Marlin in this season offers the tart ferrous quality and blood-engorged aroma of bluefin tuna.

striped marlin

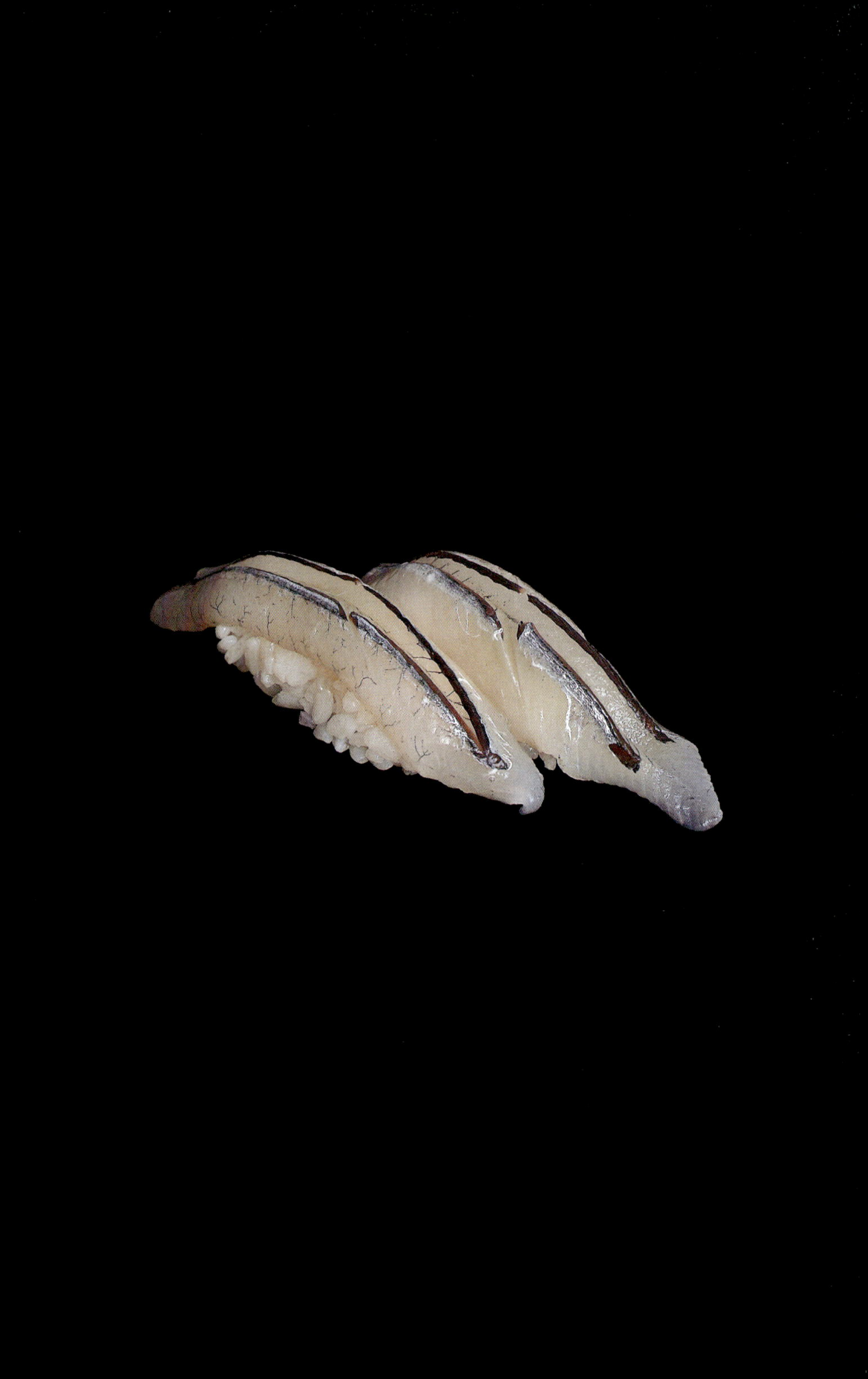

細魚
(sayori)

晩秋から春先を旨さの旬とする細魚の身には、意外な厚みが隠されている。しっかりと締まった身は、微かだが心地よい食感と爽やかな旨みを持っている。鮮度の持ちが悪く、すぐに生臭みを発っするために本来は塩と酢で軽く締めてから使われたが、最近では最高の鮮度のものを入手することが可能となり、生のままで握るのが主流となってきた。外見の美しさと爽やかな旨さとは裏腹に、腹の中は真っ黒な膜と大変な生臭さが充満している。昔はきれいで姿形のよさのわりには、腹黒い人間のたとえによく使われたという。

The flesh of sayori, best for eating between late autumn and early spring, is unexpectedly substantial for such a dainty fish. Firm and dense, it has a pleasant albeit subtle texture, and refreshing flavor. Sayori goes off quickly and swiftly acquires a fishy odor, so was originally lightly cured with salt and vinegar before use. More recently it has become possible to obtain very fresh supplies of the species, and consuming sayori raw in sushi is now the norm. Belying the fish's sleek outward beauty and bracing flavor, its gut contains a black, highly odorous membrane. In earlier times, women who were pretty and well-proportioned but 'black of heart' were often likened to sayori.

Japanese halfbeak

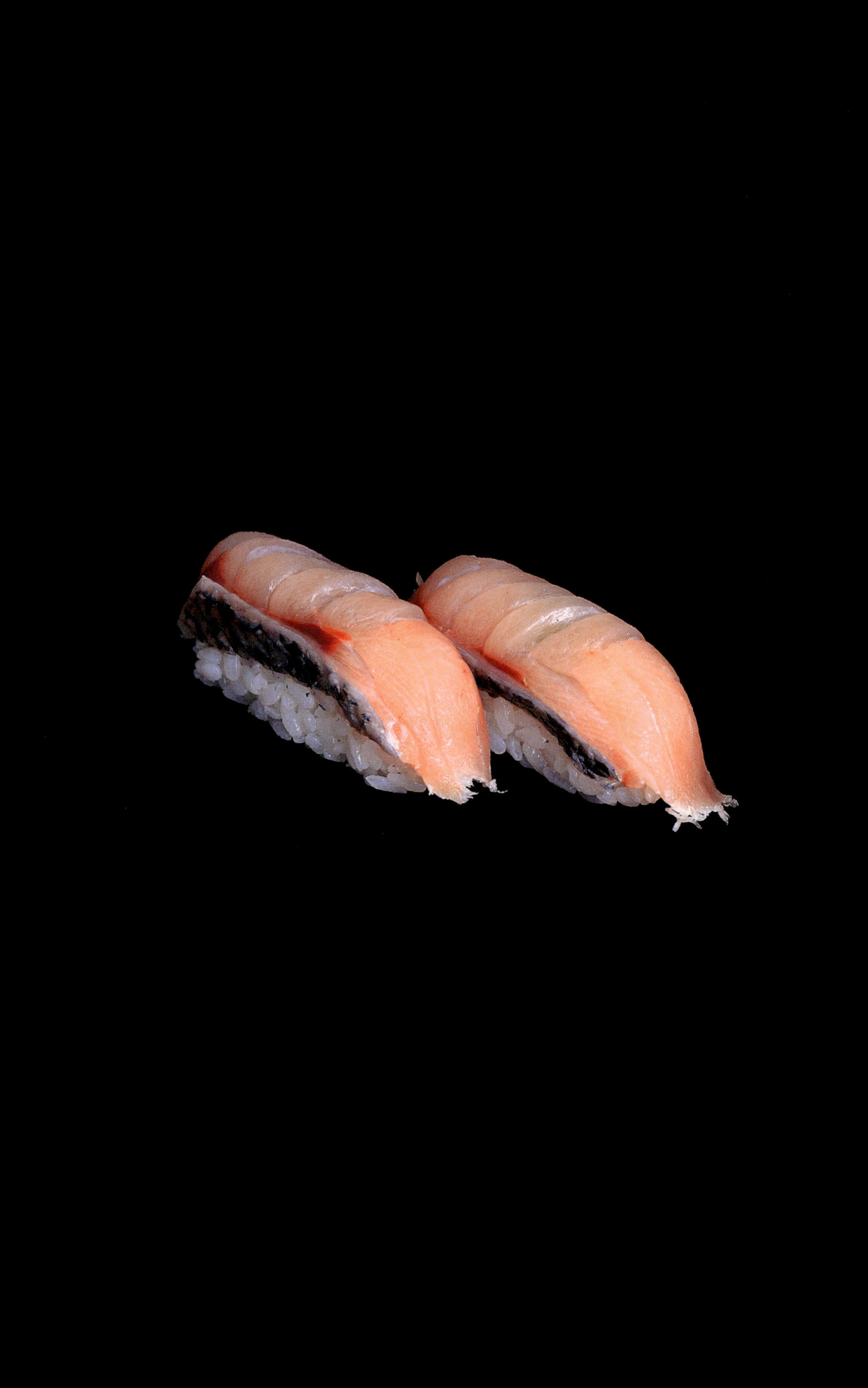

黒鯥
(kuromutsu)

黒鯥は、晩秋から脂が乗りはじめ、冬場が最高の旨さの旬となる。水深200メートルから300メートルに生息する深場の魚は脂質過多ゆえのしつこさを言われることが多いのだが、薄く白濁した脂は身肉全体に行きわたりながらも、予想に反して脂っこさは少ない。皮を上にして、皮目に熱湯をかけ、すばやく氷水に落とす。ゼラチン質を多く含んだ皮目には旨みたっぷりの脂が隠れている。軽い歯ごたえの皮が旨い。脂の乗った柔らかい身肉は噛むほどに口の中一杯に広がる甘みとなり、滑らかに包むようにして旨さを伝えてくる。

Putting on fat in late autumn, kuromutsu make best eating in winter. Fish inhabiting depths of 200–300m are often deemed heavy eating due to their excess fat, but despite being marbled with opaque fat, kuromutsu do not taste especially fatty. The fish is placed skin up and boiling water poured on the flesh just below the skin before dropping into iced water. The gelatinous subcutaneous flesh conceals a delectable layer of fat, while the skin, light in consistency, is also delicious. The tender, lipoid flesh has a sweetness that on chewing suffuses the palate with a smooth, all-enveloping flavor.

gnomefish

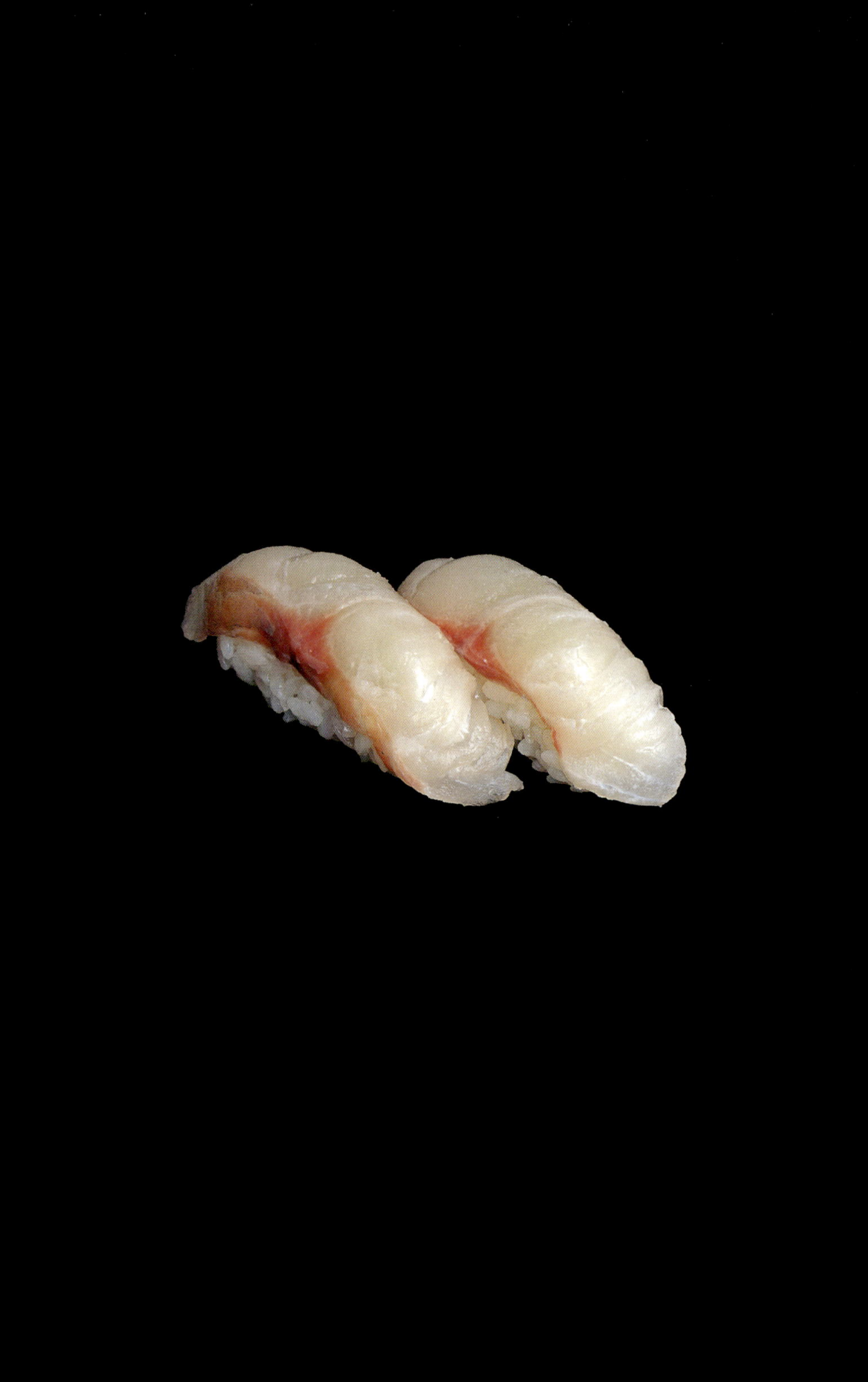

魴鮄
(hobo)

晩秋が近づく頃、築地市場には魴鮄の入荷が増えてくる。胸鰭が大きく、その内側の模様は南洋のアゲハ蝶のように妖艶で美しい。晩秋から冬に至ると身体全体に見事に脂が乗り、円筒形状の体型は丸々と膨れ盛り上がってくる。この時期に２キロ前後に及ぶ大型の最高品をすしに握ると、充分に脂の乗った魴鮄独自の旨さを楽しむことができる。柔らかだが、しっかりとした身の締まりを持ち、乳白色ににじむ脂は極めて舌触りがよく、滑らかな旨みを持っている。最高の鮮度の身質は、２日目の夜になってからも、まだ確かな歯ごたえを維持し、新たな熟成の旨さを主張する。

Hobo start arriving at Tokyo's Tsukiji fish market in increasing quantities toward the end of autumn. The hobo has large pectoral fins that on the inside are as bewitchingly beautiful as the wings of a swallowtail butterfly. Acquiring a sumptuous layer of fat from late autumn to winter that renders their cylindrical bodies plump and swollen, when top quality specimens weighing around 2kg are made into nigiri during this period, they allow diners to savor the unique flavor of the fully fat-infused flesh. The tender flesh is dense and firm, while the milky-white fat has a superb texture and smooth flavor. Even by the night after the freshest specimens are procured, the tender flesh retains a robust texture, and begins to assert a new, mature flavor.

red gurnard

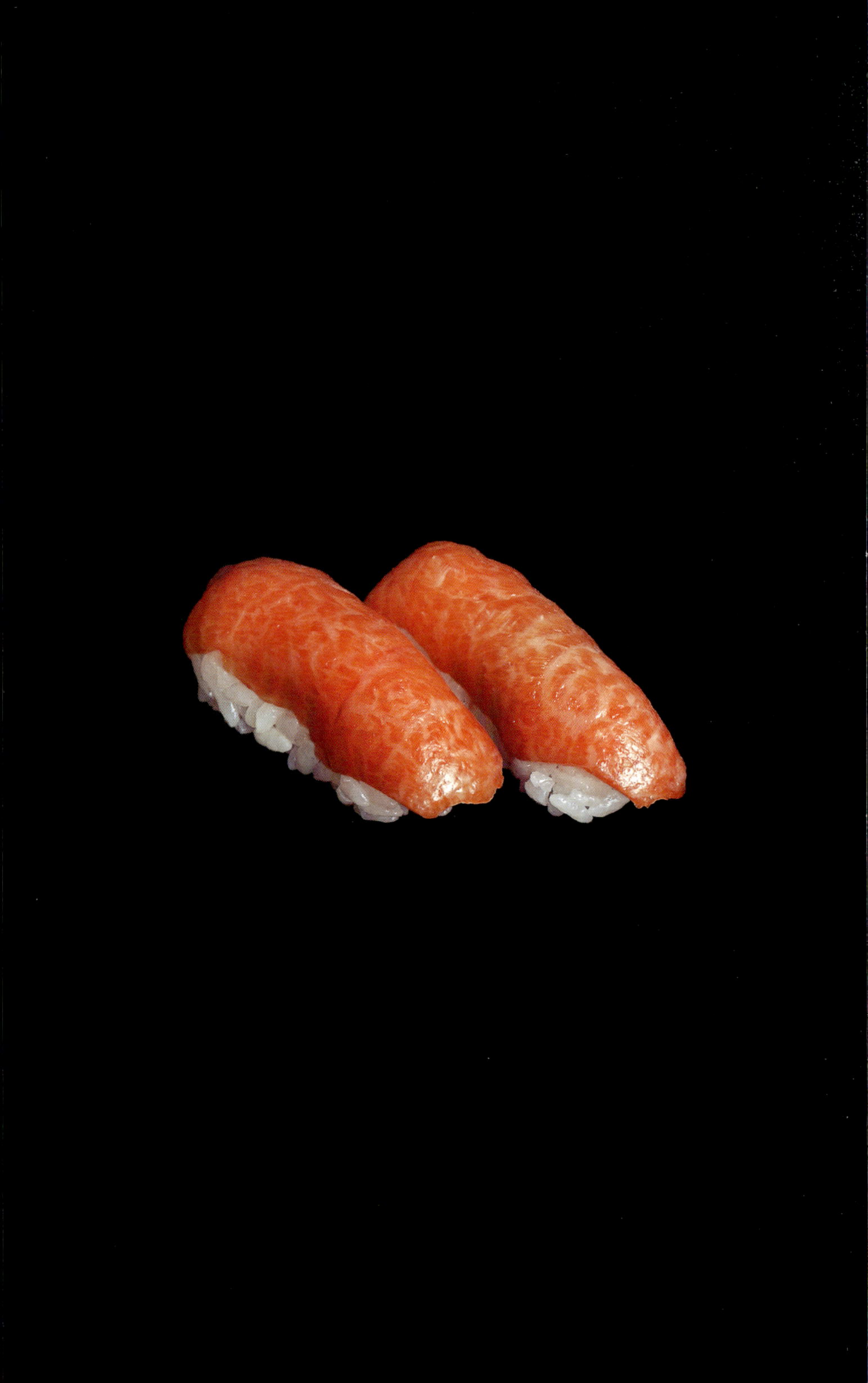

鮪
(maguro)

本鮪は密度のある身質の中に、微妙な鉄分っぽさを感じさせる旨みと、大海を回遊していく巨大な勇姿を連想させる、鮮烈な血潮の香りを持っている。そこに晩秋から冬にかけて濃くなる脂身の旨みが加わると、さらに渾然一体となった素晴らしい旨みと香りに昇華する。赤身は真紅色に冴えわたり、脂の乗りによってうっすらと白濁していく中トロと、霜降りの大トロの色彩も美しい。中トロの中では最も香りが高く、濃厚な味わいを持つ"血合いぎしの中トロ"、砂ずりの部位で、蛇腹の筋に覆われ、最も脂の強い"蛇腹の大トロ"の部位の筋さえも、まるでアイスクリームのように瞬時にとろけていく。

The dense flesh of bluefin tuna possesses a ferrous flavor, and a bloody tang that conjures up images of these giant, stately fish on their great pelagic migrations. A delectable lipid quality that intensifies from late autumn elevates tuna further to a complete, sublime package of taste and aroma. The chutoro belly meat, where the red clears to a brilliant vermilion, or is slightly cloudy depending on the fat content, and the marbled otoro, are attractively colored too. Even the sinews of 'chiai-gishi' chutoro near the spine, the most fragrant and intensely flavored of chutoro, and jabara otoro, the fattiest part of the fish, the gizzard covered in sinews, melt in the mouth like ice cream.

Pacific bluefin tuna

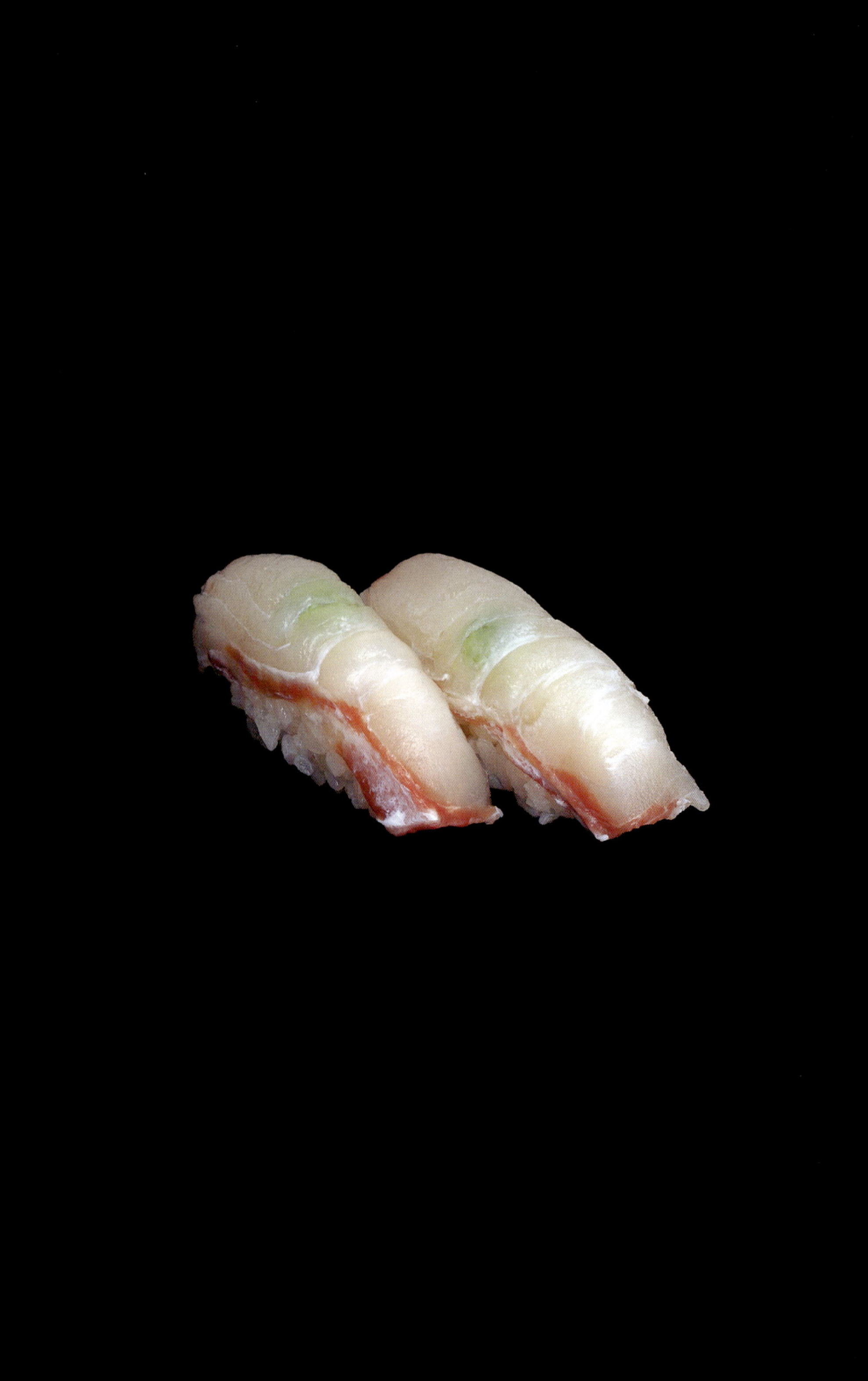

鮃
(hirame)

冬から春先にかけてが旬の最盛期の鮃は、身肉が微かに琥珀色に色づき、全体にしっとりとした脂をにじませている。脂の甘みは強めで品がよく、白身魚特有の繊細な淡白さの中に、鮃特有の旨みが伝わってくる。鰭の際にある4本の筋肉の"エンガワ"は、じっくりと噛み締めていくと、鍛えぬかれた筋肉質の脂の甘みが、口中一杯に強く濃く広がってくる。さらに薄く塩を打ち、昆布で締めることにより、江戸前ずしの昔からの仕事である「鮃の昆布締め」の握りの旨さも楽しむことができる。

The flesh of hirame, in its prime between winter and early spring, has a slight amber tinge, and is suffused with a rich oiliness. The fat is intensely sweet and refined, the distinctive flavor of hirame shining through the delicate mildness that characterizes white fish. Bite down firmly on the four muscle 'edges' of the fins and the mouth is filled with the intense sweetness of toned muscle fat. A light sprinkling of salt and kombu curing allows sushi fans to savor the delectable taste and texture sensation of nigiri made from hirame prepared using this technique long integral to the Edo-mae sushi chef's job.

olive flounder

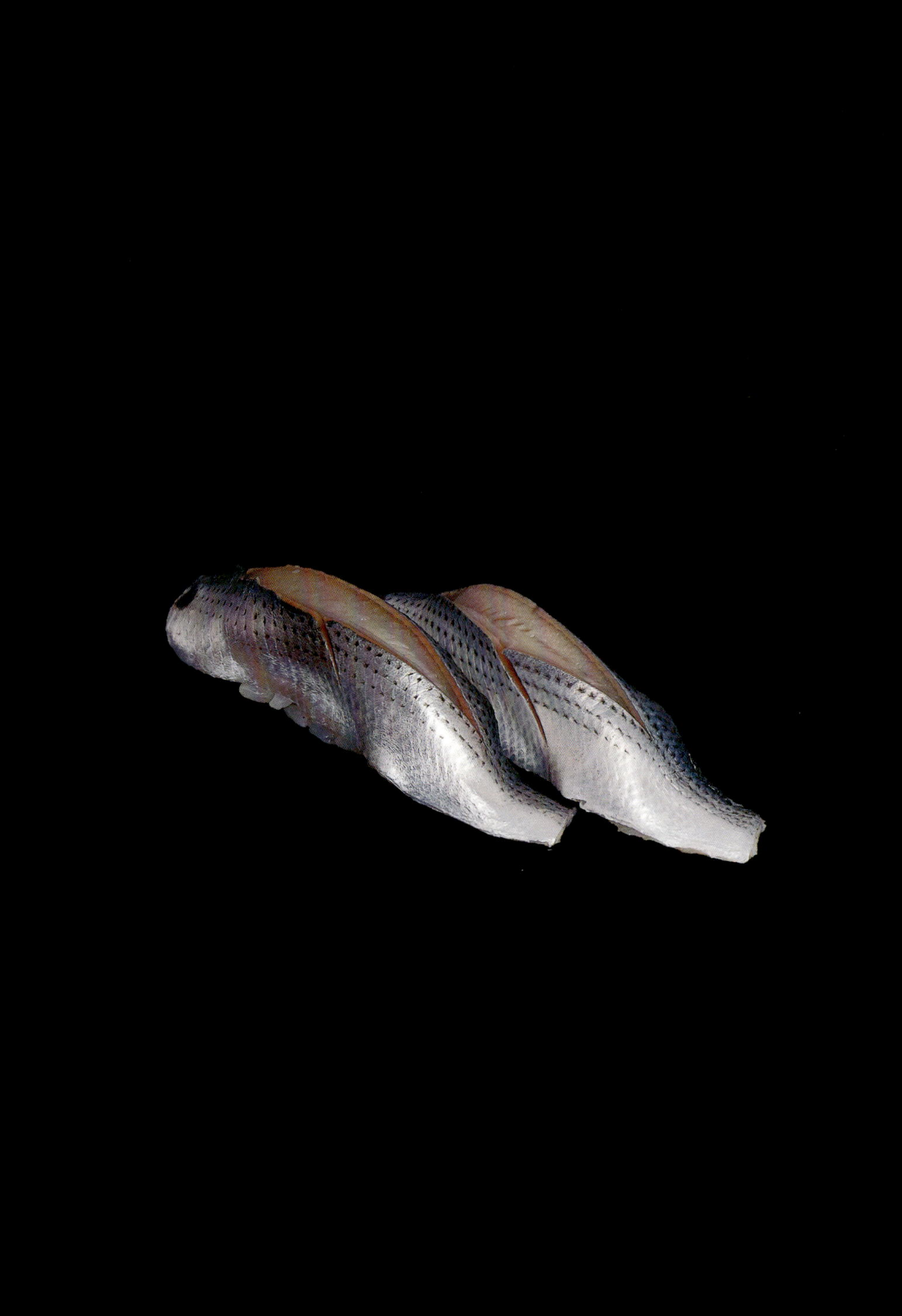

小鰭
(kohada)

小鰭の旨さの旬は中秋から初冬の頃となる。充分に脂の乗った小鰭は、塩と酢で締めることにより、小鰭特有の旨みを醸(かも)し出すことになる。季節、脂の乗りの強弱、大きさ、産地等によって締めの具合を変化させながら一年中使っていく。塩と酢で締められた小鰭は、すしに握られることによって初めて、旨さの真髄を見せつけることになる。江戸前ずしの元祖でありながら、今も江戸前ずしの究極の旨さを伝えている。幼魚の新子の初物の頃、江戸前ずしの間では、今も熱狂の世界が再現されている。

Kohada tastes best from mid-autumn to early winter. Salt-and-vinegar curing draws out the distinctive flavor of this species with its generous layer of fat. Kohada can be used all year round, adjusting the amount of curing according to the season, strength of the fat, size, and where the fish was caught. The true essence of salt-and-vinegar cured kohada only becomes evident when it is made into sushi. An 'old-timer' of Edo-mae sushi, it still offers the ultimate Edo-mae sushi taste experience. Even today, the appearance of the first kohada fry of the season sends a frisson of excitement through the world of Edo-mae sushi.

gizzard shad

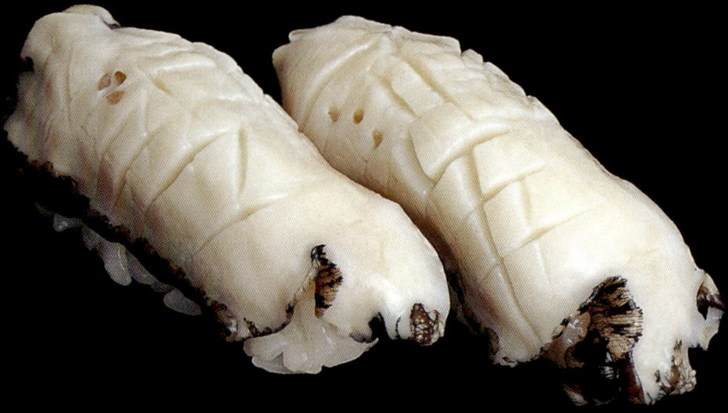

蝦夷鮑
(ezo-awabi)

蝦夷鮑は、晩秋から冬場を旬とし、他の鮑とは正反対の生態系を持ち、サイズも大きく成長しない。生食によって旨さの本領を発揮する蝦夷鮑は、身肉がよく締まり、簡単に硬くなるため、通常はその硬い食感を最高の旨さとしている。しかし、鮮度抜群の蝦夷鮑をなんのテクニックも使わずに、そっと殻から身を外し包丁を入れてやる。柔らかく歯に食い込んでいく、程よい硬さの食感は、鮑の爽やかな磯の香りとともに、甘み旨みを味わいつくす最適なものとなる。中国料理の干し鮑は、日本の業者が日本の鮑を加工したもので、蝦夷鮑は昔から干し鮑を代表するものであった。

Ezo abalone peaks from late autumn, completely opposite to other abalone. Nor does it grow especially large. Best savored raw, Ezo abalone has firm flesh that easily becomes chewy, so generally this robust texture is deemed tastiest. However Ezo abalone of outstanding freshness can be flipped out of the shell with no technique whatsoever and cut with a knife. Tender and yielding, with just the right degree of chewiness and typical abalone tang of the sea, this is the optimal way to savor its flavor and sweetness. Dried abalone used in Chinese cooking is Japanese abalone processed in Japan, Ezo abalone providing the main source.

Ezo abalone

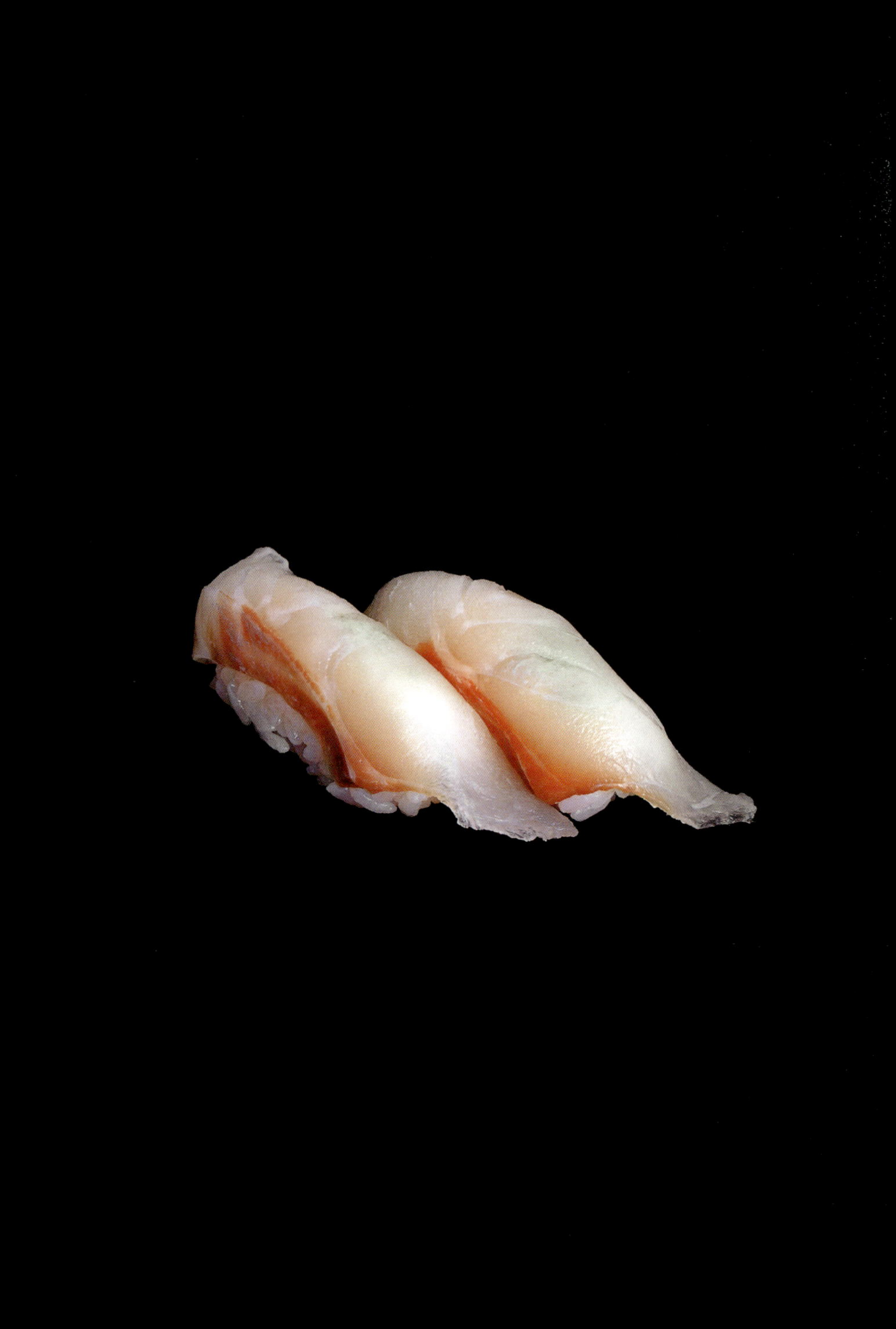

平鱸
(hirasuzuki)

晩秋に脂が乗りはじめ、冬から春にかけて旨さの旬となる。鱸と姿形が似ているが、旬は正反対なのだ。漁獲量は少なく、脂が乗った薄い琥珀色を帯びる最高品はさらに少量しか入荷しない。緻密な身肉ににじみ出てくる脂の旨みは噛むほどに増し、甘みとともに口中に柔らかく広がっていく。さらにこの平鱸の最大の旨さの特徴としては、身肉の食感の素晴らしさを挙げることができる。朝に仕込んだその夜、身肉を噛み切る瞬間には、心地よい弾力を伴う魅惑的な食感があるのだ。そして翌日、平鱸はさらに熟成し、旨みを増している。

Starting to acquire fat in late autumn, hirasuzuki is at its best between winter and spring. Similar in appearance to suzuki, it peaks at the exact opposite time of year. Catches are small, and the most prized specimens – a light amber and streaked with fat – even rarer. The flavor of the fat oozing from the delicate flesh increases with chewing, spreading smoothly around the palate with the fish's sweet taste. The most outstanding feature of hirasuzuki is its marvelous texture. Procured in the morning, bitten into that night it has a delightful texture accompanied by a pleasant elasticity. The following day, aged further, it tastes even better.

blackfin sea bass

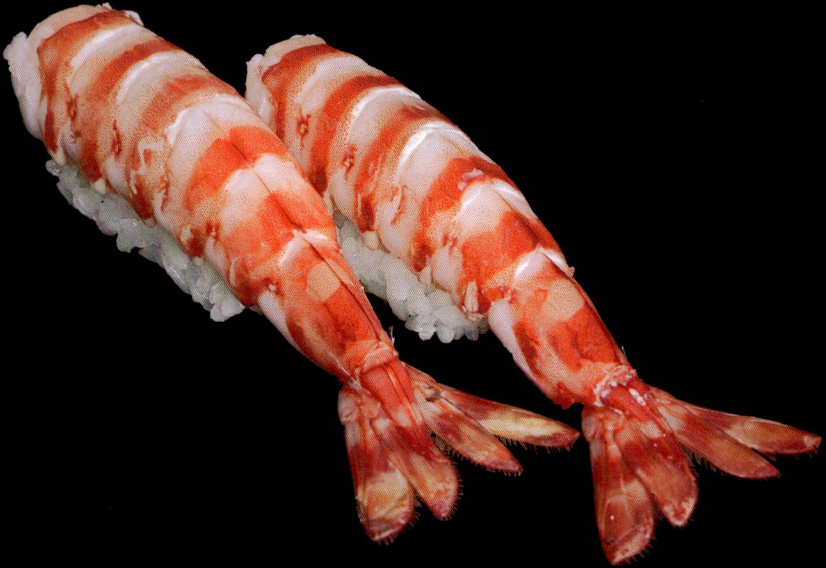

車海老

(kuruma-ebi)

車海老の漁獲と旨さの旬は産卵に向かっての初夏から夏の間だが、晩秋から冬場にかけ、もう一度旨さの旬がやってくる。水温の低下とともに深場へ移行する直前の、餌を豊富に食べ充分に太った頃だが、量は極少しかとれない。塩と酢を落とした熱湯の中で、活きている車海老を茹でる。"天然"車海老は白と鮮やかな紅朱色とをはっきりと染め分けて茹で上がる。身肉の中心は微かに半生の状態に残す。熱々の状態の皮を素早く剥き、身を開き、握り、食べる。車海老の豊潤な香りと強い甘み、身質の締まりと膨らみの食感の旨さを味わうためには、少し熱めの温度が大切な要素となる。

The kuruma-ebi season runs through summer heading into spawning, but for a time starting late autumn, the prawns are again at their finest, though hard to find. This is when they feed voraciously just prior to moving deeper as the water temperature falls. The prawns are dropped live into boiling water containing salt and vinegar. 'Wild' prawns will emerge a distinctive white and vivid red. The center of the flesh is left slightly raw and the prawns shelled quickly while piping hot, split, made into nigiri and eaten; the rich aroma, intense sweetness, and firm plumpness of kuruma-ebi best savored while slightly warm.

Japanese tiger prawn

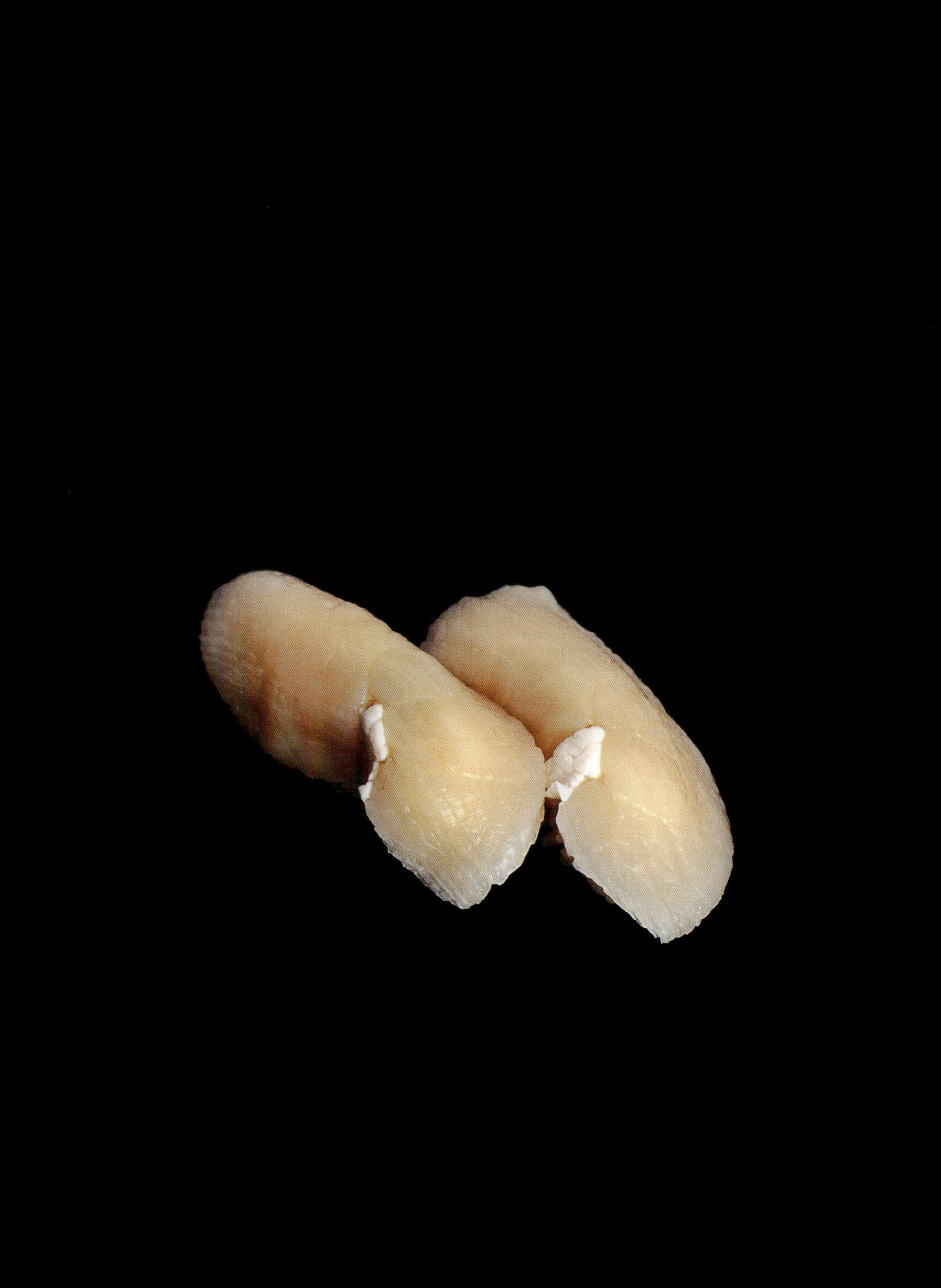

平貝
(tairagai)

平貝の旨さの旬は晩秋から春先頃までとなる。少し細長い横長の不等辺三角形で、薄い青緑色を帯びた貝殻は異端だ。帆立貝(ほたてがい)とともに中心にある大きな貝柱だけが旨さの主役となる。縦に薄めに切って握るのだが、乳白色の身は薄く透明感があり、微かに山葵(わさび)が透けて美しい。コツコツと軽い歯ごたえは単調で、甘みも薄く、すしネタの貝類の中では、最も癖のない淡白な旨みを特徴とする。しかし、この貝を塩焼きにすると、俄然馥郁(がぜんふくいく)たる旨みを発揮することになる。食欲をそそる焼いた貝特有の芳香と、グリコーゲンたっぷりの旨みはモチモチとした食感の旨さまでも加味してくる。

Tairagai with its unusual, bluish-green elongated triangular shell peaks from late autumn to early spring. Like the scallop, it is the shellfish's large central adductor muscle that is the main source of flavor. Thinly sliced for nigiri, its milky white, slightly translucent meat reveals the wasabi below to stunning effect. The mildest of sushi shellfish, tairagai has a slightly crunchy consistency devoid of complexity and just a hint of sweetness. Salt-grilled though it exudes a heavenly aroma, that mouth-watering fragrance typical of grilled shellfish and sweet, glycogen-suffused flavor also adding a delicious chewiness.

pen shell

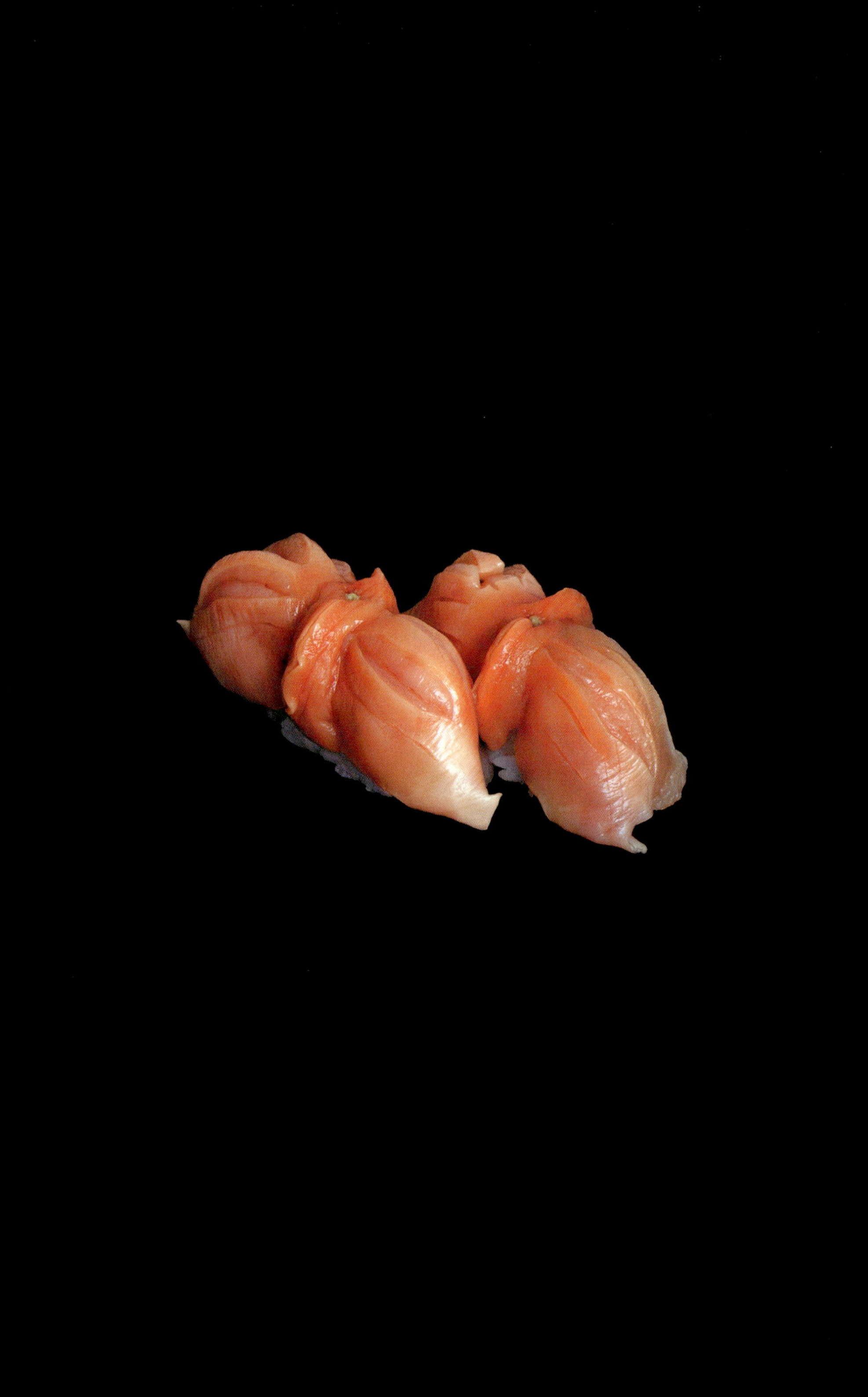

赤貝
(akagai)

鮮やかな朱色の赤貝は、すし種の中でも車海老、青柳とともに、ことさらに華やかで美しい。冬から春の頃を旨さの旬の最盛期とし、身肉が太り、厚みが増し、旨みも濃くなっている。弾けるような食感は旬と鮮度のよさの証明となる。強い磯の香りと微かな渋みは、すぐに旨みへと転化していく。外套膜の「ひも」の部位が旨い。心地よい食感と強い磯の香りは、本体の舌の部位よりもさらに珍重され、人気の高いものとなっている。旬真っ盛りの時期の、丸々と太った黒い肝は、湯通しして山葵と醤油で食すと格好の酒の肴となる。しかし赤貝は近年、漁獲量が激減している。

Vibrant red akagai, makes especially colorful and attractive sushi. Between winter and spring the shellfish grow plump and acquire a more intense flavor. An explosion on the palate – a strong salty tang and slight astringency transformed into exquisite taste – indicates ideal season and freshness. The 'string' on the outer membrane is tastiest, its pleasant texture and intense salty tang making it more prized and popular than the actual tongue. In peak season, the plump black liver blanched and consumed with wasabi and soy sauce pairs well with sake. In recent years catches of akagai have declined dramatically.

blood cockle

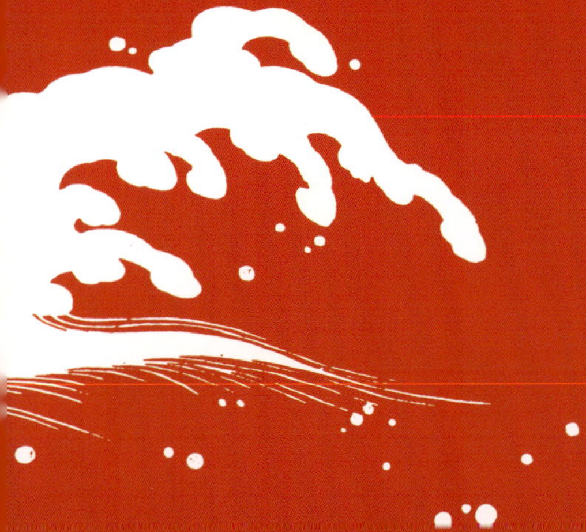

巻物

内湾で栽培された海苔の採取漁は、11月半ば頃に始まり、厳寒の時期を通じて春先まで行われ、漁師によって乾海苔にまで加工される。乾燥させることによって香りと旨みを増幅した海苔は、焼くと美しい深緑色に変化する。馥郁とした芳香と繊細な甘み・旨みもさらに強く引き出され、軽い歯切れの食感も楽しむことができるようになる。江戸前ずしの巻物は、この焼かれた海苔を使用する。江戸時代、干瓢を巻くことから始まった海苔巻は、携帯性と保存性、大勢で少量ずつ、手で直接食べられるという利便性も兼ね備えていた。そして生の鮪を巻く、鉄火巻が出現するに及んで、保存性と旨さとともに、様々な具を用いることによって、見た目の美しさも考慮に入れられるようになった。海苔巻の基本食材は海苔とシャリと山葵で、そこに芯となる様々な具を入れて巻き、醬油をつけて食べることになる。海苔とシャリと山葵と醬油は多種多様なすべての食材と、味覚上の素晴らしい相性の良さを持っている。握りずしで要求される旨さと技術上の制約から、どんなにはみ出している食材でも、海苔で巻くことによって見事に一品の巻物にすることができる。かくして珍品、奇品も含めて、多種多様な海苔巻の出現となった。素早く巻いたものを素早く食し、海苔の焼きたての食感と香り高い旨さを味わう手巻きずしの大流行を見ることとなった。

rolls

Harvesting of nori cultivated inshore begins around mid-November and continues into early spring, being processed by the fishermen into the familiar dried product. Drying enhances the flavor and aroma, toasting then gives it its lustrous deep green color, draws out its inviting fragrance, delicate sweetness and flavor, and endows it with a light, pleasant melt-in-the-mouth texture. Edo-mae sushi rolls are made using this toasted nori. Norimaki, which first appeared in the Edo period with a filling of dried gourd, offered the added attraction of convenience: being portable, long-lasting, divisible among many, and eaten directly by hand. Once *tekka-maki* rolls containing raw tuna appeared on the scene, as well as ease of preservation and superlative taste, visual attractiveness became another factor in the appeal of makimono, through the use of various neta. The basic ingredients of norimaki are nori, vinegared rice and wasabi. The neta is then added, the roll formed, and the result consumed with soy sauce. Nori, rice, wasabi and soy sauce are the perfect complements to any and every neta. With a wrapping of nori even ingredients unthinkable in terms of the technical and flavor limitations of nigiri-zushi can be transformed into stellar sushi. Thus sushi rolls now come in many manifestations, including the weird and wonderful. Another popular variation is temaki. Hand-rolled on individual sheets of nori, these cone-shaped rolls allow diners to savor sushi swiftly made and just as swiftly consumed, enjoying the texture and fragrant flavor of freshly toasted nori.

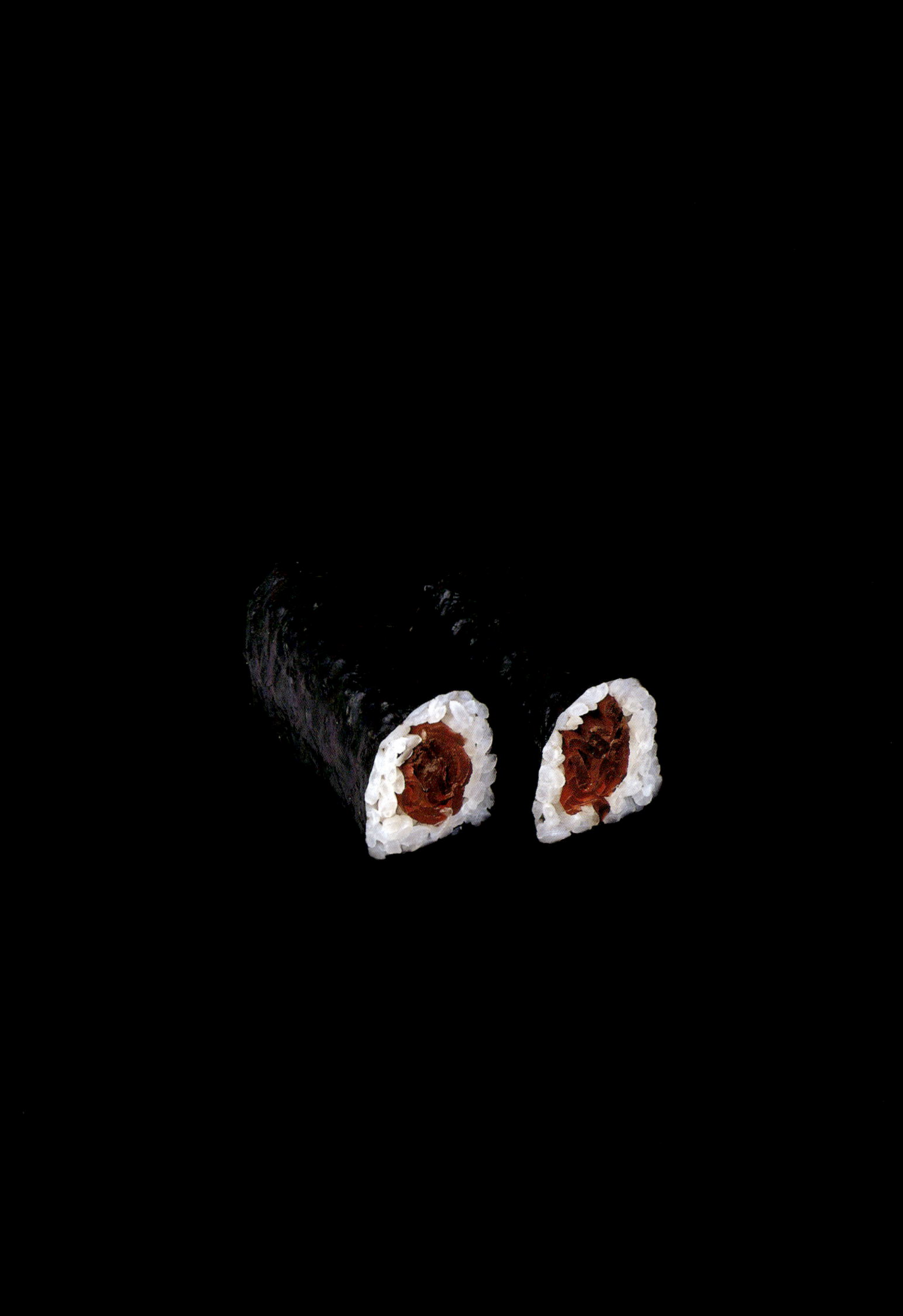

干瓢巻
(kanpyo-maki)

乾燥食品である干瓢は、塩揉みと水洗いをして柔らかく戻してから適度の硬さに水煮する。水分を絞り、醤油と砂糖を加え、甘みの勝った濃い味で、少し歯ごたえが残るように煮含める。すし屋で単に海苔巻と言えば、干瓢巻のことを指すのだが、それは干瓢が最初に海苔巻にされたことに由来する。巻かれた姿が鉄砲に見えることから「鉄砲巻」とも言われる。すしの最後に食する巻物として、安らぎと充足感を与えてくれるのだが、干瓢の味によって店と職人の技量が推測されるとまで言われる重要な巻物となる。

Kanpyo or pickled gourd is a dried food reconstituted by rubbing in salt and rinsing, then simmered to just the right degree of tenderness. Moisture is then squeezed out, soy sauce and sugar added, and the mixture slowly reduced to a sweet and succulent, al dente intensity. When sushi chefs refer simply to norimaki they mean kanpyo-maki rolls, because kanpyo was the first neta to be used in norimaki rolls. Kanpyo rolls are also called 'teppo-maki' due to their resemblance to a *teppo* or cannon. As the roll consumed to round off a sushi meal, they offer a contented satisfaction. They are however actually a key item in the makimono repertory, the flavor of the kanpyo being viewed as an accurate gauge of the ability of a sushi shop and its staff.

kanpyo roll

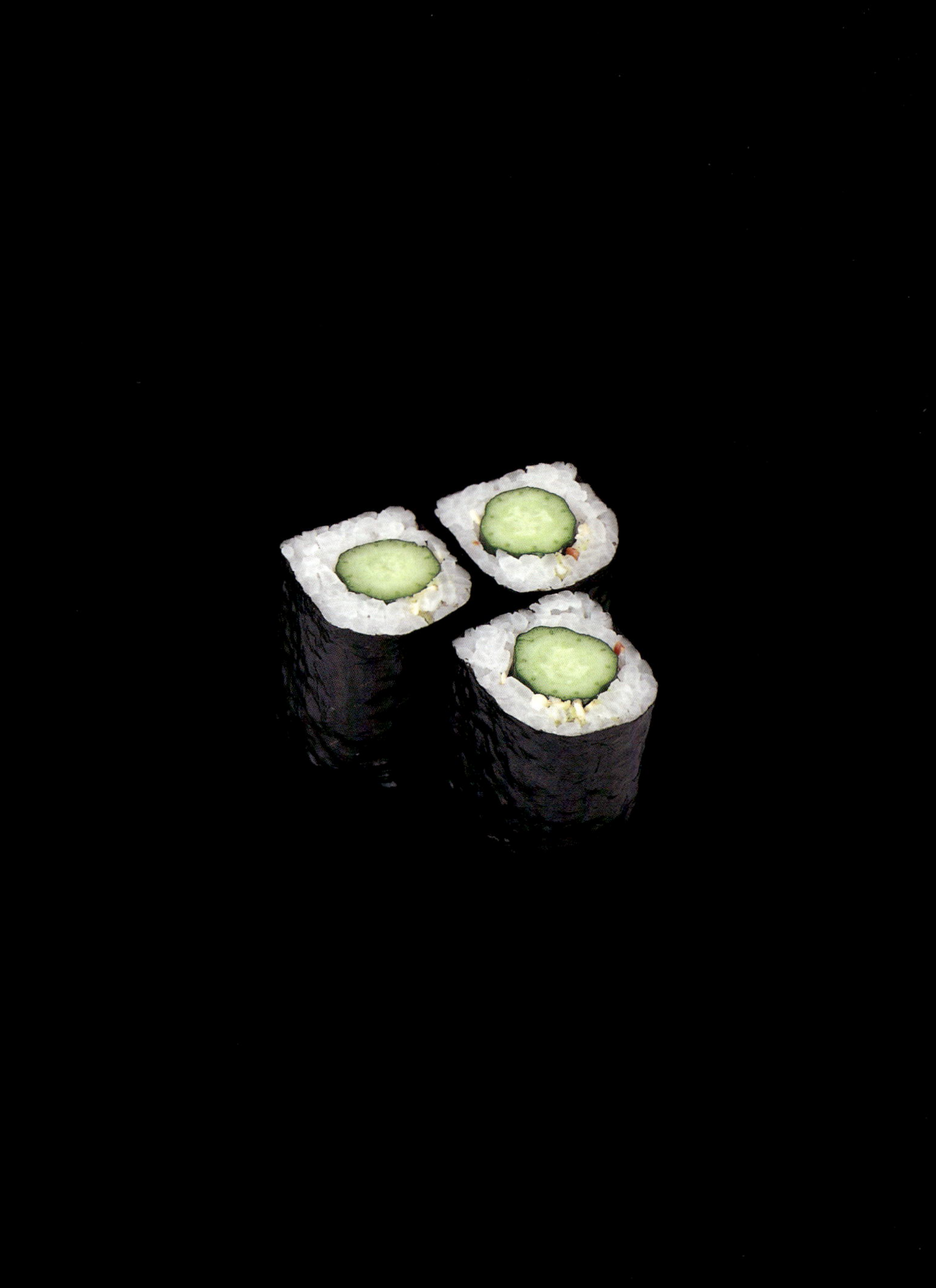

カッパ巻
(kappa-maki)

キュウリを海苔で巻いたものをカッパ巻と呼ぶ。キュウリは夏の野菜だが、近年は1年中ハウス栽培されて出回るため、カッパ巻も1年中巻かれることになった。昔は太いキュウリを細く打って巻いたのだが、近年では旨さよりも見てくれ優先で、ハウス栽培のまだ細く、小さなものを丸のまま巻くことによって、切り口が丸く美しいものとなった。炒りゴマや紫蘇の葉と相性がよく、キュウリの心地よい歯ごたえと爽やかな香りに新たな旨みを加えることになり、すしの最後の口直しとして食べられることが多い。

Cucumber is a summer vegetable, but these days hothouse-grown specimens are available all year round, and thus so is the kappa-maki roll. Once rolled using thick cucumbers cut into thin strips, in more recent years visual appeal has trumped taste, leading to the use of small, whole hothouse-grown cucumbers that provide an attractive cut surface. The cucumber is complemented perfectly by the likes of toasted sesame and shiso leaves, which add a further flavor dimension to the agreeable crispness and invigorating flavor of the cucumber, making kappa-maki a popular final palate-refresher for a sushi meal.

cucumber roll

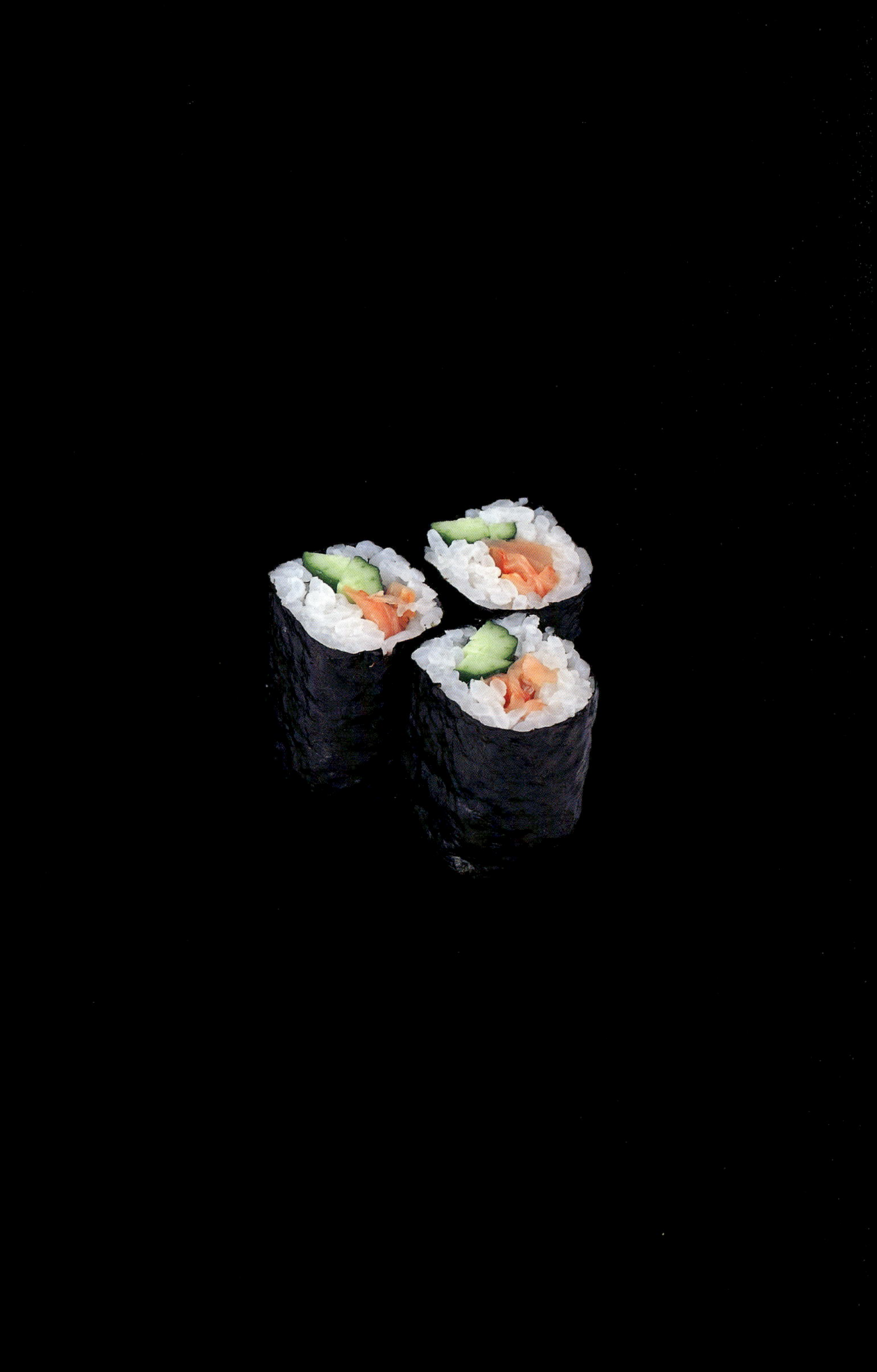

紐キュウ巻
(himokyu-maki)

赤貝の紐は、一個の高価な赤貝から1本しか採れない希少な部位で、すし通の間での密かな人気種として知られる。華やかな赤色と心地よい食感の中に、赤貝特有の磯の香りと微かな渋みから甘みに転化する旨みが、赤貝本体よりもはるかに強いのだ。この紐と細く打ったキュウリを一緒に巻くと両者は優れた相性を発揮し、紐の食感と旨みにキュウリの爽やかな香りと歯ごたえが新たに加わってくる。赤と緑と白と黒の彩りは華やかで美しく、少し山葵を効かせると、通人好みの洒落た巻物となる。

The *himo* or exterior mantle of blood cockle (akagai) is a highly prized delicacy, each precious shell having only one, and is somewhat of an unassuming favorite among sushi aficionados. Its brilliant scarlet color and agreeable texture harbor the distinctive salty tang and slight astringency-turned-sweet flavor of akagai, but in far greater concentration than the shellfish itself. Finely chopped cucumber and akagai himo make a superlative combination, the taste and texture of the blood cockle mantle further boosted by the bracing flavor and mouth feel of the cucumber. The combination of red, green, black and white makes for an attractive roll that with a hint of wasabi becomes a stylish sushi choice adored by those in the know.

himokyu roll

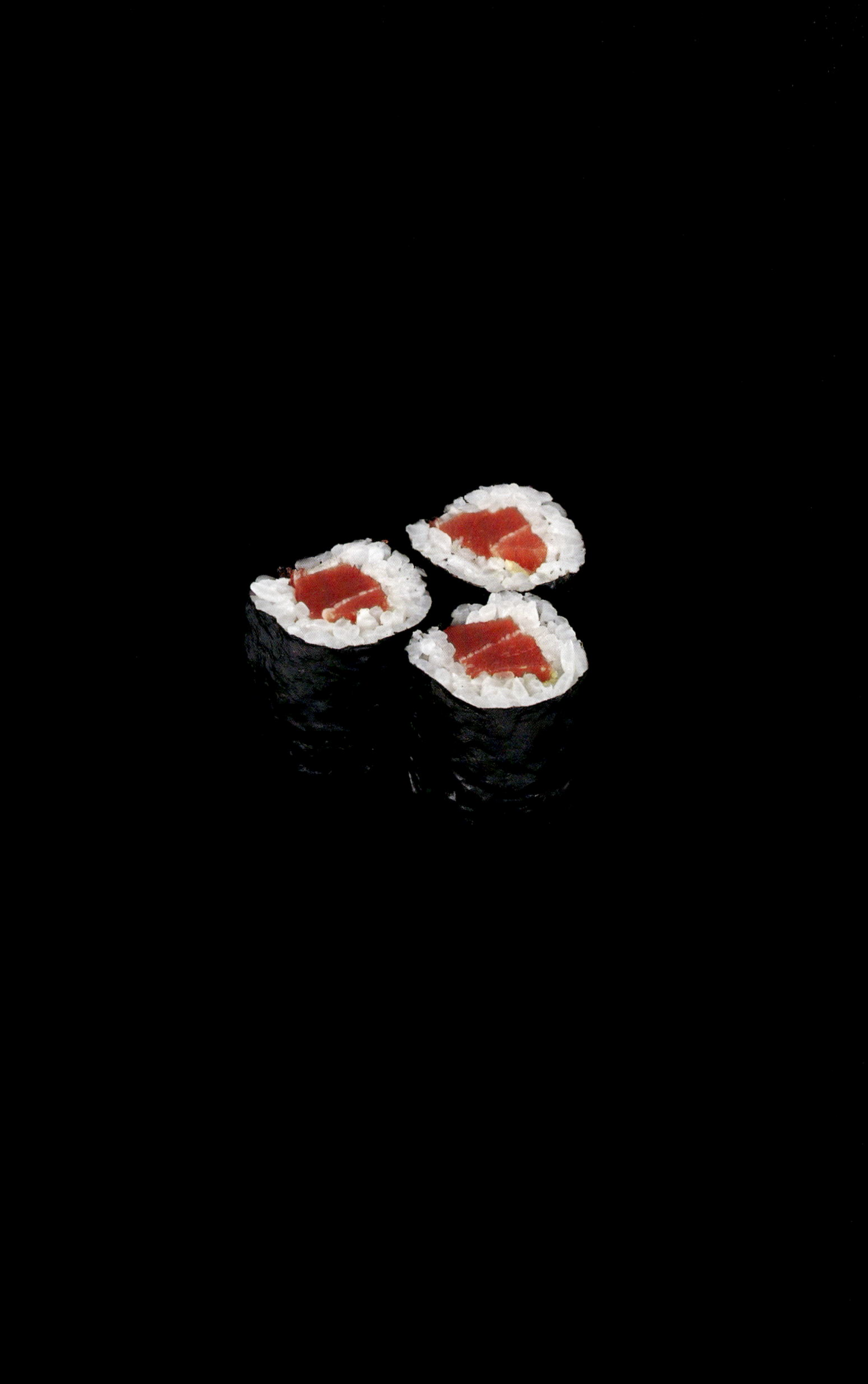

鉄火巻
(tekka-maki)

巻物の芯となる鮪の色が、真っ赤に熟した鉄棒の断面の色に似ているための命名と言われる。切り口を上にして盛りつけると、鮪の真っ赤な色合いは、シャリの白と海苔の黒との対比の中で、美しく映える。鮪の鉄分を含む立ちのぼるような血の香りと旨みは、海苔の芳香と甘み・旨みと一体となり、別格の旨さを醸し出す。赤身も旨いが、中トロ、大トロを巻くと、さらに贅沢な巻物となる。トロを強く叩き潰し、ネギと山葵をたっぷり入れたネギトロ巻は、さらに人気の高いものとなっている。

So-named because in cross-section, its scarlet tuna filling resembles a red-hot iron bar (*tekka* meaning 'red-hot iron'). Arranged with the cut surface uppermost, the bright red of the tuna contrasts brilliantly with the white of the rice and black of the nori. The almost startlingly bloody aroma and flavor of the iron-rich fish combines with the delectable sweetness of the nori to create a taste sensation in a class of its own. And while the red flesh of tuna is itself to be relished, tekka-maki filled with the medium-fatty chu-toro and premium o-toro belly meat are an indulgence one step further. Negitoro rolls, made with well-tenderized toro, scallions (negi) and a generous dose of wasabi, are an even more popular choice.

tuna roll

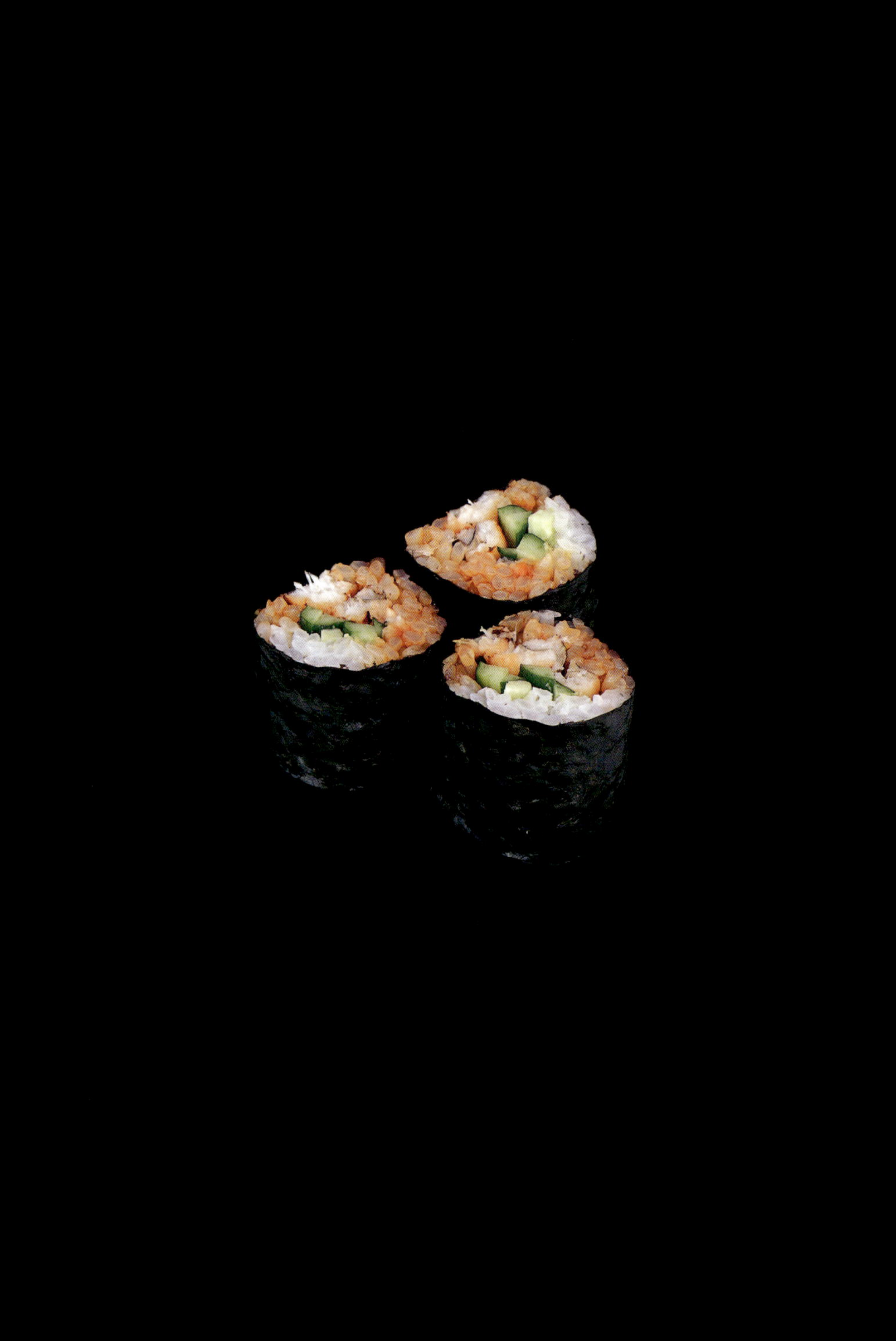

穴キュウ巻
(anakyu-maki)

煮た穴子を強火で少し焦がす。穴子にツメを塗り、キュウリとたっぷりの山葵(わさび)を入れて巻く。焦がすことによって、食感と香ばしさが発生し、脂の甘みと旨みも強くにじみ出てくる。穴子の煮汁をじっくりと煮詰めてつくられる甘い「ツメ」を塗ることによって、穴子の旨さをさらに引き立たせることができる。キュウリの爽やかな芳香と心地よい歯ごたえは、焼き穴子と絶妙の相性となる。たっぷりと入れた山葵の辛みと旨みが大きなアクセントとなり、シャリと海苔の旨みまでも改めて感じられる巻物となる。

Simmered conger eel (anago) is lightly seared over a high flame, then coated with sweet tsume sauce and made into a roll with cucumber and a generous helping of wasabi. Searing the eel adds texture and aroma, and intensifies the sweetness and flavor of the fat. Coating with the sweet 'tsume' made from the slowly simmered eel juices serves to further highlight the eel's flavor, while the crisp, refreshing texture and flavor of the cucumber make the perfect match for the grilled eel. The hotness and flavor of wasabi, included in generous proportions, add the final exquisite note to a roll in which even rice and nori seem elevated to new heights of flavor.

conger & cucumber roll

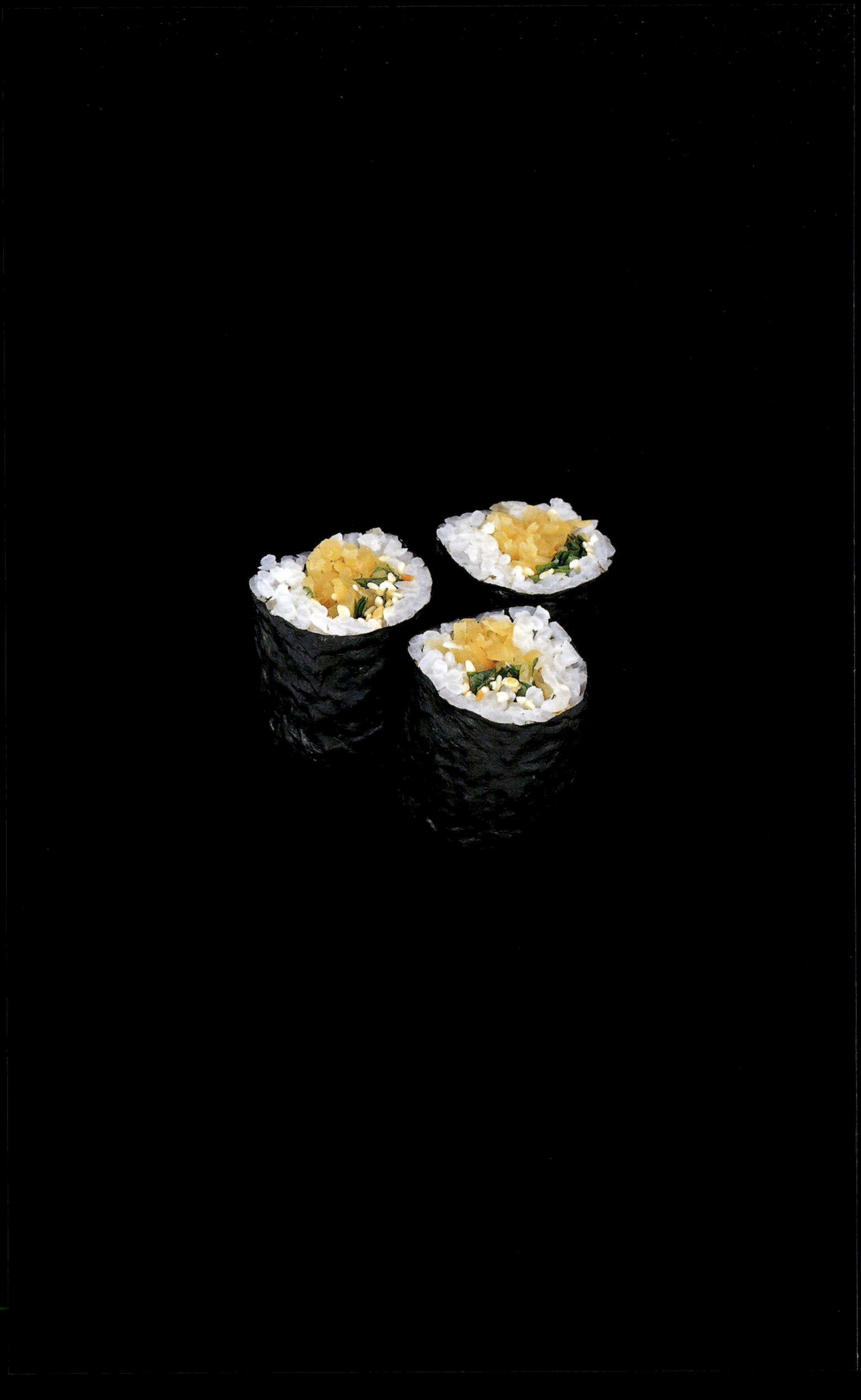

沢庵巻
(takuan-maki)

沢庵を細く刻み、炒りゴマと紫蘇の葉を入れ、山葵を塗って巻いた巻物を「沢庵巻」と言う。ポリポリとした痛快な歯ごたえと少し酸味のきいた沢庵の旨みが、ゴマと紫蘇の爽やかな香りと山葵の辛みによって、沢庵巻をさらにおいしいものにする。沢庵巻の意外な例としては、トロの鉄火巻に沢庵を細切りにして入れ、たっぷりの山葵とともに巻く「トロタク巻」がある。一緒に巻かれるもの同士のミスマッチが面白いのと、予想外の旨さのために、昔から密かな人気を持つ巻物となっている。

Takuan roll consists of takuan (pickled daikon radish) finely cut and rolled with toasted sesame seeds, shiso leaves, and a coating of wasabi. The exquisite crispy crunchiness and subtle spiciness of the radish are further enhanced by the refreshing flavor of sesame and shiso and the sharp tang and taste of the wasabi. One surprising example of takuan-maki is the 'toro-taku-maki', in which finely-chopped takuan is added to toro tekka-maki, and rolled with a generous helping of wasabi. The intriguing mismatch between the filling ingredients and their unexpectedly sublime taste when combined have made this roll an unassuming favorite for many years.

takuan roll

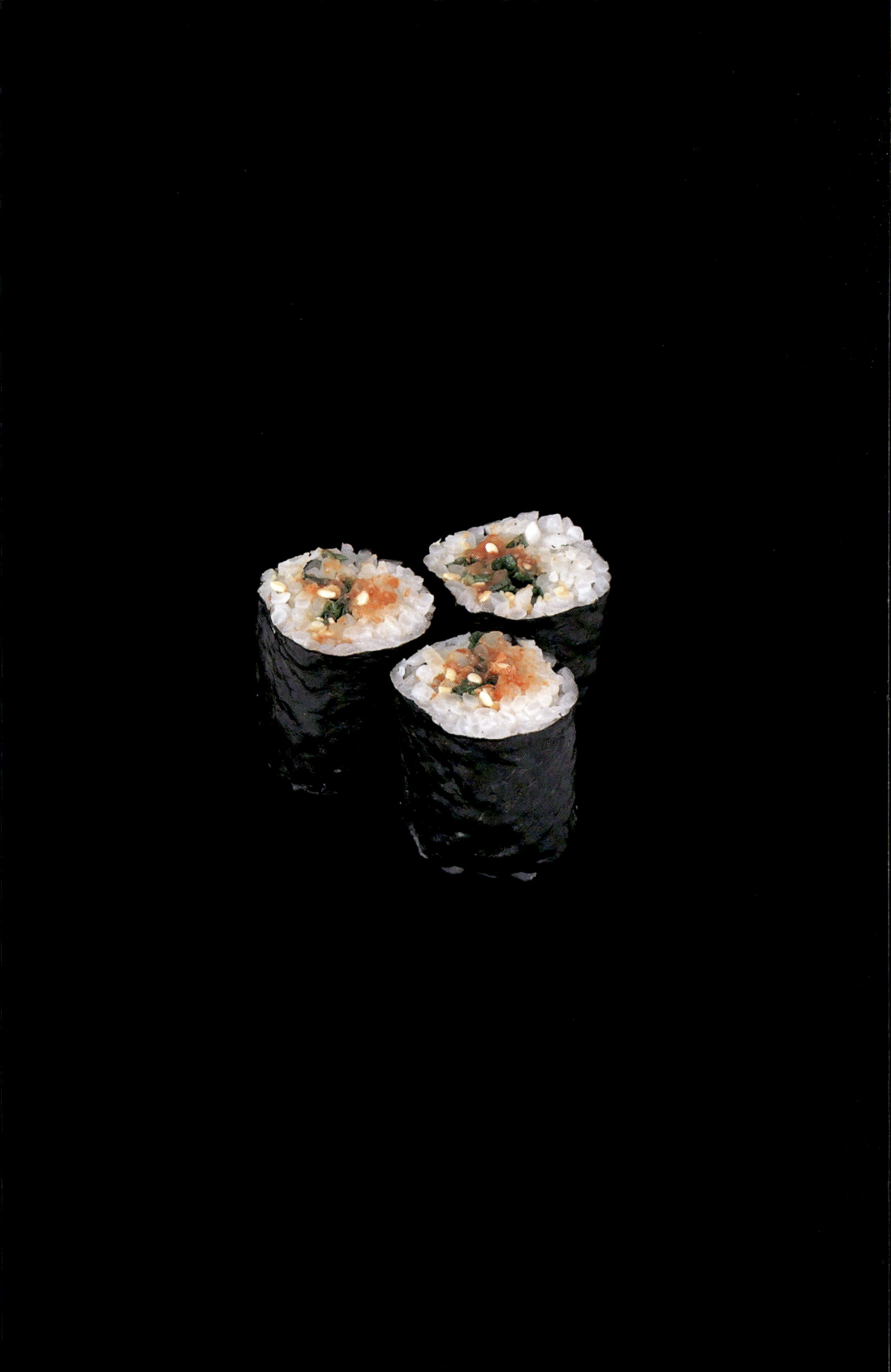

梅巻
(ume-maki)

梅干しを潰し、味醂、醤油、粉にした削り節を混ぜる。梅肉のできあがりだ。この梅肉を主役とした巻物を「梅巻」と言う。梅肉は体積が小さいために、その分だけシャリを多くして巻く。梅肉を多めに入れ、梅肉に負けないように山葵も多めに入れる。紫蘇の葉を細かく刻んだものを並べ、炒りゴマをたっぷり振りかけて巻く。梅肉と山葵、紫蘇の葉とゴマの分量がシャリとの絶妙なバランスとなったとき、梅巻はその真価を発揮することになる。すしの最後の口直しとして食される人気の高い巻物となっている。

Umeboshi plum is mashed and mixed with mirin, soy sauce and powdered bonito flakes to make *bai-niku* or 'plum flesh', the main ingredient in the roll known as ume-maki. The flesh of the plum being small in quantity, extra rice is incorporated in the roll to compensate. A generous helping of plum is included, with wasabi in almost equal measure. Finely chopped shiso is laid out, and a good sprinkling of toasted sesame seeds added before rolling rice and plum. Ume-maki displays its true worth when the quantities of plum and wasabi, shiso and sesame are in perfect balance with the rice. A popular roll often served as a palate cleanser at the end of a sushi meal.

pickled plum roll

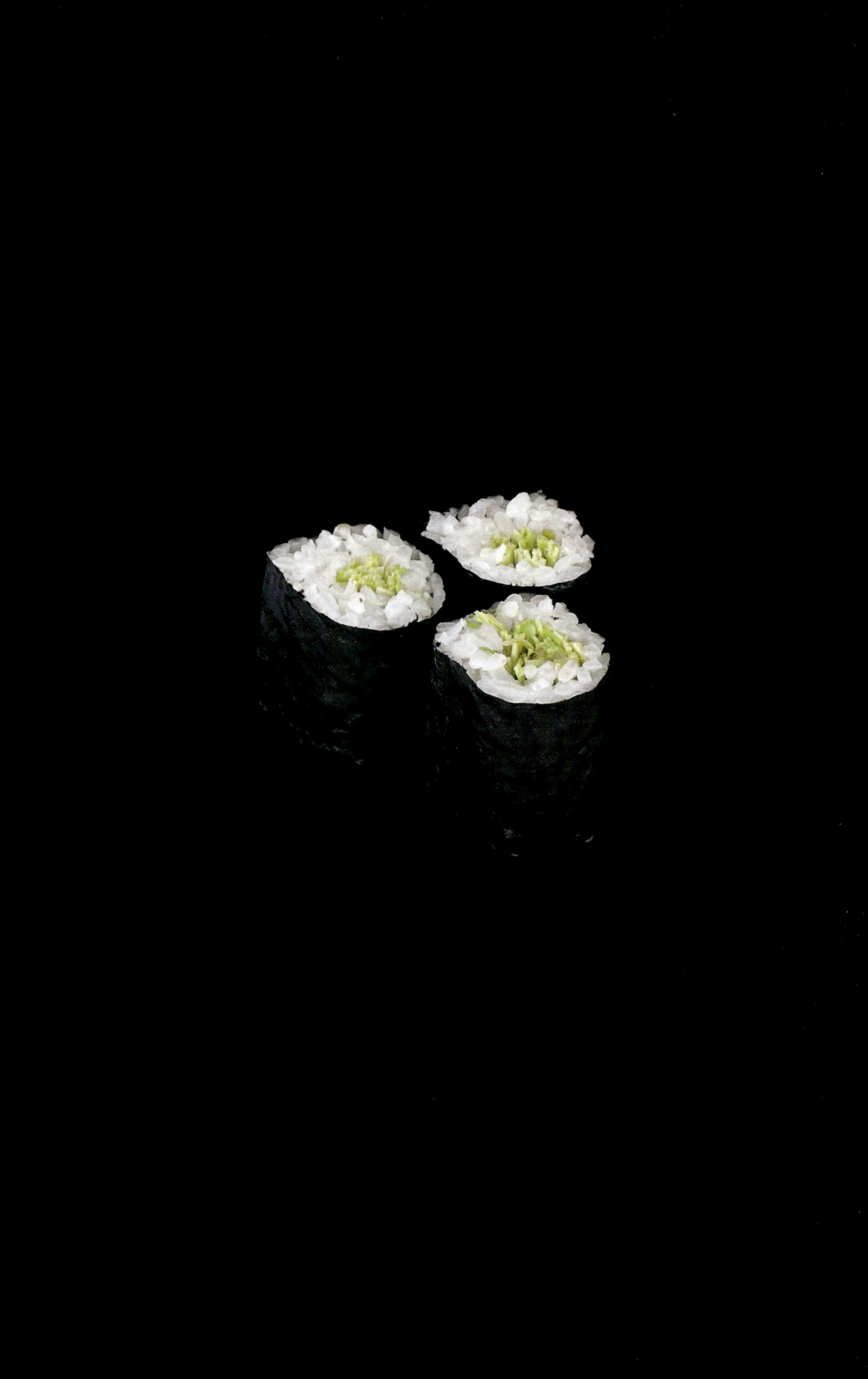

山葵巻
(wasabi-maki)

極めて細く打った極上の山葵だけを芯にして巻く。醬油(しょうゆ)をつけて食すと、噛むうちに少しずつ、山葵の甘みと香りが抑えめの辛みとともに立ちのぼってくる。山葵をすりおろさずに極細に打つことにより、強い辛みの発生を抑えているからだ。さらに噛むほどに鼻から目に抜ける辛みが徐々に発生してくる。しかし山葵巻の旨さの要点は、山葵の甘みと香りを楽しむことにあり、鮮烈な辛みは控えめにするところにある。山葵は香辛料で、本来は脇役なのだが、海苔(のり)とシャリと醬油によって主役を演じることになる。

Roll with a neta consisting solely of very finely chopped wasabi horseradish. Eaten with soy sauce, each bite gradually reveals the sweetness and fragrance of wasabi, combined with a subtle sharpness. Chopping the wasabi finely rather than grating it suppresses its spiciness, but with chewing, a hot and tear-inducing flavor sensation gradually spreads up the nasal passages. The key to enjoying wasabi-maki however is to savor the sweetness and aroma of the wasabi, minus its intense hotness. Usually a condiment relegated to a supporting role, when married with nori, rice and soy sauce, it shines at center stage.

wasabi roll

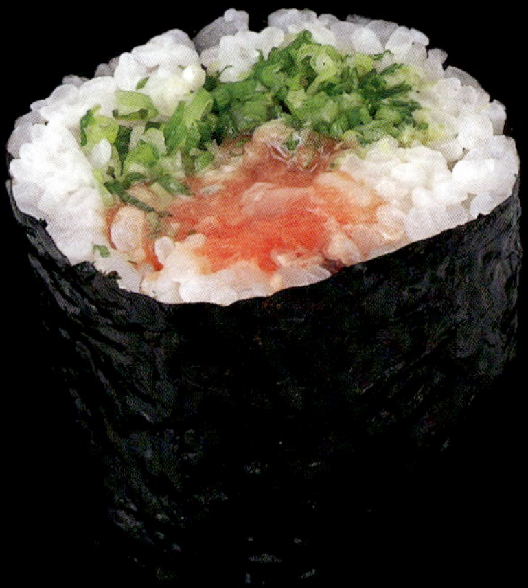

ネギトロ巻
(negitoro-maki)

大トロを、丁寧にベトベトの状態になるまで包丁で叩いていくと、邪魔な筋が殺され甘みも強く出てくる。海苔に控えめのシャリを広げ、山葵を予想以上にたくさん塗り、たっぷりの浅葱を加える。トロの叩き身の濃厚な甘みに、浅葱の意外とも思える強い辛みと香りが、山葵の辛みと旨みとともに絡みつく。さらにその上に、香り高い醤油の旨みが渾然一体となって広がってくる。トロの叩き身と浅葱と山葵と海苔と醤油は絶妙の相性なのだ。

When o-toro meat is pounded carefully with a knife into an almost glutinous state, any sinews that might detract from the eating experience are broken down and the sweet flavor of the flesh intensified. A thin layer of rice is placed on the nori, a surprisingly large amount of wasabi added, then a healthy sprinkling of chives, the unexpectedly intense tang and fragrance of the chives adding to the sweet richness of the tenderized toro and becoming entwined also with the tartness and flavor of wasabi. To this is added the flavor of fragrant soy sauce. Together toro, chives, wasabi, nori and soy sauce make a truly dream combination.

scallion & tuna roll

長山一夫（ながやま かずお）
1942年東京向島生まれ。日本橋久松町で育つ。1965年早稲田大学第一商学部卒業後、家業の春美鮨本店に入店。1973年第三春美鮨を新橋に出店。現在に至る。（第三春美鮨　東京都港区新橋 1-17-7 TEL：03-3501-4622)

Kazuo Nagayama
Born in 1942 in Tokyo's Mukojima district, raised in Nihonbashi-Hisamatsucho. After graduating in business from Waseda University in 1965, Nagayama joined Harumi Sushi, the family business. He opened the Daisan Harumi Sushi branch in 1973, which he still runs today. Daisan Harumi Sushi 1-17-7 Shimbashi, Minato-ku, Tokyo Tel. 03-3501-4622

田島一彦（たじま かずひこ）
1946年東京生まれ。1969年多摩美術大学デザイン科卒業後、資生堂宣伝部入社。2005年同社部長クリエイティブディレクターを経て独立、現在フリー。受賞歴：朝日広告賞、毎日広告賞、読売広告賞、フジサンケイ広告大賞、日経広告賞、電通賞、ACC賞、日本雑誌広告賞、ニューヨークフェスティバル等。

Kazuhiko Tajima
Born in 1946 in Tokyo. Graduated in design from Tama Art University in 1969. After working in the advertising department of Shiseido, eventually as creative director, Tajima began working as an independent art director in 2005. Among his many awards are the Asahi Advertising Award, Mainichi Advertisement Design Award, Yomiuri Advertising Award, Fuji Sankei Advertising Award, Nikkei Advertising Award, Dentsu Award, ACC Award, Japan Magazine Advertising Award, and New York Festival Award.

与田弘志（よだ ひろし）
1942年東京生まれ。イギリスの美術学校及びDavid Montgomery Studioで写真を学び、1966年ファッション写真家として独立。ロンドンにHiroshi Studioを設立し、エディトリアルを中心に活動。1972年東京に本拠を移し、雑誌・企業広告で写真を発表。講談社出版文化賞、東京ADC最高賞、毎日広告賞最高賞など受賞。国内外で多くの写真展を開催。写真集『TEA FOR TWO』『OBSESSION』、PIE BOOKSより『和菓子』出版。www.hiroshiyoda.com

Hiroshi Yoda
Born 1942 in Tokyo. Studied photography at art schools in the UK and the David Montgomery Studio. Yoda launched his career as a fashion photographer in 1966, when he established the Hiroshi Studio in London, working primarily in editorial photography. He relocated to Tokyo in 1972. His photograhs appear in magazines and corporate advertising. He is recipient of the Kodansha Publication Culture Awards for Photography, Tokyo ADC Award Grand Prize, and Mainichi Advertising Design Award Grand Prize, among others. His published books include the photo collections *Tea for Two* and *Obsession*, and with PIE Books, *Wagashi*. www.hiroshiyoda.com

Sushi 鮨
バイリンガル版

2011年9月7日　初版第1刷発行
2025年1月11日　　　第5刷発行

文　長山一夫
アートディレクション　田島一彦
写真　与田弘志

デザイン　淡海季史子
イラスト　鈴木勝久
英訳　パメラ・ミキ、カースティン・マカイヴァー
編集　高橋かおる

発行人　三芳寛要
発行元　株式会社パイ インターナショナル
〒170-0005　東京都豊島区南大塚2-32-4
TEL 03-3944-3981　FAX 03-5395-4830
sales@pie.co.jp

印刷・製本　大日本印刷株式会社

Text ©2011 Kazuo Nagayama
Photographs ©2011 Hiroshi Yoda
Book and cover design ©2011 Kazuhiko Tajima
Published by PIE International

ISBN978-4-7562-4134-4 C0072
Printed in Japan

本書の収録内容の無断転載・複写・複製等を禁じます。
ご注文、乱丁・落丁本の交換等に関するお問い合わせは、小社までご連絡ください。

※文章中の魚図は、海中の魚の位置を示しています。
右側：岸　左側：沖　上：海面　下：海底

The position of the fish illustrations within the text indicates where in the sea the species is found.
Right: Coastal   Left: Pelagic   Top: Surface   Bottom: Seabed

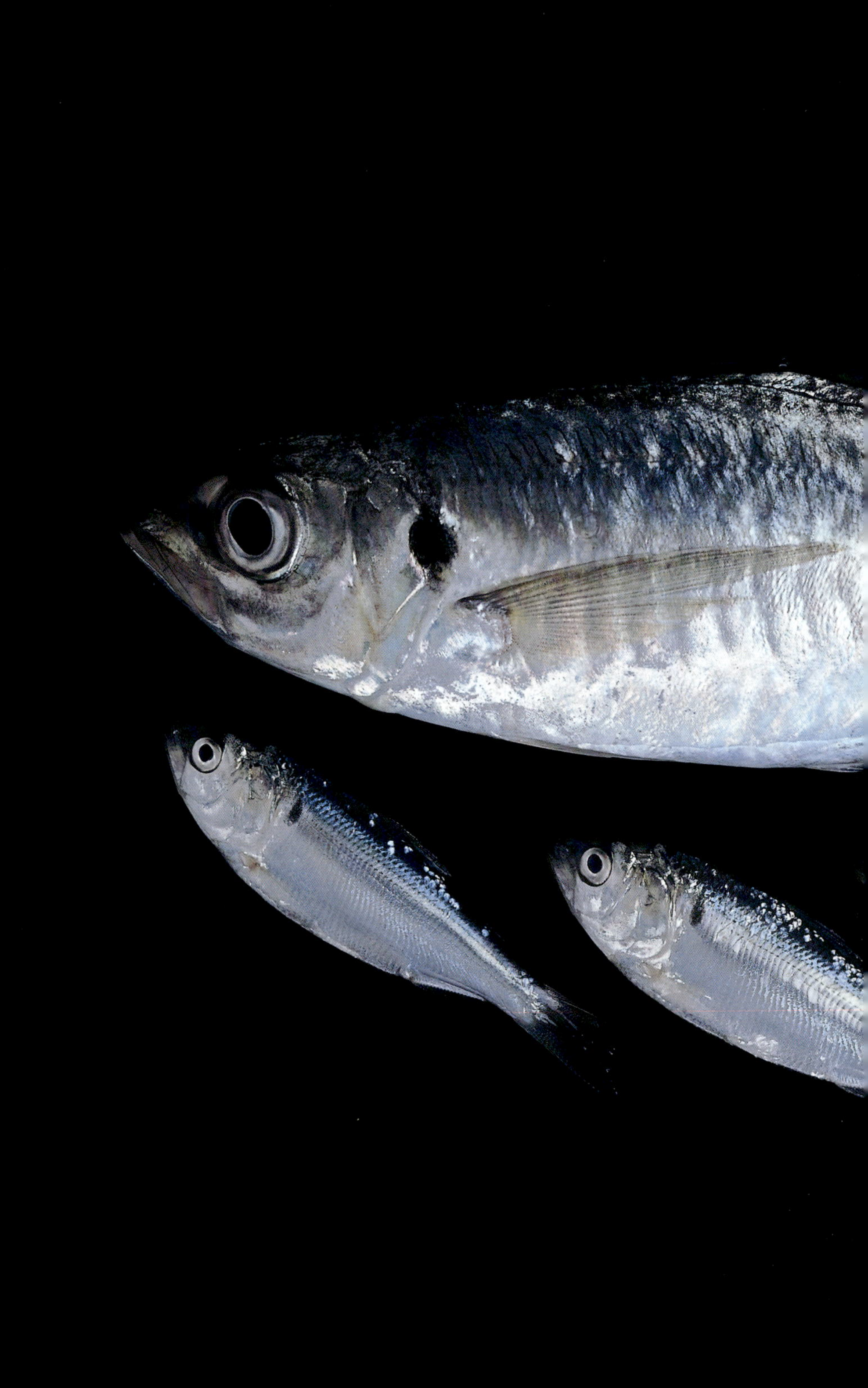